PRAYER

Hans Urs von Balthasar

PRAYER

Translated by A. V. Littledale

Foreword by Kenneth Woollcombe,
Bishop of Oxford

SPCK
LONDON

This book was first published under the title *Das Betrachtende Gebet* by Johannes-Verlag in 1957.

© translation, 1961, Geoffrey Chapman Ltd.

First published in Great Britain by Geoffrey Chapman Ltd, 1961.

Reissued in 1973 by SPCK,
Holy Trinity Church,
Marylebone Road, London NW1 4DU.

Nihil obstat: Hubertus Richards S.T.L., L.S.S.
Imprimatur: E. Morrogh Bernard Vic. Gen.
Westmonasterii, die 27a Februarii, 1961.

The Nihil obstat and Imprimatur are a declaration that a book or pamphlet is considered to be free from doctrinal or moral error. It is not implied that those who have granted the Nihil obstat and Imprimatur agree with the contents, opinions or statements expressed.

Printed in Great Britain by
William Clowes & Sons, Limited,
London, Beccles and Colchester

SBN 281 02771 4

FOREWORD

I WAS introduced to Dr von Balthasar's book on prayer by a wise Scottish priest who based a series of memorable addresses to my young students on some of its themes. He urged us to read it slowly and meditatively—to savour it as one would savour a vintage wine of rare and distinctive character—and I think he was right. It is not a book for beginners, nor is it a manual of the technique of prayer, but it is a book which goes deep into the heart of its subject and requires to be read with concentration. I have been re-reading it this month, almost exactly ten years since my first encounter with its brilliant and sensitive exposition of contemplation, and I am astonished to find how much of it has become part of my own thinking about the basic importance of this particular kind of prayer, not merely for the professed contemplatives, but for us all.

The original German title *Das betrachtende Gebet* means "contemplative prayer", or, more literally, the kind of prayer that takes a long, slow look at God. To pray thus is to expose one's human weakness and need to the limitless grace which alone can supply strength to the spirit. But it is also to recognize that a Christian is caught up into the reciprocity of giving and receiving which the theologians call the co-inherence of the Trinity. In the simpler words of Dr Austin Farrer, it is "to give God back the mind of God, coloured with our own". In a world such as ours, where the temptation is to save time by eating snacks rather than meals, to watch TV rather than to read books, to skim the headings rather than to master an argument, it is not easy to commend the long, slow look at God which contemplating demands. But the young generation has shown that it will not be content to adopt the superficialities of its parents, that it needs time to focus upon the still centre of things, and that it wants a theological rationale of the practice of prayer. Dr von Balthasar has shown us clearly why we must pray, and pray contemplatively; he has also described the character of prayer as a response from the depth of our experience to the initiative of God who reaches out to us there. It is for us to find the time and the way to respond in the power of the Holy Spirit with all our heart, mind, soul, and strength.

KENNETH OXON

May 1973

CONTENTS

PART I

THE ACT OF CONTEMPLATION

CHAPTER I

THE NECESSITY OF CONTEMPLATION

PRAYER IS something more than an exterior act performed out of a sense of duty, an act in which we tell God various things he already knows, a kind of daily attendance in the presence of the Sovereign who awaits, morning and evening, the submission of his subjects. Even though Christians find, to their pain and sorrow, that their prayer never rises above this level, they know well enough that it should be something more. Somewhere, here, there is a hidden treasure, if only I could find it and dig it up—a seed that has the power to grow into a mighty tree bearing abundant flowers and fruits, if only I had the will to plant and cultivate it. Yet this duty of mine, though dry and bitter, is pregnant with a life of the fullest freedom, could I once open and give myself up to it. We know all this or, at least, have some inkling of it, through what we have occasionally experienced, but it is another matter to venture further on the road which leads into the promised land. Once again, the birds of the air have eaten the seed that was sown, the thorns of everyday life have choked it and all that remains is a vague feeling of regret. And if that feeling becomes, at times, a pressing need to converse with God otherwise than in stereotyped formulas, how many know how to do so? It is as if they had to speak in a language whose rules they had never learnt; instead of fluent conversation, all they can manage are the disjointed, disconnected phrases of a foreigner unacquainted with the language of the country; they find themselves as helpless as a stuttering child who wants to say something and cannot.

This image could be misleading, for we cannot hold conversation with God. Yet it is appropriate, both because prayer is an exchange between God and the soul, and because, in this exchange, a definite language is used, obviously that of God himself. Prayer is a dialogue, not a monologue recited by men in God's presence. Indeed there is really no such thing as solitary speech; speech is essentially mutual, a sharing of thoughts and minds, union in a common spirit, in a shared truth. Speech supposes an I and a Thou, and is their mutual manifestation. What do we do, when at prayer, but speak to a God who long ago revealed himself to man in a word so powerful and all-embracing that it can never be solely of the past, but continues to resound through the ages? The better we learn to pray, the more we are convinced that our halting utterance to God is but an answer to God's speech to us; and so it is only in God's language that we can commune with him. God spoke first—and only because he has thus "exteriorised" himself can man "interiorise" himself towards God. Just consider a moment: is not the "Our Father", by which we address him each day, his own word? Was it not given us by the Son of God, himself God and the Word of God? Could any man by himself have discovered such language? Did not the "Hail Mary" come from the mouth of the angel, spoken, then, in the speech of heaven; and what Elizabeth, "filled with the Spirit", added, was that not a response to the first meeting with the incarnate God? What could we possibly have said to God, if he had not already communicated and revealed himself to us in his word, giving us access to and commerce with him? That is why we are enabled to look on his inner being and enter it, enter the inmost being of eternal Truth; and so, exposed to the light of God, become ourselves light and open to him.

Prayer, we can now see, is communication, in which God's word has the initiative and we, at first, are simply listeners. Consequently, what we have to do is, first, listen to God's word and then, through that word, learn how to answer. His word is the truth made known for our sakes. There is no final, unquestionable truth in man. He is fully aware of that as he looks to God for an answer and comes closer to him. God's word is his invitation to us to enter into the truth and abide there with him. It is like a rope-ladder thrown down to us in danger of drowning, so that we can climb into the ship; or, a carpet unrolled before us leading to the Father's throne; a torch shining in the darkness of a silent and sullen world, in whose light we are no longer harassed by problems, but learn to live with them. God's word is, ultimately, himself, that in him which is most living and profound : it is his only-begotten Son, of the same nature as himself, whom he sent into the world to bring it back to him. That is why God spoke to us of his Word dwelling on earth : "This is my beloved Son, hear ye him".

We are harassed by the burden of living; exhausted, we look round for a place of repose, tranquillity and renewal. We would gladly rest in God and commit ourselves to him, so as to draw from him fresh strength to go on living. But we do not look for him there where he awaits us, where he is to be found, namely in his Son, who is his Word. Or else we do seek him because there are a thousand things we want to ask him, and imagine that, unless they are answered, we cannot go on living; we pester him with problems, demand answers, solutions, explanations, forgetting all the time that in his Word he has solved all questions and given us all the explanations we are capable of grasping in this life. We do not turn there where God speaks, there where his word re-sounded in the world, a final utterance sufficient for all times, whose riches can never be exhausted.

Or else we think that the word of God has been sounding on earth for such a long time that it is almost used up, and a new word will soon be due, think that we have, in fact, the right to de-mand a new one. What we fail to notice is that it is we ourselves, we alone, who are worn out, while the word resounds as vigorously and freshly, as close to us as ever. "The word is nigh thee, even in thy mouth and in thy heart" (Rom. X. 8). We do not realise that, once God's word makes itself heard in the world, in the fulness of time, its power is such that it reaches all men, with equal directness, and that no one suffers from being remote in time or place. Certainly there was a small company who conversed with Christ on earth, and we might envy them their good fortune. Yet they conducted themselves in their talks as awkwardly and clumsily as we or anyone else would have done. In hearing and answering Christ and understanding what he really meant, they had no advantage over us; rather, in fact, the reverse, for the external, earthly aspect of the word they perceived hid, to a great extent, its divine and inner meaning. "Blessed are they who have not seen, and yet have believed", for they may find it easier to believe just because they do not see.

The disciples themselves understood the word, understood what it really meant, only after the resurrection; even then, many still doubted and showed they had failed to understand. They really understood it only after the ascension, at Pentecost, when the Spirit enlightened them interiorly on what the Son had proposed to them exteriorly. These earthly companions of Christ cannot in fact be held to have been highly privileged in any decisive sense. They happened to be present where anyone else might have been, or rather, where all of us really are. Doubtless, in the case of the Samaritan woman at the well Christ spoke to a particular person but, at the same time, he was speaking to each individual sinner, man and woman. It was not for one person alone that Jesus sat at the well, tired out : *quaerens me sedisti lassus!* and it is not just a "pious practice" for me to place myself, in spirit, alongside that woman and share her part; I not only may, I must, do so; indeed, I have long since been involved in that dialogue, without ever having been consulted. I am that harassed soul who, day by day, runs after earthly water, because it no longer understands what is meant by the heavenly water it is really seeking. Like the woman, I make the same puzzled, groping answer to the offer of the eternal fount of water till, finally, the Word has to pierce me sharply and force the admission of sinfulness. Even so, I cannot make this confession in plain language, for it must be completed by the grace of the eternal Word and Judge, so that by his unspeakable mercy it may be counted to me for justification : "Thou hast said well, I have no husband. For thou hast had five husbands, and he whom thou now hast is not thy husband; this thou hast said truly" (John IV. 17-18). Consequently, it is not enough to look on the words and events in the Gospel simply as "examples", like the examples of heroism used to incite children to imitate them. The Word who became flesh in order to speak to us meant by this or that particular circumstance any and every real, individual circumstance; saw every sinner in this repentant sinner, and in this woman listening at his feet, each one of his hearers. It is God who is speaking, and there is no such thing as remoteness in time from his word, no merely temporal relation to it. On the contrary, we find always the same perfect immediacy of communication that was given to those he met on the roads of Palestine : "Follow me !", "Go now and sin no more !", "Peace be with you !"

Indeed, the word revealed in Christ did not simply fall from heaven; the rushing stream was fed, too, from a number of sources already present. There was a preparation, a kind of crescendo leading up to the full resonance of the divine voice in the world : "God who, in sundry times and divers manners, spoke in times past to the fathers by the prophets, last of all in these days hath spoken to us by his Son, whom he hath appointed heir of all things, by whom also he made the world" (Heb. I. 1-2). However, now that the stream has become a single unity, we can see the various sources only as precursors, hurrying straight towards it, to enter and be absorbed, in the fulness of time, into the one word that says all. We cannot grasp any particular word of God without hearing the Son, who is *the* Word; nor may we rummage about in the books of the Old and New Testaments hoping to pick on some disconnected truths. We must be prepared to place ourselves in direct contact with him, this free and personal Word who speaks to us "with power". "Search the scriptures, for you think in them to have life everlasting; and the same are they that give testimony of me. And you will not come to me that you may have life. . . .'

If you did believe Moses, you would perhaps believe me also; for he wrote of me. But if you do not believe his writings, how will you believe my words?" (John V. 39-40; 46-47).

Christ gathers up in himself all the words of God lying scattered in the world; he is the burning focal point of revelation. "Through whom he made the world", says St. Paul, and therein he shows that not only the "words spoken in many ways" of the Old Testament, but equally those scattered throughout creation, stammered or murmured in it—words uttered in the great and the small things of nature, the words of the flowers and the beasts, words of overpowering beauty and paralysing horror, words manifold and confused, this word full of promise and disillusionment of human existence—that all these belong to the one, eternal, living Word become man for us; they are wholly his property, and on that account are governed by him, to be interpreted by his light and no other. None of them can be heard or understood except under his direction; none, apart from him, can be a genuine word, still less opposed to the unique word. "He that is not for me is against me; and he that gathereth not with me, scattereth." In the early stages of human history, it was possible to direct a course to him, the great river, by way of various tributary streams. The promise repeated in so many ways could be accepted by man with a faith and confidence that would dispose him to enter the unity that was to come. But now that the Son has made his appearance, the believer has to apprehend the manifold promises from the standpoint of the unity already given. He must repeatedly turn back to the centre, and set out anew to the periphery—the realms of history and of nature with their discordant and confused voices. There, at the centre, he is spoken to; it is there that he receives the definitive pronouncement: the truth about his life, what God desires and expects of him, what he is to strive for and what, in the service of the divine Word, he must avoid. That is why he must be a hearer of the Word.

Let us consider this more deeply, and more from man's own standpoint: "All things", says St John, "were made by him. In him was life, and the life was the light of men" (John I. 3-4). To say that we, together with the rest of creation, were made in the Word, is to assert not merely an original relationship but an enduring and essential "being-in" which will be fully manifested when God the Son recapitulates all the things of earth and heaven in him, the Incarnate Word (Eph. I. 10), when he incorporates all who desire it into his mystical body, and makes the blood of the mystical vine course through all the branches. The "Life" that is in the Word is not that fitful spark the children of Adam foster within them but the true, full and perfected life : "I give them eternal life. . . . I have come that they may have life, and have it more abundantly" (John X. 28, 10). He himself is this life, not simply as its channel, but bodily ("I am the life"—John XI. 25; XIV. 6) and, therefore, not solely as the source of its being but in a personal, free and spiritual manner. Inasmuch as he is the free and sovereign being, he is the "light of men". They do not have this light as something at their own disposal, as possibly they might were he merely the source of life, rather like a sap mounting from the root of eternity into individual souls in all their variety, to be turned to different account by each, according to the nature of the various branches. Many look upon divine grace as a kind of anonymous, featureless life we hold within ourselves and are able, by our own efforts, to "increase", as we can enlarge a pool by damming it or add to our wealth by saving. But this conception leaves no scope for the freedom of the Light, which never acts in the least like the light of nature and human reason. This latter indeed, is always present, and will persist in heaven; so long as there are men, we can always count on it. It has absolutely no centre of its own, but is diffused among all those who bear a human stamp.

The "true light", however, without which this other diffused light would be deceptive, is always free in its irradiation. "Yet a little while, the light is among you. Walk, whilst you have the light" (John XII. 35). Otherwise, it would not be the Word who is God, Person and Son, Lord of all who have been "created in him". If we would live in his light, we have to be attentive to his word that is ever personal and new, because free. It is quite impossible to bring forth this word out of one already at hand, known in advance and kept in store. On the contrary, it flows always new from its source in absolute and sovereign freedom. The Word of God may well require of me to-day something it had not demanded yesterday; consequently, in order to perceive this demand, I must, in the depths of my being, be open and attentive to the word. No relationship is closer, more rooted in being itself, than that between the man in grace and the Lord who gives grace, between the Head and the body, between the vine and the branch. But this relationship can only have full play if it prevails, too, in the realm of the spirit, that is if the freedom of the word is answered by a corresponding readiness on the part of man to hear, to follow and to comply. It is not just a question of what we are accustomed to call the "moral life" or life in accordance with "Christian precepts", but rather of that burning centre, the focus and vindication of all moral conduct which divorced from that centre so easily hardens and degenerates into pharisaism. What is at stake is that ever living contact with the God who speaks to us in his Word, whose "eyes like a flame of fire" (Apoc. I. 14) transpierce and purify us, whose command exacts renewed obedience, and instructs us in such a way that we seem till now to have known nothing at all, whose power sends us forth anew to our mission in the world.

If a man lacks this kind of obedience to the Word of God within him, he fails to correspond to the idea God the Father had in creating him. Whatever a man may be, bodily and spiritually, apart from this most inner and personal relationship, he is at best a mere torso; not even that in fact, for though a torso lacks certain limbs, yet of its kind it may well be perfect; while man cannot be perfect in any respect apart from this relationship. His body and soul were created in view of the perfection it brings; it is the source of the nobility inherent in his nature. Man is the being created as hearer of the Word, and only in responding to the Word rises to his full dignity. He was conceived in the mind of God as the partner in a dialogue. His reason is endowed with as much light of its own as it needs to perceive God speaking to it. His will is superior to instinct and open to the good in exactly the degree that enables him, without compulsion, to follow the attraction of the supreme God. Man is the being who bears in his heart a mystery greater than himself. He is like a tabernacle erected round a sacred mystery. He has no need, when God's Word demands to dwell in him, to take specific means to open his heart. His inmost being is readiness, attentiveness, perceptiveness, willingness to sur- render to what is greater than he, to let the deeper truth prevail, to lay down his arms at the feet of enduring love. It is true that, in the sinner, this sanctuary has become neglected and forgotten, overgrown and turned into a sepulchre or a rubbish-heap. It needs much effort, the effort in fact of contemplative prayer, to clear it out and make it suitable for its heavenly guest. But the place itself does not have to be built. It is there already, in the inmost part of man, and always has been.

For this reason the ineffable relationship of man to the Word of God is, to the endless joy and wonder of those who pray, always and simultaneously a turning inwards to the inmost I and a turn- ing outwards of the I to the supreme Thou. God is not a Thou in this sense of being simply another I, a stranger standing over against me. He is in the I, but also above it; and because he is above it as the absolute I, he is in the human I as the deepest ground of it, "more inward to me than I am to myself". And being so inward to it, he is supremely above it; his unity is above that which is merely numerical : it surpasses that of the figure one. Created being in its totality cannot be conceived except as dependent on, and penetrated by, eternal, absolute Being, neither can the created I (corresponding to the *analogia entis,* and as its supreme case, there is *analogia personalitatis*). Just as the part loves the whole more than itself, and loves itself most when it does so in the whole, and not in its particularity; so the created I loves and affirms itself most profoundly when it loves the I of God, the I that is absolute and free and opens itself to him in the Word, when he receives God's Word not as a truth alien to him, contrasting with him—heteronomous—but as the truth which is most his own, most inward to him, that lies hid so deeply (in him and in God) that the I itself has not the power to disclose it. Yet the God who speaks in me is quite other than "my best self" or the archetypal world in the ground of my soul or some other thing lying deeply embedded in nature, its tendencies and potentialities. God is the Sovereign who elects and disposes according to his will; man possesses nothing to enable him with certainty to foresee how the determinate word will be uttered to him in particular at this particular moment in his life. From his nature alone man can never divine the will of God, the purpose of his life. That would be to ask of the servant what only the master can give. "Behold as the eyes of servants are on the hands of their masters, as the eyes of the handmaid are on the hands of her mistress, so are our eyes unto the Lord our God" (Ps. 122. 2).

This looking to God is contemplation. It is an inward gaze into the depths of the soul and, for that very reason, beyond the soul to God. The more the soul finds God, the more it forgets itself and yet finds itself in God. It is an unwavering "gaze", where "looking" is always "hearing"; for what is looked at is the free and infinite Person who, from the depths of his freedom, is able to give himself in a manner ever new, unexpected and unpredictable. That is why the Word of God is never something settled for good and all that can be surveyed like a clearly defined landscape, but something that comes forth ever anew, like water from a spring or rays from a light. "And so it is not enough to have received 'insight' and to 'know the testimonies of God', if we do not continually receive and become inebriated by the fountain of eternal light" (Augustine, *Ennar. in Ps. 118,* xxvi, 6). To the lover this is immediately evident; to him the countenance and voice of the beloved are each moment as new as if he had never perceived them before. But the being of God revealed to us in his Word is ever new, not merely in the eyes of the lover, but in itself objectively; it is the marvellous object to which, for the whole duration of eternity, no saint or seraph can ever become "accustomed"—the longer they look on it, the more they desire to gaze. This gaze, this "looking", is directed towards the perfect fulfilment promised to created nature in its entirety. In seeing and hearing God, it experiences the highest joy, that of being fulfilled in itself, but fulfilled by something infinitely greater than itself and, for that very reason, completely fulfilled and made blessed.

So long as we are subject to the law of sin, this fulfilment will always have a painful aspect. We have to renounce what is our own, since this encumbers the space in us to which God's Word lays claim. The Word itself has a combative character : as "sword" and "fire", its special properties, it has to conquer in us the place without which it could not continue. On that account it seems to us, so long as we are in this world, to come rather from without than from within, to be "heard" rather than "beheld"; and we place the "seeing" more in the world to come, when the tension between the Word and the hearer shall have been surmounted. In every age, contemplation, as "vision" of divine truth, has been looked on, in the Church, as a kind of foretaste of the eternal blessedness to come. The difference, however, is only a relative one. In eternity too God, in his supremely free self-giving, will not cease to be our fulfilment and so will we, while beholding God, not cease to hang on his lips and be hearers. And even here we have no need to hear the Word in such wise that it sounds alien in our ears, instead of being what is most our own, most intimate and close, *my* truth as the truth about me and my own truth; the Word that reveals me and gives me to myself. In this Word were we created, and in it lies our entire truth, our idea, one so unexpectedly great and beatifying that we should never have claimed or believed it. In the Word of God we come into contact with this idea, and truly only there; but we cannot detach it from his Word, and take it away with us. We are truly ourselves only in him, and in so far as we are branches of his vine; only in so far as we let ourselves be formed and determined by his supremely free life. What we truly are he alone can say, and the word he spoke to the weeping Magdalen at the grave is enough : "Mary !" This proper name coming from the mouth of eternal Life is each man's true idea : it is the true I in God, given and uttered to the believer through pure grace and remission of his sins, but accompanied with the compelling might of the love which, of its very nature, demands and appropriates all. Apart from this love, man cannot be understood at all.

God's Word, as spoken to us, presupposes a Word of God within us, inasmuch as we have been created in the Word and can never be separated from our centre. It has become, in a new manner and degree, Word within us, in so far as the Word in order to reach us anew after we were alienated from it and immersed in the carnal, took flesh of our flesh, and now communicates itself to us in the twofold form of word and flesh, of Scripture and the Eucharist, of truth both spiritual and substantial. In the Eucharist (and in all the sacraments of the Church, and in the Church itself as a sacrament in its totality), we are really incorporated in the incarnate Word; we are, as St. Paul never tires of repeating, "in Christ" as in our sphere of existence. This medium in which we live goes unobserved by reason of its close proximity and unobtrusive intimacy with us; but, when we come into contact with the Word as formally expressed, whether in Scripture, in sermons, in the Church's teaching, above all in our contemplation, we meet it in its sovereign personal freedom and spirituality. Everyone who, as a Christian lives outwardly in the Church and sacramentally in the Word, must of necessity also be a hearer of the Word : the Eucharist entails contemplation. To live as a tabernacle of the Word implies living as a hearer of the Word. If we are to keep the Word within us we must listen to the Word above us.

All this makes us turn our attention to the one perfect example of Christian living, to her who realised she was hearer, bearer and fulfilment of the Word of God : "Behold the handmaid of the Lord; be it done to me according to thy word". Mary is a "prototype of the Church", and this for two reasons : she is the place of the real and bodily indwelling of the Word in the most intimate union of mother and child sharing the same flesh; and, in the spiritual sphere, she is—and to this the former is due—a servant, in her entire person, body and soul, one who knows no law of her own, but only conformity to the word of God. Because she was a virgin, which means a pure, exclusive hearer of the word, she became mother, the place of the incarnation of the Word. Her womb was blessed, only because she "heard the word of God and kept it" (Luke XI. 27), because she "kept all these words and pondered them in her heart" (Luke II. 19, 51). She is the model which should govern contemplation, if it is to keep clear of two dangers : one, that of seeing the word only as something external, instead of the profoundest mystery within our own being, that in which we live, move and are : the other, that of regarding the word as so interior to us that we confuse it with our own being, with a natural wisdom given us once and for all, and ours to use as we will.

The first danger is that of Protestantism, which has such a vivid sense of Revelation in the Word as such and is ceaselessly occupied with it. This concern is certainly to be admired and imitated by us Catholics; yet it often lacks something which would allow the study of the word of God to develop into true contemplation and vision. It overlooks the essential indwelling of the Word in the Eucharist and in the Church as in the mystical body and vine; with the result that this concern with the revealed word cannot be said to resemble Mary's.

Catholics, on the other hand, fall short—not indeed as a matter of principle, but often in practice—of a like perseverance in hearing the word. They confine themselves to the actual possession of grace as assured to them by the Church and the sacraments; and in fact, the best contemplative tradition often tends to modulate from hearing to a tranquil seeing, from submissive reception to spiritual possession (as "wisdom" and the "gift of the Holy Ghost"). The Catholic tradition of contemplation must recapture the element adopted by Protestantism as its watchword and standard, and which has become somewhat alien to Catholics: hearing the word of Scripture as the spiritual communication of revelation, alongside the "physical" form of communication in the sacraments. But this element, once regained, must be so strongly impregnated with the spirit of Mary and the Church that the effort to understand and hear aright avails, once more, to real contemplation, to an act of prayer, adoration and inmost reception, in love and service, into one's own being and life. In the pietistic movement, Protestantism attempted to recover that element, hitherto lacking, but could not really succeed in doing so, since it was unable fully to recover the positive and objective character inherent in the offices of the Church and the liturgy. So it was that the idea of "handmaid" was too promptly superseded by that of "bride" (adopted too subjectively), a word Mary never applied to herself.

The hearer *par excellence* is the virgin who became pregnant with the Word, and bore him as her own and the Father's Son. She herself, even when Mother, remained a servant; the Father alone is the Master, together with the Son, who is her life and who moulds her life. She lives wholly for the fruit of her womb. Even after she has given him birth, she continues to carry him within her; she only needs to look into her heart, to find him. But she does not omit, on that account, to turn her gaze uninterruptedly upon the child growing up by her side, upon the youth and the man, whose ideas and actions seem to her ever more unpredictable and astonishing. More and more, she "understood not" what he meant —when he stayed behind in the temple without telling her, when he failed to receive her, when, in his public life, he concealed his power and spent himself in vain and, in the end, detached himself from her as she stood at the foot of the cross, substituting for himself a stranger, John, to be her son. With all the force of her body, she obeys the word that resounds ever more strongly and more divinely but seems more and more alien and almost tears her asunder, although, in spite of all, she has given herself to it wholly and radically in advance. She lets herself be led whither she "knows not"; so far is the word she follows from being her own wisdom. Yet she is wholly in accord with its leading, so surely is the word she loves "engrafted" in her heart (James I. 21).

In the life of the Christian who tries to be a hearer of the word, this severe, relentless demand and direction will occur only if he opens himself unreservedly to contact with the word. He does this, for his part, by a loyal attention inwards, to the voice of God in his conscience, to the monitions of the "interior Master" (as St. Augustine calls Christ's indwelling in us as Word), by submission and docility to the inspirations of the Holy Spirit. Such a total attention inwards could be held to correspond, in some degree, with Mary's own interior contemplation; but it is quite distinct from her gaze directed upon the Son living bodily at her side, his actions and demands. Without some corresponding element our commerce with the word, in our obtuseness and love of ease, is likely to cease altogether; we grow increasingly satisfied with what we already know, and it becomes constantly more attenuated and elementary; our faculty of hearing is blunted, we come to expect no further word of God, no fresh demands on us. It is here that we meet with the living word of the Church: the word as proclaimed in preaching and doctrine, but, above all, the word of Scripture entrusted to the Church, the word of the Holy Spirit concerning the Son. This is God's authentic expression and presentation of the revelation of the Father in his Son and Word and, on that account, it is the spirit of the Word himself. Just as it is the function of the Holy Spirit to bring before every age the grace and the work, in fact the incarnate reality, of the Son in the Church as a whole and in its sacraments, so it is likewise his function to set before every age and each individual believer the revealed word of Scripture as one form of the embodiment of the divine Word, one aspect of the Incarnation.

In contemplating the Scriptures, not as the word of man, but of God, the Christian has the highest possible certainty and guarantee of encountering the word of God in its full sovereignty; for he thereby hears it in a spirit of worship, in the setting of the Church and the sacraments, under the guidance of the Holy Spirit who never fails in his interior motion within the Church. Scripture, indeed, is no system of wisdom, but the account of God's encounter with man, with the men of Christ's time, in whom all men are comprised; with men, too, of the ages which looked towards Christ, and (in the epistles) of the times after Christ, which, through his messengers, remain always under the living sovereignty of the Incarnate Word. Scripture is history and actual occurrence, as the life of each individual before and with God is history and actual occurrence. But Scripture contains and relates a pattern of history and events, from which each individual life draws its truly historical and "eventful" character. The contemplation of Scripture is the school where we learn to hear aright; there we make contact with the primary source of Christian life and prayer.

CHAPTER II

OUR CAPACITY FOR CONTEMPLATION

SINCE GOD himself has made us such that, to be truly ourselves, we have to listen to his word, he must, for that reason, have endowed us with the ability to do so; otherwise, he would be in contradiction with himself and so not be the truth. This power inherent in us is as deeply rooted as our very being; as spiritual creatures of the Father, we are "hearers of the Word". To this it is no doubt possible to demur on various counts. We may say that we have never succeeded in so hearing, that it does not come within our scope, that it is not meant for us with our particular characters and qualities, our occupation and manifold concerns—our religious interests do not lie in that direction, our repeated efforts have come to nothing. But such objections, which in their context may well have some slight validity, by no means affect the great, fundamental truth that God has, along with faith, given us the ability to hear his word.

Believing and hearing the word of God are one and the same. Faith is the power to transcend one's own personal "truth", merely human and of this world, and to attain the absolute truth of the God who unveils and offers himself to us, to let it be decisive in our regard and prevail. The person who believes, who declares himself a believer, thereby proclaims that he is ready to hear the word of God. If he wills to believe without inner contradiction, inwardly affirming and holding as true what he believes, then he loves and hopes as well. It needs no abstruse reflection to say that faith without love can only be a "dead" faith, bereft of inner vitality by its own self-deprivation. How can anyone seriously believe that God is love and gave himself up for us on the cross because he loved us from eternity, chose us and destined us for a blessed eternity with him, how can anyone seriously "hold as true" all this and, at the same time, withhold his love from God or doubt God's love for him? How can he acknowledge the truth of this message, the word coming from God and at the same time proclaim the contrary in his actions—at least as regards him, at least at this moment, and so long as he continues sinning? He has, indeed, this inconceivable and "impossible" power, but it is only the power to contradict what he has himself established, and so to be someone self-contradictory, who does away with himself, shatters his own being. Once a man has given his assent to faith in any way at all—if only in the vague sense of conceding in principle to the truth of God (or of some Absolute, something divine or all-embracing) a preponderance over his own personal truth— such a man assents to this truth, loves it and hopes in it; he is, either explicitly or implicitly, a hearer of the word.

Yet the supreme point of his being can be overclouded in various ways. He may live so continuously with it concealed from view that he may almost forget its existence. He may live among distractions, in a continual hurry, or in a state of secret despair over the rightness and the importance of all he does and the possibility of ever doing the one essential thing; and this despair may come to infiltrate his whole interior life, infect his prayer, and stamp him as one resigned in a false and sterile sense to a wretched state, enslaved by his own nature. Yet all this does not prevent his faith persisting alive within him, and offering him insistently the possibility of bringing it to fulfilment. The banquet of faith lies ready prepared, whether the guest comes to it or withdraws on all sorts of pretexts or excuses. The entire objective world of God's word, that is to say of God's love drawing near to man, opening out to him, seeking to be understood and grasped, is always at hand; of itself it never fades into the distance, even though man, immersed in the world, shuts his eyes and plays the absentee. No doubt, in the actual world of grace, there are valid experiences of absence, but these are themselves forms and modes of love; such are the experiences of the prophets of the Old Testament, of the Son of God on the cross and in the darkness of the descent into hell, and of all those who, in their different vocations, are followers of the Son. These are the redeeming ways of love following the sinner in his steps to catch up with him and bring him home. It would be blasphemous to equate these experiences with our sinful refusals, and to ascribe to our own indolence and distaste for listening to the word any positive meaning within the world of faith and its truth.

To be convinced that we are capable of hearing the word of God, it is only necessary to open our eyes and see what faith is. Faith is twofold: an act and its content or object; it is a holding-as-true and a held-as-true. The two are inseparably conjoined, since the holding-as-true, the disposition to let God's truth and love prevail is the way, indeed the only way, in which we can participate in the content; expressed concretely, it is the grace, contained in God's self-giving to us, of our corresponding gift of self to God. God showed such trust as to create the world, to endow Adam with sovereign freedom, to deliver his only Son into the hands of sinners, to set up the hierarchical Church as the sign and place of his kingdom among men. He entrusts himself to us in all this without the least misgiving, he is the Faithful in eternity (Ps. 88), and so gives his truth (*veritas*) the character of a venturesome, faithful love (*fidelitas, emeth, pistis*). Furthermore God confers his spirit, the spirit of venturesome love upon the inmost being of the man he has in view, whom he speaks to and wishes to win over, giving it to him as a bond between them; this bond is faith (*pistis, fides*). All the concrete and objective acts and signs of God in history that man's faith must "hold as true" are simply acts and signs that tell of God's daring trust, presenting it to us as worthy of belief. God does not show us an abstract, theoretical, lifeless, "dead" trust, nor does he enclose the divine wisdom in so many propositions and precepts and leave it at that; he allows it to take flesh in the movement of history, of real life, with all its attendant risks. He cannot be content with a "dead" faith as man's response. The living God is present in the world and is personally involved for man's sake; he claims a response that engages the whole person, one given by man in his entire life as hearing the word and answering its demands.

But to respond in this way, as a believer in God's word, a man must be at home with the word. He must know it intimately. He must, in hearing the word, be attentive to it and not merely aware that he is spoken to—not like someone standing in a wind and feeling it blow upon him—but summoned to understand what is being said to him and to act accordingly. So it was that the boy Samuel was instructed by Heli: "Go and sleep; and, if the Lord calls thee again, thou shalt say, Speak, Lord, for thy servant heareth" (1 Kings III. 9). So it was that Mary heard the word of God from Gabriel, ready and eager to respond to it: "How can that be"—that is, how should I act in that way—"for I know not man?" (Luke I. 34). In the same way, Paul, in his fear at the Lord's revelation that cast him to the ground, heard as one ready to correspond: "Trembling and astonished, he asked, Lord, what wilt thou have me to do? Then the Lord said to him, Arise and go into the city, and there it shalt be told thee what thou must do" (Acts IX. 6-7; XXII. 20).

Contemplation, then, in the context of revelation, does not simply mean gazing on the Absolute, abstracting as far as possible from all relationship with the world, in order to perceive it in the greatest possible purity and detachment. It is a meeting with the Absolute—an encounter which is never found in so vivid and compelling a form outside this context—a meeting with the God who reveals himself in the setting of the world and its history, and whose gaze is fixed on man; on man in general, though he never exists except as an individual man at a particular moment in history. It is this particular, irreplaceable person that God speaks to and thinks of, "this" man with his own particular truth—situated, indeed, within the general truth of the covenant—a truth which expresses God's special historical relation to him: which expresses the covenant between God and this particular member of the people of the covenant that *I* am. For what I am accustomed to describe as God's will over my life, as his providence as well as his claims over it, is inescapably situated within the great context of the covenant of God with his world. That is God's unalterable relationship to the creation, and there is no other access to him but by returning along that path. But the content and form of the covenant are outlined and defined by the word of God, so explicitly that the word not only proclaims, but actually is, the covenant and its grace. Christ, as the Son of the Father, is the final end of the Old Covenant and the summing-up of the New and Eternal; he is the incarnate fidelity of God to the world (*pistis*), and as such the "origin and crown of faith (*pistis*)" (Heb. XII. 2). In him the gift of faith made us by the Father becomes the gift of the power to answer in every possible way, hearing and understanding, obeying and living by this understanding.

These are the theoretical and practical foundations and presuppositions of contemplative prayer. We will now briefly develop them.

1. Its foundation in the Father.

We can attend to God's word and hear it because the word of God is open to us. The majority of Christians do not realise that this by no means follows from the nature of things, but is one of the miracles of God's love. It should, in fact, astonish and delight us daily as a man may be transported by the love of the woman he loves. But there is a difference. In this instance it is God, the eternal and absolutely Other, having no need whatever of created love, owing no such intimacy to any of his creatures, who lays himself open and surrenders to us, gives himself by inviting, exalting and ennobling us to a participation in his own divine nature. We say this glibly enough, because we are accustomed to these expressions; but our hearing and contemplation of the word should wean us from our habits of thought and make us conscious of how prodigious the summons is. The word addressed to us by God is a word of love, uttered loud and clear in the full light of day, and almost menacing, so as to rouse man from his dreams and make him inwardly alive to what sounds in his ears; but it is also a secret whispered in the night, gentle and alluring, impenetrable, incredible to the most robust faith, a mystery no creature will fathom. For these voices come from eternity, sounding and echoing through all that is good and true in the inner world. Without depriving the things of the world of meaning or worth, it imparts a new and unfathomable dimension to them which breaks open what was closed, makes relative what seemed definitive, gives deep significance to what is simple, alleviates the painful and softens the tragic elements of life.

Renunciation can now mean enrichment beyond measure; dying can mean entrance to eternal life; acknowledgement of one's misery and guilt can be the act of casting oneself into the arms of eternal mercy and knowing oneself saved. The world of love and its mysteries is opened to us, stretching ever further beyond our sight till it reaches its ultimate source in the divine life that has neither beginning nor end. Between the beginning without beginning that lies in God's eternity and the end without end that is there too, and nowhere else, extends the minute segment of our finite being taken up and accepted. It has value in God's eternal life; through the free gift of his grace it stands in his presence; through the miracle of his merciful election it is, with all its roots and the earth that clings to them, "transplanted" from its native soil and being into the garden of his wholly other, eternal Being.

This image and similar ones are used to express as vividly as possible the incomprehensible leap and breach between one sphere of being and another—a breach which, however, shatters nothing and is therefore felt as a rapture of love. The highest flights and ecstasies of contemplation encompass regions no more remote than those attained, in principle, in the primary act of divine grace. They only help to reveal, in some degree, and supplement our knowledge of what has already been affected in everyone who has received grace, in the simple believer. Such experiences give us some realisation of what God has already wrought in them from the very beginning. We say, from the very beginning; for, although grace has a relative beginning in time—first of all in baptism and, more relatively still, when given anew in the sacrament of penance—this beginning is grounded in an absolute beginning, which reaches back to the eternal beginning of the divine eternities. Then it was that God looked on us and knew us (though as yet we had no existence in time), like the sun lightening up a landscape, giving it colour, warmth and fecundity, penetrating all things so deeply as to empower them to grow, flower and bear fruit of themselves; but, all the time, they do so only by grace of the sun, which is the indispensable condition for such actions and the medium in which they exert them.

When God looks on man there is nothing passive in his gaze—otherwise, it would not be divine—he does not "read and mark" but is creative, productive of very being through his absolutely free decree. "As thou art in my eyes, so hast thou value for me; no other truth than this has any value either for me or for thee or for anyone else." When God's love is turned upon his creature it is an act of perfectly free pre-election (predestination) unlinked to anything prior, whose absolute, irreducible liberty is reflected clearly in each particular act of divine love towards us in time. It is reflected, above all, in the act of grace calling us, where the eternal election becomes actual and perceptible to us in time; and again in the equally fundamental act of justification, which indicates decisively the realisation, in us, of the divine intention of grace. Between calling and justification, there is certainly something like a response on the part of the creature, an incipient assent, that is taken up into the final miracle of transformation by grace from which proceeds complete assent to the grace-given love of God uttered out of a living and loving faith. But this contribution on man's part, as his own "meritorious" act, depends wholly on God's free, loving decision to admit and receive, assess and value man's being and act within his own divine "milieu", which is of an altogether higher order. This "milieu" is, admittedly, "exterior" to the simple created "nature", because infinitely transcending it; but, once opened up to and shared by the creature, it sanctifies him inwardly and makes him bear fruit in acts and thoughts which, though originating from God's freely-given love, are his very own fruits and works.

If this divine plan to exalt and ennoble the creature is the crown of the providential design of the Creator, it is understandable that the simple "nature" of the creature stands in relation to this decree as clay to the potter's hands (Is. XLV. 9; Jer. XVIII. 6; Ecclus. XXXIII. 13; Rom. IX. 21 ff.). It is still uncertain what ultimate meaning and value will be given to it before God; man's existence will still fluctuate expectantly, till its final, supernatural meaning and purpose is accorded to it, indicated and imposed out of the freedom of God's word of grace. Man's nature necessarily retains something of this fluctuating expectancy, inasmuch as its final meaning and purpose surpass his natural powers and vision, and in consequence faith appears and is experienced again and again as the unexpected, neither derived from, nor rooted in, his nature. The natural man, as a spiritual creature, is impelled to know himself, to understand and estimate his worth. But these basic spiritual acts, this entry into himself, do not immune him in self-sufficiency. What they presuppose is the clay in God's hands; they must remain open and prepared for God's judgments which may prove to be quite different. As God judges me, so I am. *Cogitor, judicor*: *ergo sum*. The creature originates from the unfathomable freedom of God; its being takes its rise from the loving look with which God chose it. This is made known to us in time by the fact that God calls and justifies us, and final fulfilment is reached with the sovereign act of judgment in which God receives the creature out of time into his own eternity, there to "glorify" it. Certainly, in this judgment, the whole conduct, both good and bad, of the life lived will also have its say and enter into the reckoning; but this conduct will not be decisive taken in isolation (otherwise no creature could sustain the judgment), but only as inserted into the very Word of God, which is his Son. It is in the Son that man is predestinated and elected. In the Son he is called and justified; in the Son, to whom all judgment is committed, he is judged and glorified.

Salvation, however, with all that it comprises, derives from the Father as Creator. It is he who, in creating man's nature, prescribes and bestows its final end. He did so out of love, not from necessity or mere justice, as though the greatness and dignity of the created spiritual nature demanded such an end. It was for this supreme work of love that he delivered up his eternal Son, so as to elevate our nature in accord with its heavenly end. This he accomplished in the Person of him who, as God and man, binds heaven to earth, and whom he sent "in the likeness of sinful flesh", in whose flesh he "condemned sin" (Rom. VIII. 3). Henceforth, the "counsel" of the Father is revealed in its full breadth. "For whom he foreknew he also predestinated to be made conformable to the image of his Son, that he might be the first born amongst many brethren. And whom he predestinated, them he also called; And whom he called, them he also justified. And whom he justified, them he also glorified" (Rom. VII. 29-30). So the life of the believer is one single utterance of praise to the Father, whose sons we have become in Jesus Christ. "Blessed be the God and Father of our Lord Jesus Christ, who hath blessed us with spiritual blessings in heavenly places in Christ. As he chose us in him before the foundation of the world that we should be holy and unspotted in his sight, in charity. Who hath predestinated us unto the adoption of children through Jesus Christ unto himself, according to the purpose of his will, unto the praise of the glory of his grace" (Eph. I. 3-6).

Our praise, gratitude and worship do not spring solely from our existence—though we can never thank God enough for it; our existence itself was only given to us because of a thought in God's mind prior even to that of our existence—"Before the foundation of the world". Indeed, our whole being is immersed in the ocean of the Father's love, who creates nature and its laws to act as a foil to set off his miracles. When we contemplate the word of God, we must let ourselves be gripped by this primary truth, namely, that the whole compact mass of created being and essence and the everyday world we are so familiar with sails like a ship over the fathomless depths of a wholly different element, the only one that is absolute and determining, the boundless love of the Father. We must try to experience the freedom of this love, not merely the freedom which is the opposite of necessity, the contingent nature of our own existence, but that more profound, wholly new and other freedom that corresponds to the "free good pleasure" of the Father. And so we, his creatures, are reckoned his intimates, and by his free decision we are reckoned, from this very beginning, as his "sons", intimates and "co-heirs" of his Son. This follows, according to a logic, a system of thought and reckoning, whose inner coherence, exactness and justice comprise and presuppose grace and all its accompaniments, a logic which applies even to the most formal elements of the grammar of God's language.

Once we have suspected or felt the mystery of our existence, the necessity of prayer and, especially, of contemplative listening in prayer, becomes evident. For the relation between God and creature is now seen to depend on the marvel of God's incomprehensible love, and shows him, in setting up this relation, as the Lover absolutely. Then the creature itself is seen as a sustained utterance of prayer; and man only needs to know, in some degree, what he really is, to break spontaneously into prayer. That is what is meant by the use of "blessed" and "blessing" at the beginning of the epistle to the Ephesians quoted above : "Blessed be the God, and Father of our Lord Jesus Christ, who has blessed us (endowed us with grace) with spiritual blessings in Christ". This twofold blessing—in prayer, and in the gift of grace—which constitutes the essence of the relationship between God and man, becomes clearly evident in the incarnation of the Word of the Father. He appeared in the sign of blessing—Mary is the "blessed" purely and simply

(Luke I. 42); the Messias makes a symbolic entrance into Sion as the "blessed" (Matt. XXI. 9; Luke XIX. 38), and, with him, the whole kingdom of God : "Blessed is the kingdom coming to us" is the cry of the people meeting him—and his departure is in the sign of blessing, answered by the corresponding blessing on the part of engraced man : "Lifting up his hands, he blessed them. And it came to pass while he blessed them he departed from them, and was carried up to heaven. And they adoring went back into Jerusalem with great joy. And they were always in the temple, praising and blessing God" (Luke XXIV. 50-53). The Son is sent "to bless you" (Acts III. 26). He is the Father's subsistent word of grace and prayer sent to the world, and he makes possible the words of prayer with which the world answers.

Since our existence is based on this "blessing", there is really no necessity for any special way or endeavour to pass from nature to the supernatural. We have, in fact, already received the *parrhesia* from God—another key-word in the language of revelation. Originally it meant the privilege of free speech belonging to full citizenship and so came to mean the right "to say all" and, the corresponding interior attitude—the "franchise" of the word, but also "openness to the truth", whereby the truth itself contains the element of openness and free self-giving on the part of the thing known. In Scripture, however, what is primarily disclosed is God himself who, emerging from his invisibility and remoteness, "shines forth" (as Psalm LXXIX. 2 says, using the word, *parrhesia*). Not only does he become accessible, but as Proverbs I. 20 says, using the same expression, as Wisdom, he "preacheth abroad, uttereth his voice in the streets; at the head of multitudes crieth out, in the entrance of the gates of the city uttereth his words".

The word, *parrhesia,*—derived from "*pan*" (all) and "*rhe*" (the root of "to speak") and signifying omnipotence of utterance—when used of God, is related to the key words "parousia" and "epiphany" (manifesting, shining forth from hiddenness), and to "splendour", "glorification" (*doxa*), all of which indicate the manifestation of the glories of the divine essence and activity hitherto veiled (in the remoteness of the Father, in the Son's form of a servant). But the parrhesia of God only becomes comprehensible to us in the parrhesia given by him to us, the elect and redeemed, raised to the status of citizens of heaven. This signifies a free, unconstrained, unabashed and quite fearless quality in our filial approach to the Father, a complete confidence and naturalness in one who has an innate right to stand before him and speak to him, to look him in the face without apprehension;—the very opposite of the cringing attitude encouraged by an absolute ruler only to be approached with servile or obsequious manners, a strict and formal ceremonial and a prescribed pattern of address. The door stands wide open, and invites God's children to enter, wherever they may happen to be. Man himself is not the door, but Christ, the Son of the Father and his own Word. For he has become man's brother and neighbour; and, when he invites and introduces men to the Father, he introduces them as his play-fellows, informally, or rather as his own brothers in the flesh. "Father, I will that where I am they also whom thou hast given me may be with me, that they may see my glory which thou hast given me, because thou hast loved me before the creation of the world" (John XVII. 24). "In that day you will ask in my name; and say not to you that I will ask the Father for you, for the Father himself loveth you" (John XVI. 26).

The manifestation of God's truth, love and life to man is but the counterpart of the election, calling, justification and glorification of man by God. Viewed in that perspective, it is the tremendous gift of grace to men of "good will". Christ bore our reproach on the cross, the reproach we could never of ourselves expiate of our want of love towards God and man, wholly unfitting us to live in the company of the eternal Love. All the attempts we might make to remedy this unfitness by "works" would be of no avail; God himself had to purify us in the blood of his Son and endow us with a clear conscience and "confidence to enter the sanctuary" (Heb. X. 19). Peace with God in a good conscience is a gift of grace

so incomprehensible—since it overturns all the laws of ethics—
that man is completely ignorant how it comes about. He ought
really, as things are, to have a permanently bad conscience; his
own heart is his accuser. But more powerful than all reproaches
is the defence of our "advocate with the Father, Jesus Christ the
Just" (1 John II. 1); and as a result, our own psychological and
ethical disquiet cannot prevail against the profound peace which
is given us in the grace of God. "In this we know that we are of
the truth and in his sight shall persuade our hearts. For if our
heart reprehend us, God is greater than our heart and knoweth
all things" (1 John III. 19-20). This wonderful discovery is no
licence to go on sinning; on the contrary, it is a most pressing
invitation now, at last, to love. Yet this love, any more than the
parrhesia given to us, is no longer seen as the fruit of our own
effort; for it is the acceptance of life freely given, the abiding in
the place to which man has been raised by grace, the garnering
of the riches spread before his eyes.

Thus *parrhesia* is one with prayer. The way to the Father is
open and so is the heart of man (in the sense of "good conscience");
the way between them is open, and that way is prayer. Prayer
rests on the assurance that we speak to a God ever ready and attentive to hear us. "We have confidence (parrhesia) towards God,
and whatsoever we ask we shall receive of him (1 John III. 21-22).
"This is the confidence (parrhesia) we have towards him: that
whatsoever we shall ask according to his will, he heareth us. And
we know that he heareth us, whatsoever we ask; we know that we
have the petitions which we request of him" (1 John V. 14-15).
Parrhesia is the intimacy that comes from love, the right which
love gives to share in all the other's goods.

We can now see the twofold presupposition—objective and subjective—of hearing the word, of Christian contemplation: the
divine truth must be open to man, and man's heart and mind
open to God. The latter is grounded in the former, and for that
reason parrhesia is something imparted to man, given in advance,
something objective. "Which house are we, if we hold fast the

confidence (parrhesia) and glory of hope unto the end"
(Heb. III. 6). St. Paul regards God's openness to us as the word
of God personally uttered, as the countenance of Jesus Christ,
which is the manifestation, the image, the splendour of the
Father, hidden indeed, but now disclosed to the world. His exposition of the parrhesia, in 2 Cor. III. 12—IV. 6, illuminates the
recesses of the Christian mystery. Moses, after beholding the
majesty of God on Sinai, veiled his face which reflected that
majesty, when he came down from the mountain; in the Old
Testament the objective revelation is always veiled, and so is the
heart of the people receiving it. The parrhesia was still lacking
to the Spirit of God and liberty. But "we all beholding the glory
of the Lord with open face are transformed into the same image
from glory to glory, as by the Spirit of the Lord"; as Christians,
we are given the property of "openness", of resplendency un-
concealed, before the rest of our fellow-men and the world.

Christian preaching really means the parrhesia of God's word
in Christians directed to the world, principally through the
apostolic office and function. "We renounce the hidden things of
dishonesty, not walking in craftiness, nor adultering the word of
God; but by manifestation of the truth; commending ourselves to
every man's conscience in the sight of God. And if our gospel is also
hid, it is hid to those who are lost in whom the God of this world
hath blinded the minds of unbelievers that the light of the gospel
of the glory of Christ, who is the image of God, should not shine
unto them. God who commanded the light to shine out of darkness hath shined in our hearts, to give the light of the knowledge
of the glory of God in the face of Christ Jesus". Thus St. Paul's
contemplation is itself part and parcel of his action, just as the
light on Moses's countenance, as he came down from the mountain, attested and reflected his speaking with God. Looking on the
open light of God—and the light is Christ, the Word and Image
of the Father—the Christian himself becomes open, and light,
not, however, to make himself known, but to preach "Jesus Christ
our Lord, and ourselves as your servants through Jesus".

There we see the whole of Christianity presented as "parrhesia", and St. John confirms St. Paul when he speaks of Christ referring to the descent of the Holy Ghost who was to explain and make clear all the mysterious sayings and parables uttered by him on earth (John XVI. 25 ff.; XVI. 13), and again when he describes this, clarifying and explaining it, like St. Paul, as an effect of the glory of Christ, indeed as the glory itself.

It is, of course, true that the contemplation of "the glory of the Lord with face unveiled" remains in the darkness of faith, "for we walk by faith and not by sight" (2 Cor. V. 7), and "hope for that which we see not" (Rom. VIII. 25); and at the second coming of Christ, our "seeing" will be "face to face" when "I shall know even as I am known" (1 Cor. XIII. 12). Yet, in the contemplation of faith, what is believed, hoped for and loved is already present. For, by faith and baptism, we are dead to sinful nature, buried with Christ in his death, risen with him in his resurrection, borne up to heaven in his ascension, where we await with him his re-appearance so as to appear ourselves with him. St. Paul's doctrine (Rom. VI. 5 ff.; Eph. II. 5 ff.; Col. III. 1-4) is no mere figure of speech, but expresses the very essence of grace. By grace, indeed, heaven is opened up to us, given to us in such wise that we are at liberty to lead our life on earth in the strength of the eternal life yet to come, but already present, to live by its power and its truth now at our disposal. Moreover, it is our duty so to live in gratitude for the grace received.

There is therefore no question of any personal certainty of salvation. Man can turn away from God again, and neglect to give his life the "splendour" of the open manifestation of Christ; and that would show that his contemplation of Christ's splendour was not serious and lasting. Yet that is no reason for watering down all that the word of God declares about the openness of the eternal world of the Father to those who believe, or for only seeing the openness in the future, as something promised and spiritual, rather than present, accomplished and incarnate. We are not to think of ourselves as merely striving to live in this light and so to rise from the natural to the supernatural, from earthly to heavenly things, but as already living and loving by it—living in the world of nature by grace from which all derives, loving, in the light of heaven already opened, the earth bathed in its splendour. This the believer is well able to do, since in fact, he must do so.

2. Its foundation in the Son.

Fundamentally, what makes us capable of the contemplative faith which hears and sees is grace as election, calling, justification by God the Father. From it we derive the power and liberty to contemplate the truth open to us.

The manifestation of the truth of the Father is the Son. In him the Father beheld us from eternity and was well pleased. In him the Father predestined and chose us to be his sons, joint-sons with his one eternal Son, who, from the beginning of the world, pledges himself for his estranged creatures. In him the Father justifies us, for he views and values us in the light of his Son's justice that pays our debts in full; this justice he reckons ours and gives it to us to be our own. Finally, it is in him that the Father glorifies us by making us participate in his resurrection, setting us by grace at his right hand, the natural place of his Son.

In the Son, then, heaven lies open to the world. The commerce between heaven and earth, the ways of descent and ascent, are made possible by him, principally by his incarnation (John I. 51). To those who contemplate in prayer, this assumes two forms, seemingly incompatible, in reality complementary : it seems as if the infinite riches of God were focused on a single point, the humanity of Christ, but so that in him alone lie hid "all the treasures of the wisdom and knowledge of God", "all the fulness of the Godhead dwells corporeally", for in him is found the eternally-loved Son whom the Father's voice expressly designates, saying : "Hear ye him". Here, too, in the "fulness of time, all that is in heaven and on the earth will be recapitulated in the Head, which is Christ"; and all the ways leading from heaven meet at the one "door" through which all must pass to reach the Father; all the ways, too, which throughout history have led to the centre, whether signed and posted as in Judaism, or overgrown and half concealed as in paganism.

The fact that all the ways to God and all the relations of men to God without exception are orientated towards the one Mediator may seem to us, particularly to those who practise contemplative prayer, an extreme violation of the liberty, dignity and independence of the individual. Indeed, it is bound to seem so, so long as the contemplative fails to perceive that the oneness of the Mediator (I Tim. II. 5) is set up by God himself as the counterpart of the oneness of God the Father. All that proceeds from the one mediator necessarily bears the stamp of unity which turns us to the Father, a unity, that is universal and integrating and, therefore, catholic—"One body and one Spirit, as you are called in one hope of your calling. One Lord, one faith, one baptism. One God, and Father of all, who is above all, and through all, and in us all" (Eph. IV. 4-6).

But, at this point, the pattern is inverted. The point on which everything is focused is no longer the Son on earth, but the Father in heaven, to whom the Son, raised up, directs all things, bearing them along with him. Henceforth, it is not only the whole immensity of created things that is orientated to the Father through the Son, but the infinitely greater fulness of riches the Son brings from heaven and spreads out before the eyes of man as treasures of eternity. These, however, by their very multiplicity and complexity, may well perplex the contemplative with his thirst for unity, recollection and vision in depth. His perplexity may grow when faced with the varied aspects of the Church and its history, dogmas and institutions, definitions and pronouncements. Together they form a kind of barbed fence which makes it hard for the contemplative to find God, precisely because nowhere outside the Catholic Church is there such strict insistence on literal formulas and their binding character; nowhere is it so difficult to see through and pass beyond the finite, concrete form to the infinity of God, which is what the contemplative seeks.

But this is precisely where Christ in his twofold movement—coming from and going to the Father—comes to our help and makes contemplative prayer possible.[1] For, in taking flesh, he brought the riches of heaven down to earth, spread out the fulness of the indivisible unity of God in a multiplicity of aspects in time and space, expressing it in terms of human existence with all its changes, its growth and striving, its activities, in its living and dying, expressing it too in a variety of formulas and concepts, images and judgments. Were it not for this, no other form of contemplation would be possible than that of a negative mysticism, seeking to reach contact with God beyond all that pertains to the world, with God as the wholly Other, beyond the range of our thought, vision and understanding; a form which entails of necessity a profound and wrongful disparagement of the world and all creation.

Natural mysticism and religion, which starts from man and is directed towards God, is an *eros* whose impulse is to take flight from and transcend utterly the things of the world—necessarily, indeed, and inculpably so. But in its desire to reach beyond the things that point the way to God, only seeing them as that which is not God, it is in constant danger of losing the two, both the world and God as well—the world, because it is not God, and God because he is not the world, who without the aid of the things of the world which mirror him, can only be experienced as absolute void, *nirvana*. Christ, however, returns from the world accessible to our senses and mind to the Father, and for the first time, opens the true way to contemplation. He does not abrogate the images and concepts which tell of the Father, which he first devised when a man living among men. On the contrary—and this is the great theme of Pauline theology—he transposes them from the earthly, literal, level to the heavenly, spiritual level, from the sphere of prophecy to that of fulfilment; and we who die, rise again and

---

[1] This will be discussed in detail in Part III on the tensions inherent in contemplation; it only calls for mention here.

are carried to heaven with him, are empowered by his movement from the world to the Father to accomplish with him the transformation of the old world into a new, spiritual and divine one.

No mystic of the negative theology has ever traversed the "dark night of the senses and the mind", which is the way to the Absolute so completely as Christ in the terrible desolation of the cross, in which not only the world sank away before his dying eyes, but God himself withdrew and abandoned him. Neither has anyone experienced the movement from appearances to reality in more blessed fashion than he did in his ascension from the world to the Father, transcending all that is ephemeral and passing over into the eternal. But this death of his was no turning from the creature to gain God; it was God's rejection of all in the world that was not willed by God and did not conform to him. Nor was the ascension a turning away from the world, whether from indifference or revulsion, to possess God alone; it was a beneficent departure with a promise of return before long, a departure to prepare a place with the Father to be occupied by men and the world as a whole, changed, indeed, and purified, but not repudiated or destroyed. And as a sign of his fidelity to the world, Christ, in leaving it, promised to send the Holy Ghost from heaven, who, now that the Son's contemplation is finally perfected, is to sow its fruits in the hearts of those who believe.

What, then, makes contemplation possible is not a mere dialectic or synthesis of its two constituent factors. Their union is, indeed, extremely difficult or even impossble for the natural man to achieve; though he may well be able to deduce it from the very idea of what contemplation is and from his own aptitudes, and so to postulate it as his own idea. (Hence the mythologies which represent God in concrete forms taken from the visible world, and the subsequent dissolving of these forms, these images of God in legend and art, in an ascending movement of thought—in Buddhism, Plotinus, Porphyry, etc.). Were this all, Christ would be seen simply as the perfect man perfecting others, bringing all the strivings inherent in human nature to fulfilment. That, however, is not the core of belief in Christ, but rather that the two movements—the concretising of God in the created world, and the carrying up of this whole world back to God—are brought about in the *Person* of the Son, the Person who *is*, from eternity, the Word of the Father and, also, the primary idea *wherein* the entire world was conceived and realised. Thus in representing the Father in concrete form, we can never for a moment leave the Son out of account. As he is the eternally beloved of the Father, so is he sent and authentically accredited by the Father; in contemplating him, we see the Father, and no way that passes him by can lead us to the Father. The inclusion of the world in God cannot be effected except through him who was the primary idea before the creation, and on whose account the world as a whole and in all its parts appears as it is and not otherwise. For "in him were all things created in heaven and on earth", "all things were created by him and in him; and he is before all, and by him all things consist."

Yet he is the primary idea "before the world" only because he was already, from all eternity, "the image of the invisible God", the first begotten of God. As such, he is fitted, not only to mirror the infinity of God in the finite world, and to include the finite in the infinite, but also to bring about the transformation of the old world into the new, of death into resurrection, in a drama which is his exclusively, the drama of his own death and resurrection. "In whom we have redemption through his blood, the remission of sins. . . . In him it hath well pleased the Father that all fulness should dwell, and through him to reconcile all things unto himself, making peace through the blood of his cross, both as to the things that are on earth and the things, that are in heaven" (Col. I. 14-20). This drama, in which God's design for the world is realised, in which all the individual meanings contained in nature and the human world are accomplished—that is, in that mode of transcendence we spoke of above—this drama is an act and a manifestation of pure and absolute love, of God's love, and therefore of an eternal and boundless love. But this love, far from being a universally pervading medium in which everything dissolves in a vague emotionalism, is shown in a clearly delineated figure, occupying a definite place in history (in no other way can the personality of the Father appear in the world), taking visible form in distinct words, acts, sufferings and miracles. Consequently every beginning of love that reaches out from the world towards God must let itself be transformed and integrated into the drama of this unique, distinct Person, so as, in him, to penetrate to heaven itself (Heb. IX. 25)—that is to say, to be delivered from the dim colourlessness of all that is merely of this world, and take on a splendour of its own, worthy to stand alongside that of God himself.

Certainly this would be quite impossible, were Christ a mere man, for then he would always be the "other", a more perfect man than the rest of us but still on the same level of being. But, since he is also Son and Word of God, he has the power to incorporate us as his "members", to integrate our finite personalities—without destroying or even lessening them—into the life of his infinite personality. Existence in the Son, as members of his mystical body, is, therefore, far more than a simple possibility of access to God based on "merit", even though the merit be infinite. It is, rather, this very access itself, because it brings to completion the whole drama of reconciliation in both head and members at the same time. "For it became him for whom are all things and by whom are all things, who had brought many children into glory, to perfect the author of their salvation by his passion. For both he that sanctifieth and they who are sanctified are all of one. For which cause he is not ashamed to call them brethren. . . . We are made partakers of Christ" (Heb. II. 10-11; III. 14).

The question, how can we hear the word of God? is now answered. We can, because we are in the Word of God; because the Word that was made flesh takes us up into himself, and gives us a mode of existence. It is no mere "supernatural elevation" of a vague, general nature that is imparted to us by grace, but a share in the personal existence of the eternal Word of God. He became "flesh" like us, that we might become "spirit" in him; and, for

47

that reason, he "is able to help us" to attain our "heavenly vocation", because he "has become in all things like his brethren"
(Heb. II. 17—III. 1). The grace the Father gives us has a Christlike character; it assimilates us to the Son without doing violence
to our human nature, because the Son himself has become man.
In the one Person of Christ, the election, calling and justification
of the individual man is likewise personal. In other words, the
Father's grace offered to him and received has a uniqueness deriving from and stamped with the uniqueness of the Son, and this
unique character is divine and supernatural as well as human and
natural, since it proceeds from the grace of the God-man, and is
given in view of it. This character is, on the one hand, made to
man's measure, and, on the other, has a "form" that is sonlike and,
as such, wordlike. "Form" is a word used for want of a better to
express that mysterious reality which is the ideal archetypal image,
in Christ, of the redeemed and believing man, and, therefore, also
his true individual self, according to which the Father now looks
upon and appraises him, and by which he, as a believer, is summoned to live. By believing, he enters upon this his own "Christ-
self"; St. Paul calls this "putting on Christ" (Rom. XIII. 14;
Gal. III. 27), "putting on the new man" (Eph. IV. 24; Col.
III. 10). It is this he has in mind, when he says: "Put you on,
therefore, as the elect of God, the bowels of mercy, benignity,
humility, modesty, patience.... As the Lord hath forgiven you,
so do you also.... Let the peace of Christ rejoice in your hearts,
wherein also you are called in one body.... Let the word of Christ
dwell in you abundantly" (Col. III. 12-16).

This "form" of the Christian—which is, at one and the same
time, a pure grace of the Father, his membership of the mystical
body of Christ, in fact the man himself taken in his entirety, though
in the context of redemption—this form may be called his
"mission". To this he should constantly apply all his natural
capacities, so that in this surrender to God's service he may find
his own supreme fulfilment as a person in a manner surpassing
his natural and imperfect potentialities. It is through this that his

nature is unfailingly possessed of powers exceeding those proper to it, and so enabled to become truly fruitful. In it, too, man finally (in faith) comes to an understanding of himself, since the mission itself has a Christlike form, a form corresponding to the word or logos. The man obedient to his mission fulfils his own being, although he could never find this archetype and ideal of himself by penetrating to the deepest centre of his nature, his super-ego or his subconscious, or by scrutinising his own dispositions, aspirations, talents and potentialities. Simon, the fisherman, before his meeting with Christ, however thoroughly he might have searched within himself, could not possibly have found a trace of Peter. Yet the form "Peter", the particular mission reserved for him alone, which till then lay hid in the secret of Christ's soul and, at the moment of this encounter, was delivered over to him sternly and imperatively—was to be the fulfilment of all that, in Simon, would have sought vainly for a form ultimately valid in the eyes of God and for eternity. In the form "Peter" Simon was made capable of understanding the word of Christ, because the form itself issued from the word and was conjoined with it. Whenever Simon follows the light of "Simon", his own self, he will always be wrong and dangerously so; he only acts truly when he "takes no heed to flesh and blood", but is obedient to his mission, through which he knows the Father's will.

Once we see this, we must admit the possibility of a real hearing of the word, and so of contemplation. The necessary pre-condition is that we be able to see in Christ two aspects—to see him as the "other" man, the Thou within history, on whom we "fix our gaze" (Heb. III. 1; XII, 2), and to whom we surrender ourselves in love; and also as the Son and Word of God, who is no finite Thou marked off in contradistinction to us, but the origin and ground in which our whole being with all its roots is fixed, from which it draws its sustenance and derives all its best and characteristic features. Here the trinitarian background of faith is fully evident—we are rooted in the Son analogously to the way in which the Son is rooted in the Father. "I in them and thou in me"

(John XVII. 23). Thus our Christian life proceeds always from the Word, as it always proceeds from grace, since "Word" and "grace" are simply two aspects of the one revelation of God in Christ. Whoever has God's word addressed to him has received the offer of this grace; or, rather, he is enveloped by it, he is ever confronted by the word, and this is the case even with the man who declines it, who is unwilling to believe the word—he is nevertheless marked out by grace. The person who contemplates has not to strive laboriously to enter a region wholly alien to him, alien, that is, in so far as God's word is not of this world, and so can never be discovered in the categories and ordinary rules of human reason; in a profound, supernatural sense, he enters into himself. He realises that archetypal sense wherein our "being in the world" is ever embedded with grace, and against which the sinner rebels, which he stifles and "detains" within himself (Rom. I. 18). And as, in contemplation, man turns back to the truth of his existence—not his own truth, indeed, but God's—he comes to live, in faith, by this truth. He is able to do so only because he has been given the ability. He does not need, as would one living by the rules of ethics, to think out how he can bring the (unreal) realm of values into the realm of actuality, or whence he can derive the strength so to do; for he draws on the fulness of God's power, in which he is embedded and "rooted". The question is not how he will come to realise the good by his own efforts, but how he will realise himself by the power of the Good and in accordance with the law of his own reality already there.

Seen in this light, the Christian life is the reversal of all forms of natural ethics, and contemplation helps us to *realise* this reversal and is necessary to it. Contemplation, indeed, is itself subject to the law of reversal; for, while approaching the word and seeking to understand it (*credo ut intelligam*), it derives from a previous, original hearing and understanding of the word (*intelligo ut credam*), even if this first understanding were no more than the creature's repose in being understood by God. The absolute amazement of nature at hearing a single word of God—whether a teaching or a miracle of Christ, in action or suffering—our nature's striving to adjust itself to this unheard-of thing and to live accordingly, all depends upon an ultimate repose and assurance. In that and in no other way was the wonder of God to touch me; I had no claim to it, either as creature or as sinner, yet, from eternity, I was conceived in the mind of God that I might grasp this even "older", eternal word of love, which, though pure grace, is more interior to me than I to myself, more reasonable than my own reason, so that the act of obedience in faith is more truly reasonable than the most reasonable act could be. In this were not the case, such obedience would be a prison in which human reason and freedom ought never to be confined; it would be what Kant calls heteronomy. But the word of God is never something encountered empirically in the world around us (something "Ontic", in Heidegger's sense), something *a posteriori*, for which a resultant and equally empirical *a priori* entity, a corresponding faculty of perception, needs to be postulated. On the contrary, the act of faith is man's acknowledgement and agreement that he has been, from time immemorial, encased in the love of the God revealed to him, and this faith comprises everything in the historical sphere that the believer encounters *a posteriori* as "facts of revelation".

It is not, however, as if these facts, centred on the incarnation of the Son, were in any way derivative or secondary compared with an all-embracing inner grace. The two are strictly complementary and neither is thinkable apart from the other. Both are necessary modes of manifestation of the one, free and sovereign occurrence of the divine self-revelation; for, in the mere concept of the creature, it is impossible to find the fact or the exigence of such a revelation, or even any presumption of it. Christ appears in the centre of history as a personality confronting me in a manner wholly free, fully contingent. He is always to me the sign most actively opposed to the constant tendency of my philosophical reason to deduce my religion from my own inner self. He shows me continually that the Christ of the heart, the "inner teacher" (St. Augustine), God's interior truth that enlightens me, is something

fundamentally other than the "depths of my soul", than my archetypes and profoundest categories, classifications and ideals. Not-
withstanding the efforts of rationalists, the truth of the facts
vouched for by Scripture and tradition is not to be assessed by the
measure of reason; it makes us ever aware that the act of reason
must have, as its indispensable accompaniment, an attitude of
prayer and adoration. The rationalism of the Enlightenment
(Lessing and the rest) issued necessarily in pantheism (the German
idealists) where prayer had no place and contemplation was de-
graded to an inventory of reason's possessions.

If we avoid this error, and preserve a sense that all things have
been thought, loved and created in the Word of God, then the
whole world, within and about us, becomes necessarily an associated object of contemplative prayer. Christ, indeed, is not to be
seen in isolation, in abstraction from world-history; he is only to
be understood as the summit of an entire history of salvation—
Adam, Noah and Abraham—which continues in the Church and
the world up to the end of time. And just as he cannot be detached
from the world he came to redeem, neither can the world be considered apart from him, for in him it has its "subsistence", and,
therefore, also its explanation and justification. But the contemplative Christian's view of the world and history must never be
detached from the Christian responsibility for the world already
implicit in the very origins of the act of faith. "The expectation of
the creature waiteth for the revelation of the sons of God"
(Rom. VIII. 19). Since, and in so far as, we, who enjoy the grace
of sonship, respond rightly in our loving and living to the summons of the Word, the Son, so the whole meaning of the creation
shines forth resplendently, and every creature, through the intermediary of believing man, receives an "apocalyptic" share in the
truth as revealed.

Certainly, the Christian may make the laws of nature and of
history an object of his contemplation, and even consider them
as laws of ascending development towards freedom and the spirit;
but he must not succumb to the deceptive splendour of this vision,

and, instead of the word of God, unconsciously take the words of created nature as his object. Those who consider Christian contemplation outdated and turn to the values of the world to give them fresh force are victims of an illusion. Only "in Christ" do things attain their ultimate meaning and end, and whoever is to help them thereto must himself be "in Christ", striving his uttermost to achieve the supreme freedom—of the sons of God—which alone can raise things along with him into the sphere of freedom. If, where secular truth is concerned, it is man through his whole existence who gives a meaning to things, and so helps them to reach their secular truth, this is still more true in the region of faith. But his faith, if it is to be effective in the world, must be active in itself : it means altogether renouncing one's own particular truth and placing one's faith at God's disposition, however crucifying that may be for man in his natural and fallen state. Man to-day is more conscious than at any other time of his responsibility for creation as a whole, and so is liable to the temptation of seeing himself as God's steward over the world, as its final truth. For that reason, he needs unremitting contemplation of the word of God more than ever, in order to bring both himself and things to their true and final perspective.

There is one more thing to be said in this connection. Christ, as God made man, is the revealed truth both of God and of the world, nor can he be this otherwise than as the mighty Word upholding all things (Heb. I. 3). Consequently, all the rigidness and opposition, all the misleading and frustrating finitude of the particular truths we meet with, are dissolved in him as in the one Truth, and, being a divine Person, he can never be transcended. The Christian may even be tempted to envy other religions, and forms of contemplation, which are not bound, as he is—with no hope of change—to a definite group of finite words and formulas in a "Holy Scripture"—a definite group of statements, situations and events in sacred history, a definite set of propositions defined by Councils and Popes and to be accepted by faith as true, a seemingly finite world of truths round which he revolves. Even though he may come again and again on new and interesting combinations, he may seem, fundamentally, like a prisoner at his exercise, unable to escape. Thus a feeling of oppression may seep into his contemplation. Is not a Buddhist or a Taoist infinitely freer in his contemplation, above all more tranquil, since he can draw away from tiresome multiplicity into an all-embracing One, while the Christian can never get beyond the stage of concern with the manifold? He would seem to be wholly bound to the one Scripture (among so many other "sacred writings"), to the one Church (among so many other communities which sincerely seek salvation), indeed to the one Redeemer, who, however sublime and elevated, is nevertheless one among several others : in fact, though his historical influence has been immense, surely it must, according to the laws of history, one day be exhausted and make way for new and unexplored perspectives. Thus stated, the Christian attitude seems petrified in two ways. For it clings to certain historical occurrences held to be absolutely final, while at the same time subjecting them to a forced spiritualisation, so that they can be held absolutely valid in relation to the rest of history, including that of our own time, though only through a symbolic and prophetic interpretation.

This impression is bound to arise whenever we fail to make faith the basis of our living and thinking. The contemplative is constantly exposed to this danger but, in withstanding it, he fights his way back to this basis. What he has to do is to reflect composedly on all that he stands to gain from this apparent loss of spiritual freedom; for it offers him the power to resolve the isolated truths of nature and the supernatural, of the world, of history and the Church, in the breadth, the freedom, the mystery of a beloved Person, who, though human like us, is no finite person, but divine Love itself. The Someone, to whom all particular truths return as to their native dwelling-place, is no mere Other, whom we may one day tire of; he is the eternal Thou, who, for that very reason, spans the dreary barrier between me and the not-me, and is the support and protection of each individual person. Only thus can the contemplative movement in all non-Christian religions—the movement of self-sinking from the many into the One, from becoming into Being—be achieved; access to the One becomes possible without turning away from the manifold and the world. All becomes steeped in the perfume of the One, which, alternately appearing and vanishing, reveals itself in the Many—*currimus in odorem unguentorum tuorum.* But the truth which the eternal Son asserts himself to be is itself a truth of self-surrender, of transparency, a truth leading beyond itself in self-effacement; the Son, indeed, is the way to the Father. He is the perfume of the Father in the world. He is the Ultimate and, at the same time, he is not. He is absolute—as God—and, as absolute is relative; for, being the Son, he is a relation proceeding from the Father and returning to him.

3. Its foundation in the Holy Spirit.

Contemplation is also made possible for us through the Holy Spirit. All that has so far been said about grace applies to the communication of the Spirit in so far as he comes to us as one with divine grace, not only offered but accepted. It is the whole man (though, primarily, his spirit, his personality) that enters the sphere of the inner life of God ("partakers of the divine nature", "entrance . . . abundantly into the everlasting kingdom"—2 Peter I. 4, 11) and this is normally described as the gift of God's Spirit to the spirit of man; as the pouring of the divine Spirit of love into our hearts (Rom. V. 5), as the "sealing" of the inmost core of our spirit through the Spirit (Eph. I. 13). It follows that the sending of the Word of God (the Son) and the imparting of the Holy Spirit are but two phases of a single happening, in which divine life and truth are brought to man. Man is not to be raised to the true life apart from and against his own volition; he must both understand and desire it. But the one man who accepted to be ruled by God was the man who, on his entry into the world, was resolved to fulfil God's will (Heb. X. 5-7); as the new Adam, he is the origin and representative of every assent to cross and resurrection.

Before his death on the cross, the Spirit rested on Christ alone (John VII. 39), and where the believer was concerned he was "not yet given". The Spirit only "came" at the "last" self-giving of Christ (John XIII. 1) which was, at the same time, the gift of his flesh and blood, the communication of eternal life (John VI. 54), the gift of his life both temporal and eternal for and to his sheep (John X. 17, 28), the gift of his inmost (temporal and eternal) spirit (John XIX. 30), which was accomplished once again in the gift of the water and blood from his opened side (John XIX. 34). Spirit, water and blood thus bear a single, common "testimony" to the truth of our divine sonship (1 John V. 5-9). Thus the Word that the Father utters in the world and which is his Son is fulfilled in such a way that, in giving his life, he gives us his flesh and his Spirit, incorporates us in him, and draws us into the divine love of the Trinity through the two forms of his being as Word. When the risen Christ repeats the action of the Creator, and "breathes" on those who believe, this communication of his human and divine *pneuma* completes, in sensible form, his revelation as Word. It is the "sacramental" sign of what was, in principle, accomplished at Easter and was to become ecclesiological reality at Pentecost. It also assumes an eschatological form in the judgment on the antichrist whom "the Lord Jesus will kill with the spirit of his mouth" (2 Thess. II. 8).

The Son's ascension into heaven made the outpouring of the Spirit possible in all its forms. Christ's gift of his bodily and spiritual life to his own, reveals the incarnational aspect of the communication of the Spirit : we enter into the inner being of God through the wounded side of the Father's Son and Word. His whole life with his death was his self-revelation and self-giving to us, and it alone can teach us that the Spirit of God is the Spirit of love; there we are shown the extreme of self-giving, and there the Son proves his love in the outpouring of his blood, the immolation of his flesh. Transcending the bounds of finite life, the Son

returns to the Father, with whom, from eternity, he breathes out
the one Spirit in mutual exchange, and the outward sign of the
Son's return to the Father is, in accordance with his promise, the
Spirit sent at Pentecost. The withdrawal of the sensible form
"frees" the Spirit, and the ascension is the consummation of
Christ's death. Borne aloft (*raptus*—Apoc. XII. 5) to the right
hand of the Father, the Son's glorified humanity participates in
the eternal "expiration" of the Holy Spirit, and the fruit of that
outpouring of the Spirit is Christ's mystical body on earth.

At this point, the relationship alters again. Hitherto it was the
Son, the Word, who breathed forth the Spirit, and was seen as
Lord of the Spirit (2 Cor. III. 18), indeed as "Spirit" himself;
for, by contrast with all finite, earthly and "fleshly" words, the
eternal Word of God holds within himself the depths, the vital
power and strength of the Spirit of God (2 Cor. III. 17; John
VI. 63). And so the Son, having fulfilled his work on earth,
breathes upon us and sends us forth to the Father. Then we can
see that the grace communicated to us by the Father was already
"Spirit", not merely a new act superadded to the creative action
of the Father, but an opening out of his inner divine life. Moreover, we should not look on this as a participation "first" in the
Son's generation from the Father, and "then" in the breathing
out of the Spirit from both, but always as a participation in the
entire Trinitarian life eternally completed in the Holy Spirit. In
this way, we are brought through the Spirit of grace into the
mystery of divine sonship, and we may even follow those theologians who say that we share by grace in the Son's generation
from the Father. In this sense we may say that the Spirit, as proceeding from the Father, becomes manifest in the history of salvation before the Son himself : in the Old Testament, as the Spirit
of God; given to the prophets and poured out in the whole of
creation, as Wisdom; and in the New Testament, as the Holy
Spirit coming down on the Virgin Mary to bring to her the Word
and make this Word flesh, and finally, "Spirit" once more.

The Holy Spirit is already present at the very outset of the revelation of the Word—"God has sent the Spirit of his Son into our hearts" (Gal. IV. 6). He alone can bring about the entry of God's Word into mankind, into history and nature; and so only in the Spirit can man receive, contemplate and understand the Word. For every real encounter with the Word presupposes a whole-hearted assent and acceptance on the part of man, and the assent on the part of Mary became, through her initial state of harmony with the Spirit and his descent on her, the source of the Incarnation of the Word. It was in the Spirit that she uttered her consent, an utterance that is the source of all Christian contemplation; it made her pregnant with the Word, made her treasure up all the words and ponder them in her heart (Luke II. 19, 51). Now, for the first time, it becomes clear why the Word uttered and given us by the Father is capable of being understood, not only on the human, but on the divine level, and indeed is a Word awaited in faith and unfolding itself there as in a resting-place already prepared. It is because the Spirit that brought us the Son from the Father had already ensured that our hearts were disposed to receive him. The feminine, marial element in faith is a complete openness and readiness for the "divine seed" that is to come, and it is also the contemplative element implanted deeply by the Holy Spirit in every act of faith.

Through the gift of faith we are taught the truth concerning the Son by the Holy Spirit. The background of this teaching consists of an omniscience already given with grace, and, as such, it is incapable of any complement or addition, for it is the presence of the omniscient Spirit (his "unction"—1 John II. 27). But the Spirit leads us by degrees into the depths, already opened up, of the truth of God present within us, and this by explaining, interpreting, incorporating Christ's revealed words in the heart of the believer. The Spirit alone knows "the inner things of God", and "searches all, even the deep things of God", but in principle, he has revealed these depths to "those who are spiritual", the "spiritual men" who "possess the Spirit of Christ". They have access to these things and, with them, to all the mysteries which "eye has not seen nor ear heard"; and, for that reason, no one who has not received the Spirit "can understand because it is spiritually examined" (1 Cor.II. 10-16).

The depths of the Godhead are opened to those endowed with grace, and they are also made capable of scrutinising them in the Spirit—"we have received the Spirit that is of God, that we may know the things that are given us from God" (1 Cor. II. 12). What the prophets and evangelists, St. Paul and St. John, declare to us is, indeed, the word of God, but the word as understood by them and for which they take responsibility—"my speech and my preaching was not in the persuasive words of human wisdom, but in showing of the Spirit and power; that your faith might not stand on the wisdom of men, but on the power of God"; "we speak wisdom among the perfect ... the wisdom of God in a mystery, a wisdom which is hidden, which God ordained before the world, unto our glory" (1 Cor. II. 2-16). And, paradoxically, it is precisely this basic revelation of the "depths of the riches of the wisdom and of the knowledge of God" by the Holy Spirit that makes the contemplative cry out in wonder and adoration : "how unspeakable are his judgments, how unsearchable his ways" (Rom. XI. 33); it disposes him to be more and more profoundly and humbly "taught of God" (John VI. 45) and to be led by the Spirit whose guidance continues throughout eternity.

Contemplation must always be a renewed "hearing" of what "the Spirit speaks to the Church" (Apoc. II. 7; etc.), a new hearing of what he unfolds inwardly to the contemplative mind in its own spirit of faith as member of the Church. These two forms of the Spirit's action are not wholly coincident, but are intimately connected and interpenetrating. The Spirit *"speaks"*, principally as the prophetic Spirit of Old and New Testament prophecy, when he draws forth and explains new and unsuspected elements from the depths of Christ's revelation, by means of the charismata given to individuals for the sake of the community; whereas he principally *"understands"* when he explains, assimilates and incorporates within the hearts of men the prophetic element in Scripture, Tradition and the life of the Church. The "mysticism" of interior contemplation, considered as the unfolding of the gifts of the Holy Spirit in the faculties of the soul raised to the supernatural is based, consequently, on prophecy, and can itself take on a prophetic, that is a charismatic and missionary, character in the Church. And in view of the mutual dependence and interpenetration of the prophetic and the mystical elements it is idle to set off the charismata and the gifts against one another, and to assign their order of priority.

Every word of God is set in a framework bounded by Spirit and spirit; the Holy Spirit of the prophets and the Incarnation carries the word from the Father to men, and it is the same Spirit that interprets its spiritual and divine meaning in the souls of men, so bringing man's spirit back to the Father by means of the word. For that reason, no interpretation that is purely earthly of this world (what St. Paul calls *sarx,* "flesh") can lead to the Spirit, still less may the Christian seek to perfect in the flesh what he had perforce begun in the Spirit (Gal. III. 3). The true Spirit of God is always recognisable in that he brings and interprets to us the Incarnate Word—"every spirit which confesseth that Jesus Christ is come in the flesh is of God; and every spirit that dissolveth Jesus is not of God" (1 John IV. 2). Everything, then, depends on this, that the Word should be recognised as coming from the divine Spirit, but assuming real flesh (this is what St. John most emphasises); and then, as going from his mortal state to that of his resurrection, ascension and the sending of the Holy Ghost, in which state he has become spiritualised and only to be comprehended in the Spirit of God—and this is the aspect emphasised by St. Paul.

Thus, the Spirit who leads us into all truth is at once Christological and Trinitarian; for he brought about the incarnation of the Word, and his will is that, in this, Christ should be believed and acknowledged as a divine Person, inseparable from the Father and the Spirit. Finally, through him the Son's return to the father issues in his becoming the Head and life-giving source of the

Church, in the outpouring of his life in the sacraments, Scripture, the liturgy and preaching, and in the whole of Christian living. Thus the Holy Spirit is always and inevitably bound up with the Church—the spirit of unity in the supreme degree (Eph. IV; I Cor. XII). Apart from these relationships the Spirit of God is never present in prayer and contemplation. Whatever depths be reached by human contemplation, if they are not, explicitly or implicitly, bound up with the life of the Trinity, the God-man and the Church, they are either illusory altogether or diabolic.

As we have already seen in speaking of the Word, the action of the Spirit does not make for multiplicity, but rather draws all multiplicity into unity. As spirit, he stands in sharpest contrast to the very principle of the material, literal world. He is, in God, the expression of the unity and the uniting of Father and Son, whose "spirit" is shown forth in their common and single spiration as itself one, equal, divine and personal. The mysteries of the Spirit are, to the human mind, absolute paradoxes of a unity which does not abolish differences—neither between the divine Persons nor those between God and creatures—but utilises them to create forms of unity that are far more subtle than any conceived by monists, pantheists or idealists. Non-christian mysticism and contemplation almost always aim at a speedy and experimental realising of unity, but the unification that the Spirit effects and is then experienced in Christian contemplation is on an infinitely higher and more wonderful plane. For the Spirit, as the absolute, free and divine subjectivity, is able to take to itself created subjectivity and to inform, indwell and inflame it so long as is needed for it to blossom out, through the medium of the divine Spirit, into a mode of being, in acts and states, of which not even the rudiments were present in created being.

The qualitative difference between the Christian revelation, and so of Christian contemplation, and all other possible forms of religion and contemplation then becomes evident. Outside Christianity, whenever the idea of an infinite I indwelling in the finite I is seriously pursued, it inevitably leads to pantheism; the transition from a finite (empirical) I to the absolute, of necessity becomes a kind of blessed self-annihilation (cf. Fichte). In the Christian setting, on the contrary, an indwelling of the kind can be fully accepted without any dissolution of the finite personality; rather, it fulfils itself in a most mysterious way by being raised above itself to God. Here too there is a "mystical" death of love, but it is, at the same time, a real, indeed bodily, resurrection in God. Such an indwelling by the Spirit of God presupposes the mystery of the Trinity in its fullest sense, the wonderful mutual indwelling (*circumincessio*) of the divine Persons without any infringement of their individual personality. And since all the profound mysteries of Christian contemplation centre on the indwelling of the Holy Ghost in the soul, it is evident that the very possibility of Christian contemplation rests on the doctrine of the Trinity.

The mysteries we speak of are not merely of the domain of theory and theology, but preeminently of the practical order. It is by no means a matter of indifference, in regard to the acts performed in contemplation, whether I consider myself as seeking in isolation, though admittedly aided by the grace of God, to gain some understanding of the mysteries of revelation, or whether I am certain, through faith, that my faltering attempts are reinforced by the indwelling wisdom of the Holy Spirit, certain too that my act of adoration, petition and thanksgiving is supported and informed by his own infinite and eternal act, and that this is all the effect of that ineffable union that has already raised up all human action and existence and steeped it in the stream of eternal life and love. Our human frailty and ignorance are always, in our living faith, compensated by divine omnipotence and omniscience, and it is essential to the contemplative act of faith to hold on to this. "We know not what we should pray for as we ought, but the Spirit himself asketh for us with unspeakable groanings; and he that searcheth the hearts knoweth what the Spirit desireth; because he asketh for the saints according to God" (Rom. VIII. 26-27). The Spirit is not just by our side or above us, but truly within us, calling the Father, who "searches the heart" and hears him.

The Christian is never to think that this indwelling allows him, in quietistic fashion, to cease his own supplication so that the Spirit alone may pray in him. This is never suggested by Scripture insisting, as it does, on "prayer in the Spirit" (Eph. VI. 18; Jude. 20), which with its own particular force and personality is borne up on high by the all-encompassing action of the personal Spirit. This activity on the part of man might well be called passivity in so far as its surrender to the Spirit gives preponderance to the latter, just as inner learning in the Spirit takes the form of attention to his inspirations and illuminations. Yet this passivity under grace must never be confused with a purely natural "laissez-faire"; in fact, the intensified fervour due to the presence of the Spirit gives powerful impetus to the created soul. The action of the Spirit in pointing the way, stirring her heart, thinking, willing and praying in unison with the soul, springs from the inmost core of the soul's life; and, by this action, which as a general rule is not directed to the Spirit himself (whose primary aim is the glorification of the Father and the Son), the contemplative is placed in the closest intimacy with divine truth.

Man in prayer does not merely come into the presence of the truth and contemplate it as an object; he lives, as St. John loves to repeat, "in the truth" itself (John XVII. 17, 19; 1 John II. 21; 2 John III. 4; 3 John IV), he "stands in the truth" (John VIII. 44), he comes "from the truth" (John XVIII. 37; 1 John III. 19). On that account, there is a direct connection between "Spirit and truth" (John IV. 23-24); the Spirit is the "spirit of truth" (John XIV. 17; XV. 26; 1 John IV. 6). To pray in the truth does not mean to begin by viewing it in a kind of detached way, as if we were first, by reflection, to convince ourselves that the Word of God we are actually contemplating is the truth, and then to assent to it on that ground. It means, rather, to set out from the affirmation of it as something already given long ago, and to give up and reject whatever in us militates against it. It is to live in the knowledge that the truth, which is the Spirit dwelling in us, is more interior to us than we are to ourselves, since, in God and in his truth, we were predestined and chosen, before the foundation of the world, before our own creation, to be his children, pure and unstained. Consequently, whatever in us disaccords with this is but a later encroachment in opposition to our real truth, and so an internal contradiction which cancels itself.

The only analogy nature seems to offer to this intimacy with the divine truth is the union of the sexes, though the analogy holds only if we omit the time-interval between the union of the two persons in one flesh and its result in the birth of a child. So from the union between man in the state of grace and the Holy Spirit there issues a fruit of incomparable richness, in which it is impossible to distinguish what comes from man and what from God. The "fruits" of the Spirit in the soul opened out to him are the newly created dispositions and acts resulting from the union of God's life with man's, fruits which, when fully matured, leave the place of their nurture, the branch which bore them, and begin a new life, a life in the Church and as part of it. St. Paul, after enumerating the fruits of the Spirit, continues: "if we live in the Spirit, let us walk in the Spirit" (Gal. V. 22 ff.), and then adds admonitions on love between members of the Church. The essential thing is that the origin of this fecundation is the ineffable embrace between God's Spirit and man's, in which the latter experiences, in faith, the real nature of the divine wisdom (which is one with love), experiences so strongly the Spirit invading and possessing him that his response and self-giving follow spontaneously. This response is not "ecstasy", in the sense of violent enthusiasm or a transcending and a rejecting of one's one created reality in order to live outside oneself in God; these two elements may indeed be present, but they are not the core of the experience. Rather, it is primarily adoration of the infinite holiness of God present in the soul, and this adoration implicitly contains assent to being wholly possessed by God for his own purposes; it is "ecstasy", indeed, but the ecstasy of service, not of enthusiasm.

Intimacy with the Spirit of truth does away with that objective attitude to the truth which views it impartially from the outside, passing judgment upon it, and substitutes one that can only be described as an attitude of prayer. It is one of total prayer, in which seeing and self-directing to what is seen, receiving and self-giving, contemplating and going out from self, are all present indistinguishably at the very core. No other attitude to the eternal truth is in accordance with reality or truly objective; even the speculative, theoretical standpoint adopted in faith, theology and the Christian life generally, necessary as it is, derives from this, and so shares in its character. It is true that reflection on divine truth spurs on the believer to renewed prayer and that, normally, acts of the will, such as self-giving, love and confidence, follow on the insights gained by the understanding. Yet it is still true that the understanding could gain no contact with this truth, without some rudimentary, inchoate "experience" of its divine quality, and so from an implicit attitude of prayer. This attitude alone is what impels man to concern himself with divine truth on his own account and to communicate it to others.

As regards the truths of this world, an attitude which stands apart and judges (with proper humility and receptivity) is perfectly appropriate; but the Christian must always bear in mind that the things of this world have their place in the order of salvation, and therefore are not to be considered and dealt with apart from the truths perceived in prayer. "Every creation of God is good . . . it is sanctified by the word of God and prayer" (1 Tim. IV. 4-5). For this reason, contemplation of the Word which sanctifies is necessary, if we are to use God's creatures for God's purpose. And our use of them, however much it may require the full play of our human faculties, must proceed "from the truth" and "in the truth", and so take place in a setting of constant, habitual prayer, in an attitude of reverence and adoration before that divine truth in which all worldly truths, even the most profane, are rooted. That is why St. Paul urges us to pray without ceasing (1 Thess. V. 25; etc.).

Whoever is conscious of the presence, at the centre of his being, of the ever active stream of God's truth and love is impelled to turn back to it again and again to purify, renew, tranquillise himself there. He knows that he can shoulder the burden of his Christian responsibility for the world without danger only so long as he is inwardly, and in relation to God, a child unreservedly open to the Word of the Spirit, living in intimate contact with the pure spiritual food and in the experience of "the goodness of the Lord" (1 Peter II. 2-3), one who has "tasted the heavenly gift, made partaker of the Holy Ghost, tasted the good word of God" (Heb. VI. 4-5). Whoever is to testify to others the truths of the Gospel can do so only if he possesses within him the continuous testimony of the Holy Ghost. "The Spirit giveth testimony to our spirit that we are the sons of God" (Rom. VIII. 16). "It is the Spirit that testifieth that Christ is the truth . . . He that believeth in the Son of God hath the testimony of God in himself. . . . This is the testimony that God hath given to us eternal life, and this life is in his Son" (1 John V. 6, 10-11). Thus the Spirit appears as the herald of the divine life in man which makes its own presence manifest. This life is the Son given us by the Father, and the truth of this life is the Holy Spirit, who both proclaims it and causes us to know it (he is the "communication"—2 Cor. XIII. 13). We are not to regard this witness as a second Word of God, but as the most express form of the Father's own revelation of the Word; for, when the Son's course is finished, the Father breathes out his own and the Son's Spirit into the spirit of his children. The Spirit is the implanting in the soul of the Word, the seed of the Father. In this consists the testimony of the Spirit, the final condition that makes contemplation possible.

We have now seen what makes contemplation possible, in so far as it is prepared by God—by the Father, who predestines, chooses and accepts us as his sons; by the Son, who makes known to us the Father, and gives him to us in his self-giving unto death and the Eucharistic mystery; by the Spirit, who brings and makes known to our soul the divine life.

But there still remain other conditions to be considered. The contemplative is not an isolated individual. He is a member of a community constituted by the hearing of the Word, a community which has the Son's assurance that it hears aright, that it hears even in every failure to hear. Whoever belongs to it can, ultimately, never have failed to hear, never have failed to see what is of decisive importance for him. Contemplation, therefore, is always a repetition in the individual of an act that has already been accomplished in the Church. It is never, even when it takes place in the "chamber" spoken of in the Sermon on the Mount, an act cutting man off from his associates, but one which brings him ever anew into the centre of the Church and its life.

CHAPTER III

THE MEDIATION OF THE CHURCH

NOWHERE IN the Christian life is the believer more an individual than in contemplative prayer. In the performance of the liturgy he is a member of the community; he joins with others in the same words of thanksgiving, petition and adoration. In his private vocal prayer too, he makes use of formulas, or at any rate forms, taken from the prayer of the Church. But in contemplation he is intent on hearing an utterance of God never given before. He is "this" person, and none other, whom God now addresses : he is at the temple gate receiving what is given him; spiritually blind and lame, he wants to be healed; a disciple listening to the Master. He must really desire to be "the individual", and not try, through fear of personal contact, to shelter behind the anonymity of a member of the Church. The wonder of this form of prayer is that it can and should offer the same personal contact with the Lord as men had during his life on earth; so that Scripture or any other medium of grace—such as a prayer from the liturgy, a saying or example of some saint or lover of God, or created nature as pointing to Christ—becomes as real a medium of communication as the air transmitting the voice of the Son of man to the ears of those who heard him.

None the less, this medium belongs to the Church, the community. Grace, which empowers us to be hearers of the Word, is always given in and through the community; it is, indeed, God's love, but the incarnate God's, whose will it is to do nothing otherwise than in communion with his brethren. So, without impairing the fulness of personality on both sides, the community is an essential factor in God's Word and in the hearer of it—in the Word which is authentically spoken only in the setting of the guiding function of the Church, the bride of Christ; in the hearer, especially the hearer in spirit, whose perceptions are sure, clear and free from error only when he is in union and community with the original hearer of the word, the infallible Church. In the Church the two sides are closely intermingled, and that makes her the medium between the word and the individual who hears it. The Church being the original, authorised hearer of the word, in its full sense, is the authentic interpreter of it to the individual. Two factors in the Church must always be held in mind together. The first is that she is the original contemplative who sits at the Lord's feet and listens to him, and as virgin and mother opens her heart to receive and bear the seed of the word; she does not possess the word as something stored away, but received it in contemplation from the very outset—in the full assent of Mary and of all who comprise the living Church, and co-operate by their prayer, faith, hope and love, to form, feed and sustain the essential source of her life. The second factor is that she receives in her inmost being, as a nuptial gift of the Incarnation, the assurance of her eternal, unfailing fidelity; and it is on this account that she is a mediator enabling the individual, who has no such assurance, to hear rightly. The institutional Church herself depends on prayer in love, but the Church's prayer, likewise, depends on the institutional Church.

The Church's inner spring of life is the prayer of Mary and of all who pray in sincerity and obedience; and so the word of God, when it comes to the isolated person praying as part of the Church, comes attended, as it were, with an innumerable host of others praying with him. The word that comes to me now is the same before which innumerable others have bowed the knee, which they have heard with all their heart, which had the power to perfect them, to convert them, to remake their lives. The Lord promised to appear, when he came again, in the clouds of heaven, surrounded by the angels and saints. It is in this company that he comes now in prayer. And just as there is a Church that descends together with the Word, so there is a Church that ascends to meet him (1 Thess. IV. 17); and both together make up the one *Catholica*.

This social aspect is already indicated in many parts of the Old Testament, where the hearer of the word is, at one and the same time, the individual and the people as a whole. Normally, it is the individual within the people, although, by way of emphasising the symbolic and representative character of the messianic people, there are also individual hearers outside it. There is always a particular individual at the origin of the community which is to be the "hearer"; God did not choose a "collective", but a man who heard the word with his whole life, and made him the "father of the believers", and of him a people more numerous than the sands of the sea. This was exemplified in his covenant with Noah, and more explicitly in the case of Abraham. And then, when his offspring and his people had multiplied, those who are sent to it to speak in God's name are always men who have previously heard the word as individuals, men who, like Moses and Ezechiel, have had to pass through the school of solitude to prove their capacity to be hearers. But these solitaries, though often groaning under the burden of the word and their task of proclaiming it to a stiff-necked and recalcitrant people, despite their longing for an ordinary life, never think of dissociating themselves from the people and its destiny. No one ever becomes a hearer of the word for his own personal benefit; he is always aware that the end in view is a common obedience to it, and that in preaching the word to the people he shares responsibility for the way they respond. No doubt, God expressly exempted Ezechiel from such responsibility, when he pointed out the limits of human endeavour and the freedom of each hearer to align himself with the word or to refuse it. The prophet is sent to those who, it is known beforehand, will refuse to hear: "for all the house of Israel are of a hard forehead and an obstinate heart". None the less, the messenger has to oppose their obstinacy with all his might and is steeled by God for this purpose—"Behold I have made thy face stronger than their faces, and thy forehead harder than their foreheads. I have made thy face like adamant and like flint" (Ez. III. 7-8). The prophet commits himself irrevocably to proclaiming the word in truth; ultimately no one but the hearer can be responsible for its acceptance.

But the hearer of the message can rarely be identified as a particular individual and is more often an element in the people, which is divided into those who hear and those who do not. The source of the decision is only indirectly perceptible, as a function—it cannot be measured statistically, for it is dependent on the incalculable power of faith—a function within the assent or the refusal of the people. It is the consciousness each man has that he has to answer, not as an individual, but as a member of the community, that gives him his dignity as a hearer of the historical and social revelation of God.

It is therefore a misconception of the nature of contemplation in its New Testament phase to regard the individual and not the people of God as the hearer. This tendency is evident in Protestantism, even in its best representatives, like Kierkegaard. For it is as part of the people of God that the individual Christian exists in the first place, and the individual who prays does so as one of them. Recent developments in the theology of contemplation, have emphasised the social element in the act of contemplation. St. Athanasius was fully aware that the lonely struggles of St. Antony, the father of the monastic life, were of decisive importance both for his spiritual sons and for the whole of Christendom; and Origen thought likewise as regards the true theologian, who hears and rightly understands the word of God, and his own spiritual conflicts. These struggles were fought out in solitude for the sake of the people of God. Yet the Greek idea of contemplation—*monos pros monon,* alone before the alone—prevailed for centuries over the social aspect. Intercession for others was certainly acknowledged, as was the fruitfulness of action proceeding from a contemplation in itself barren; but it was not so clearly seen that

71

the act of Mary of Bethany in simply hearing and adoring was at least as fruitful for the Church as a whole as the activity of Martha.

In the Middle Ages it was realised, from time to time, that the contemplative has a function analogous to that of the Mother of Christ, inasmuch as he receives the seed of the word into his soul and gives it birth, thus discharging a function in the Church though it may not be easy to elucidate. But the social aspect of contemplation only became prominent in our own day, in the theology of St. Teresa of Lisieux, among others, who saw in the ecclesial function of the contemplative as in the action of the priest and the sacraments and preaching, the mainspring of the whole life of the Church. St. Paul's conception of the part played by the different members of the mystical body does not in fact allow us to be content with the rather superficial idea that the prayer of the contemplative possesses a special "merit", applicable to the rest of the body. The contemplative act, consisting, as it does, of a loving reception of the Word into the soul, is fundamentally one with the act of Mary the Virgin-Mother and the Church, herself too virgin and mother; and so it has a far deeper meaning than the one just indicated. The contemplative, in fact, participates mysteriously in the very being of the Church, and so in that essential action of hers which reaches out to all her members without restriction, animating them by faith, hope and charity. It is the mystical, "Marial", element in the Church which distinguishes it from the people of God in the Old Testament; and this, together with the social factor in the hearing of the Word, indicates the essential function of the hearer as productive of the Church, the bride and bearer of the Word. What the contemplative, in his solitary encounter with the Word, comes to grasp and understand is incorporated with the understanding of the Church. All that he, in his contemplation, adores in so far as he understands something of the unfathomable mystery of the Word received, and all that he leaves unprobed out of respect and awe before the mystery, enters as a living element into the Church's own adoration, and thus instils in others the desire and practice of prayer. No doubt, these effects, owing to their widespread distribution, escape exact detection. Contemplatives are like great subterranean rivers, which, on occasion, break out into springs at unexpected points, or reveal their presence only by the plants they feed from below.

From the ecclesial element present in the individual's solitary act of contemplation there follow various consequences of importance for the contemplative. He cannot look upon himself as marked out to receive the Word mainly as a result of his own characteristics and aspirations. He must make way within himself for a sense of the interests and needs of the Church as a whole. They may concern him personally only slightly or interest him only remotely; the subjects to which his attention is directed will be of importance either for the Church in general or for someone to whom he may communicate the outcome later on, in the course of conversation or some other form of contact. This aspect is of particular moment as regards the contemplation of the priest or the layman called to the apostolate. It is an attitude which will always lead him to ask himself what, on this matter, is spoken to the Church as such, what it is that the Church as such has to elicit from it. There is no call for the individual to be discouraged by this necessity, or to sink his personality altogether; on the contrary, it should rouse him to broaden its scope to the fullest extent, make himself fully objective in his outlook, and generalise his own particular situation, and so allow the Word in the Church the greatest possible effectiveness. Even if he has to forego subjects which appeal to him more and apply himself to things and their implications that have greater objective importance, though uncongenial to his mind, he is by no means the loser; in fact he stands to gain much; for the newly opened-up regions may well turn out to be those he will subsequently most delight to explore and abide in.

Owing to the ecclesial factor in contemplation, it may often happen that the contemplative may be given insights, and experience difficulties and trials, not intended for him personally, but for persons unknown to him, whether accustomed or not to the practice of prayer. Or again it may be for the sake of a definite individual, who is helped by the contemplative assuming a burden intended for him. This may be something borne by the contemplative which the other ought by rights to endure as a punishment, and that as a result he can accept with alacrity and joy; or some particular spiritual experience or insight accepted and endured by the contemplative on another's behalf, to whom the fruit is communicated by a kind of spiritual osmosis made possible by their union in the Church.

The contemplative, for his part, gains, from his bond with the Church, a discipline and firmness in all he does which he would never receive apart from it. From her perfect acquiescence within the ecclesial setting Mary too derived a certain simplicity and directness which well became her as the partner of the Word of God, so precise in his action, and as the archetype of the Church. The vague and indefinite character which, outside the Church, is held to attach to contemplation, and which is probably inevitable in any kind of general interpretation of the symbols and signs of the world, is quite out of place in the mutual contact of the heavenly bridegroom and his bride, the Church. The Church has to correspond with her bridegroom, and she is enabled to do so in virtue of the word spoken to her. The individual too has to correspond in the same way, but from within the Church. He must receive his Communion at the time when Communion is being given, and have finished his examination of conscience and acts of contrition, when his turn comes to confess. He may not (which is no disadvantage) take up much of his director's time with his own problems, to the detriment of the community. And just as his way of life is formed by the practices of the community as ratified by the Church, so is his spirit formed by the preaching he hears, the doctrines he believes, and his constant readiness to accept inwardly any new decisions of the teaching authority.

The Christian enters on contemplation tempered by this discipline. In this field, too, the Church expects of him something definite, something duly accomplished in the ecclesial setting, even if this is mainly a docility in following every inflection of the word and inspiration of the Spirit. When Mary sat at Christ's feet, listening to his words, she was not indulging in a kind of lassitude or an agreeable reverie. Nor was she intent on acquiring ideas that suited her, that she thought herself capable of evaluating, ideas of the kind she might expect to pass off, later, as her own in conversation with others. She was wholly alert and receptive to the word, prepared to give herself to it fully, without preferences of her own, without picking and choosing or making conditions. Her disposition was one of calmness and recollection, prepared to adapt itself to whatever was required, observing the slightest sign given by the Master, and following him in his greatest designs.

The Church does not insist that the beginner in contemplation should already possess a perfect mastery of it in its ecclesial aspect. She allows him, as in the period of the novitiate and of his formation, some years of apprenticeship. But even then she insists on supervising the practice of each individual, to see that he makes proper use of the time allotted and to find out if he has acquired the requisite breadth of outlook, a real contact with the divine Word, a sufficiently deep sense of worship, an awareness of his function in the Church as a whole. And the individual, for his part, has, in the appropriate degree, to submit his contemplative practice to the maternal control of the Church; it is under her gaze that he will pursue his contemplation, the better to learn how to see as she sees. All contemplatives have to act in this way, not only religious and priests. Everyone is exposed to the danger either of not taking a wide enough view at the outset, or of allowing it to be narrowed with the years, and of sinking into a routine he finds more or less satisfying and agreeable. The Church it is who opens up God's immensity and guides men into it. Her direction is acknowledged to be necessary when God calls anyone to the mystical way, but particularly so when he has to tread an entirely personal road, on which the confessor or director cannot follow him, except in very rare instances. But the fact is, as we have already said, that mystical prayer is simply experimental knowledge of the same mysteries of faith that the ordinary person of prayer lives in the darkness of faith; for everyone baptised into the Church, whatever his own stage of development, shares in the mysterious, intimate nuptial union between bride and bridegroom. Consequently, even for the ordinary contemplative in simple faith, the direction of the Church, who is the bride, is indispensable. The mysteries belong to him only because they first belong to the Church; and he can only receive and understand them in faith because the Church has received them beforehand and understood them by her docility and willingness to hear.

At this point, another consideration arises. The Church communicating with the Word of God is the one, sole bride of Christ, and, therefore, is essentially solitary. She has but one interlocutor, namely God; nor, in her intercourse with him, is there any other partner, such as the rest of mankind, who have not the faith. They can be the subject of the dialogue, but they take no part in it themselves. The exalted state of isolation above all other beings, in which the meeting of the bridegroom and the bride takes place, is a manifestation of the divine solitariness. There is nothing comparable with the divine essence, which infinitely surpasses all multiplicity, since what is multiple has always something with which it can be compared and shares a common foundation; and this "incomparability" is shown exteriorly in the exclusive character of the love which chooses some and not others. Love is not divided and distributed. "One is my dove, my perfect one, a garden enclosed, a fountain sealed up" (Cant. VI. 8; IV. 12). There is but one bride of Christ, and each and everyone who wills to share in the mystery of being the object of God's love must be of her and in her. Whoever is chosen to be loved by God is in the bride as a "part" of her, or rather as an incarnation of her, with the result that her unique mystery shines forth in the depths of the soul chosen and endowed with grace, the soul that believes and loves, and its truth becomes more and more luminous. For the Church is not just one person among others, nor a suprapersonal institution, what remains when we abstract the members from a community, namely its framework, laws and customs. Nor is she merely a kind of lifestream surging up from the roots into the branches; the analogy of natural organic life gives at most one, and that not the decisive, aspect of the Church's unity. The Church is a living unity formed through the imparting of the unique life of the Spirit of God *above, in* and *out of* the individual persons incorporated in her. It is a life which neither hems in nor threatens their uniqueness as creatures, but, on the contrary, makes them enter by grace into the uniqueness of God and so brings about their fulfilment. Whenever a man encounters God in faith and love, the divine uniqueness is reflected from the Word and falls upon him and he becomes a member of the one bride, the Church. No analogy in the natural order can adequately clarify this mystery. It has to be experienced and known of itself through the Church's life in the individual and the individual's own life in the Church.

Those in the Church who give themselves to prayer realise the need to withdraw into solitude in order to pray effectively. Psychologically this is essential if they are to meditate undisturbed by the feverish bustle of the modern world. Most suitable is the quiet of one's own room, undisturbed by the presence of others, where it is possible to adopt, in perfect freedom, the posture and attitude found most appropriate and conducive to progress, such as kneeling down or stretching out one's arms. Where that is not possible, the necessary quiet and solitude may be sought in some part of a church where no service is taking place. Only in exceptional cases should a room be chosen that is shared by others unless one is so accustomed to a particular person that his silent presence is not a source of distraction.

More important than exterior solitude is the consciousness of interior solitude, of that solitude within the Church's framework that we have described above. This kind of solitude does not consist in the individual foregoing his own personality and letting it become absorbed and dissolved in a total Truth, thinking so to find redemption. It is rather an alert presence and preparedness of the entire personality for the service in love of the mystery of the encounter between Christ and the Church, a mystery wholly surpassing his own nature. Now, at this moment, the complete solitude of my being before God is the place where this encounter is to be accomplished. Here and now, God, in his revelation, speaks, not to anyone at all, but to me. The love which chooses the elect casts its beam on me. For me Christ is born; for me he dies on the cross. It is to prepare a place for me that he ascends into heaven; and, to take me there, he will come again in glory. The contemplative must constantly stress and keep vividly before his mind this element of the here and now, and rule out any idea that he is simply one of a number of people all going in the same direction, who would advance just as well, perhaps better and less encumbered, without him. "Thou art the man", said the prophet to David, pointing at him. The Word of God in his solitary splendour within the turmoil of human history turns to me his countenance radiant in the vision of the Father, and speaks to me personally. As in all human love, only more so, I am entirely without concealment, I cannot hide behind anyone else; each time is the first and last, and the assent spoken in love has the freshness of the day of creation. Men smile at the illusions of lovers; they see through the love that seems to itself to be different from any other, ascribing it to a trick of nature; they have grown accustomed to the ways of love. The love of God permits no such interpretation; it is no roundabout way nature takes to gain her ends, but the direct way between the one God and his creature he here and now addresses. For whoever really desires it, grace has the power to restore him, at each moment of his life and commerce with God to this pristine freshness.

The person who knows himself called has to embolden himself to act the "role" of the Church (this is what the Fathers of the Church called *"personam Ecclesiae gerere"*). As he can never be this "person" himself, he must act in the consciousness of performing a purely vicarious service. The individual is merely the servant, the handmaid; the Church alone is bride and mistress. And since even the Church calls herself the servant of the Lord, the individual's status as servant is correspondingly lowered. Yet, however lowly, he has to perform this function; he must represent the "person" of the Church in his own person; servant as he is, he must take on the role of bride. And the Lord in his grace, we might almost say in his blindness, overlooks the difference, lets himself be deceived, and raises him from the ground as if to him was due the throne of the "one dove", the "bride without spot or wrinkle". It is, too, a part of the perfect service of the unworthy servant to be at the disposition of his Lord; not, indeed, in affecting modesty, retiring and protesting he has no such right; nor taking credit to himself and wanting to know better than the Lord; but, in a sentiment of profound awe, letting him prevail. "Be it done to me according to thy word" is the answer of the "handmaid" now standing in the place of the Church and, indeed, predestined to it from eternity.

The contemplative will have much to endure—his sudden precipitation into the very breast of God; the cataract of graces breaking, seemingly without reason, on his total unpreparedness; the solitude, at once terrible and blessed, into which, raised to be the chosen bride of Christ, he finds himself thrust without support, bereft of any analogy and standards of comparison to help him; destined to be mother of the eternal God, and, thus exposed before heaven and earth, answerable for all who dwell in them, conscious of his unshared, freely accepted responsibility. Perhaps it may only be for a moment, but a moment which only a miracle prevents from being mortal. Once it was Mary alone who was thus placed, and there was no one able to help her. For she was the archetype of the Church. But every contemplative must pass through something of the kind, at least once, when he has to swear fealty to the word of God, unconditional submission; but perhaps often, for the bridegroom bends down over the bride over and over again, just as he did the first time. Later, there follows the injunction to turn towards the community—"behold thy cousin Elizabeth". In the Church, solitude does not isolate one from the community, it is not loveless and heartless. God brings together those in solitude in various ways, in prayer and the apostolate, in ordinary life, in the liturgy, in work and family-life, in friendship and in contacts which, however fleeting, may bring strength for years. He brings them together, those solitaries who all bear in their lives the image of the Church, the virgin-mother, and in that image they know one another. They are in the bride, at the disposition of the bridegroom, whose seal they bear stamped on their whole life. The Church is not merely at their side, for they are within her, a part of her.

CHAPTER IV

THE REALITY OF CONTEMPLATION

1. Totality.

IN THIS chapter we are still concerned with contemplation as an act—leaving its content for later consideration. We have seen what is required for its possibility, and now we can examine the respective roles of the Church and the individual.

The individual prays as a part of the Church and his effort, however simple and humble, is indispensable.

It is not enough for him to "hear"; for if hearing does not lead to an active response to the word, he has not heard at all. It is not enough for him to let the Holy Spirit pray in the depths of his soul; he himself has to pray for, whether his prayer be vocal or contemplative, God awaits the act of the individual.

Never, perhaps, has St. Paul's saying been so apposite: we do not know how to pray. We live in a period spiritually arid; the images of the world that spoke of God have become obscure signs and enigmas, the words of Scripture are mauled by sceptics and rationalists, men's hearts, in this robot age, are crushed and over-ridden, and they no longer believe in contemplation. When people turn to prayer, they start from a feeling of hopelessness and futility; they drag along the ground and despair of ever rising. They are drawn to anything and everything negative, to doubt the existence of God, to withstand him to the face, perhaps to hate him for letting the world go on as it does, and because, exalted as he is, he feels no call to intervene; because secure in himself he abandons his children in the dark and anguish of a boundless universe, leaving them no other hope than nothingness, no other consolation than certain death. The temptation to

negation and despair is so great, it presses so heavily upon those
who still remain sensitive to the question of the meaning of life that
they need to use all their strength to go against the stream.

It is here that the thought of the Church at prayer comes to
the rescue. Prayer and contemplation are not just possibilities, but
realities in the Church. And between the great, unfailing prayer
of the Church and the hesitant, groping prayer of the individual
there is an unbreakable bond. There are millions of people in the
world who pray, but all their isolated prayers are gathered up into
the one, all-inclusive prayer of the Church, the bride, whose prayer
makes them all one with that of the head and representative of
mankind before the Father. The Church gives the individual's
contemplation not only form, but reality. There is one place in
God's creation where the world holds uninterrupted intercourse
with God : the place where, thanks to the power incessantly poured
out from on high, the earth opens itself to heaven, to the heaven
which holds itself open to the earth—and this is the eternal Son,
given to us by the Father, to lead creation back to the Father, as
the bridegroom brings home his bride. The earth is open to heaven
at the will of the bride who conforms to the love of her Lord and
adopts it as her law, taking the words "on earth as in heaven"
quite literally.

This simple fact is of the greatest significance. Assent to the will
of heaven is what we ask in the preceding petition, "thy kingdom
come". The Father's will is always luminous and transparent,
simple and easily understood by the upright of heart, and, at the
same time, immeasurably rich and overflowing, being the will of
the infinite God and likewise of all in heaven who will as he does;
they all share in the loving will of the Father that is to be realised
in the Church praying on earth. The individuals who pray too
often forget this in their contemplation. There are, of course, some,
the mystics, who are conscious of the presence of certain heavenly
figures—angels or saints, the Mother of God or the Son himself.
But apart from them, those who pray act as if alone in the presence
of God, of God in his solitude, as if they were always alone with

God, and had to put themselves in accord with his word and law. This is a false conception from both points of view. The individual contemplating in his room is not separated from the choir of the Church at prayer, but, as we shall show later, celebrates her liturgy in a different form, no less real and effective. In contemplating the divine word he does not encounter a word detached and abstracted, or isolated from the living fulness of those already existing in the kingdom of God to come. For since Christ, and through him the Trinity, is present to him so, if he wills, are all his brethren both living and dead, those in whom the Kingdom of God has actually come or is to come in the future. A community without number, to which he belongs, from which he can never be separated, has already realised what he is striving for and is approaching—namely full assent to the will of the Father. In this assent alone can his kingdom come. And all those who have heard and uttered this assent, and continue to hear and utter it—both in eternity and in time—are joined through him in the will of God. What was once an act of assent on earth, for example that of Our Lady at Nazareth or on Calvary, now fulfils the will of God in heaven and contributes to the kingdom of heaven; it can equally be a help to the contemplative, easing his task, and encouraging him, or sometimes perhaps an imperious demand. My own mother, perhaps, or some saint to whom I have a particular devotion, a friend now dead, a priest or nun, a martyr, may communicate with me through some passage in the Gospel, and may make me realise what is really at stake. We are accustomed to consider the "merits" of other people's prayers and sufferings in a purely generic and sacramental sense as the Church's "treasury of merits". We do not take enough account of how strongly the communion of saints intervenes in contemplation, in an entirely personal and individual manner.

It is this living kingdom of heaven that is concerned with the changing things of time and fosters all kinds of ideas, intentions and projects in the Church on earth. The truth of the kingdom of heaven is not set high above the earth like a firmament of stars, or Plato's eternal ideas; it is something personal, clearly defined, intensely alive; it confronts every situation as it arises afresh, and in a new fashion. Some quite precise task may be the will of heaven for me to-day; and if I feel this and act upon it, I increase the effectiveness of the kingdom of heaven in the world. The will of heaven cannot be conceived as though it were the will of earth. Heaven has very different views; what seems to us important is to it insignificant, and vice versa. What we avoid may, in its eyes, be useful, necessary; what we regard as central is to it peripheral; and what we fail altogether to discern is viewed by it, as the focal point of human life.

The contemplative is not required to take a general view of all these heavenly designs and their relationships, or to become an associate of Providence, and still less to assume its function, taking the reins in his hands and making important decisions. His role is quite different. What is demanded of him is that he should be supple and pliable in the hands of God, as clay in those of the potter. His love for God must take the form of obedience, the obedience of a bride, obedience as member of the Church, of the body to its head in heaven, to whose will and intimations he must be responsive at the slightest suggestion. Obedience does not desire to see, and so contemplation on earth is not primarily a matter of "vision". But neither is obedience mechanical; it results from understanding in love, and has to be one in sentiment with the will of the person commanding. The light and spiritual understanding given in contemplation make for a deeper penetration of the individual by the divine will.

The concept of the will, in this connection, is not to be taken in the sense of a faculty of the soul distinct from the intellect, as if the theology of contemplation propounded were a "voluntaristic" one. "Will", here, signifies that the heavenly, eternal world is one of intense life and spontaneous activity, that it puts forth power to achieve its purpose, and needs the prayer, the consent, the readiness of the Church and the believer, to attain them. "Be it done to me according to thy word" is an utterance that opens the sluice-gates of heaven, so that the "clouds may rain on the just one". "Thy will be done on earth as it is in heaven" is a wish, not that ensures that God's moral law is observed, but that opens up the world of time to the invasion of the whole reality of the kingdom of heaven. Christians often fail to understand that this reality is eternal and so does not belong to some future time, and that what we pray for, whose "coming" we implore, is not something as yet inexistent; they tend to think of it as a temporal value in the historical order, as though it could only participate in our present existence through our prayers and exertions. It is, on the contrary, the eternal reality which we, the ever unreal, must allow to pervade us with its own being and prevail. What is envisaged by contemplation is the eternal reality of the heavenly kingdom, which by its means becomes a reality in time, in the world and among men.

Catholic Action too, rightly understood, is based on this conception. We must not look on contemplation as concerned exclusively with the eternal, and action with the temporal; that would be to sunder what forms a single unity in Christ, and should become ever more so. Unfortunately this unity has always been insufficiently perceived in traditional spirituality and to-day, in the age of Catholic Action, is still not always seen as imperative. It is not we who build up God's kingdom on earth by our efforts, even when these are sustained by grace; all we can do by praying aright is to assure that the kingdom, both in ourselves and the world, deploys its power and activity to the full. Everything that we can bear witness to concerning the reality of God derives from contemplation : Christ, the Church and ourselves. But no one can proclaim the contemplation of Christ and the Church in an effective and lasting way, unless he himself participates in it. No one can speak meaningfully of love if he has never loved, or of the least problem of spirituality if he has never met with it personally. Nor can the Christian exert an effective apostolate, unless, like Peter, he announces what he has seen and heard. "We have not by following artificial fables made known to you the power and presence of our Lord Jesus Christ, but we were eye-witnesses of his greatness. For he received from God the Father, honour and glory, this voice coming down to him from the excellent glory. This is my beloved Son, in whom I am well pleased. Hear ye him. And this voice we heard brought from heaven, when we were with him on the holy mount ... whereunto you do well to attend" (2 Peter I. 16-19). But where do we find Thabor mentioned in the programmes of Catholic Action? And who speaks of seeing, hearing and touching what cannot be proclaimed or spread abroad by activity, however zealous, unless it has first been experimentally known? Is there any mention of the peace of eternity beyond all worldly strife, and of the utter weakness and helplessness of crucified Love, of love "emptied" even to nothingness, to becoming "sin" and a "curse", and from which all salvation flows to the Church and mankind? Those who have not experienced this through contemplation are always impeded in speaking and even acting in its regard by a certain embarrassment and feeling of guilt, though the feeling may be covered up in a buzz of activities which are mistakenly imagined to be spiritual.

At times, the Church's receptivity to the kingdom—the deep-lying mystery from which her fruitfulness derives—becomes manifest—for instance, in a saint, whose soul has gazed so long and deeply on the light of God that it has come to hold within itself an almost inexhaustible store of light and love, and so can offer lasting force and sustenance. There is no religious order that has not been born of contemplation and long exercised in it, whether its subsequent action continues to be contemplation or is of an apostolic and pastoral nature, or both together. But at a particular time in the past the entire kingdom of God, which was to flow out over the ages—for centuries, as in the work of St. Benedict—was comprised in the contemplation of its founder, as in a single seed. "The Order of Preachers is presented to us as the charity of St. Dominic spread out in space and time, his contemplation become visible" (Bernanos). Of course, this effect is not to be measured in human fashion, as if the founder and his perceptible action were great and powerful in proportion to the number of his spiritual offspring. Its fruitfulness lies in the quality of his mission, which, being charismatic, brings to light, at least partially, the hidden fruitfulness of all missions in the Church.

If we fail to see that the realisation of the kingdom on earth, which is the aim of the active life, is rooted in the act of contemplation; if we separate the two, and see in prayer at best a source of strength for action or a source of merit for its success, then both contemplation and action are deprived of something essential. As regards action, this is evident enough. As for contemplation, it comes to be seen primarily as repose from the fatigue of earthly concerns, or else as a gazing upon the things of eternity, truths and ideas that are good, true and beautiful whether they are realised on earth or not. Contemplation of that sort lacks the element of urgency, which derives, not from earthly needs (and so conducive to earthly activity), but from the very nature of the kingdom of heaven. For the kingdom is in process of "coming", it is "in travail", it breaks out and rushes in forcibly, as can be seen from the whole character of the Gospel, which, for that reason, is so charged with "power", and which—as we should see well enough, if we were not so familiar with it—breaks over our heads like an apocalyptic tempest. The gospel can indeed be interpreted as pure love and pure grace, but only appears such when viewed from afar, as with St. John who spoke of it thus in the remoteness of old age, or with St. Paul, who was not present at its proclamation. But the Church adapts herself to the tremendous, driving will of heaven to realise itself on earth and offers herself as the place where heaven and earth come together. Indeed, she is the very point of contact of the two, the point where earth becomes heaven (in the Church triumphant, especially in its members already risen), and heaven earth (in the sacraments, in the authoritative utterances of the Church and its hierarchy, but also in all the souls which, through the mediation of these, become participants in the kingdom). It is at this central point that the contemplative takes his stand.

2. Liturgy.

This enables us to see straightaway the connection between the
Church's liturgical prayer and contemplation, and to ensure that
the two are not separated in practice. The liturgy is the service
of prayer rendered by the Church to God, whereby, in utter self-
oblivion, she seeks only to glorify God in adoration, praise and
thanksgiving. These include the prayer of petition, which is an
acknowledgment of the void into which the splendour of grace
may pour itself, so that the effusion of grace is an inducement to
a renewal of praise, adoration and thanks. In this sacred service,
the Church has her gaze fixed on God; it is a service in the spirit,
one of insight and understanding (Rom. XII. 1): a contemplation
of the truth of God, and an opening out to his word which, with
the reception of the word, forms the chief act of the liturgy. From
this point of view the liturgy may be divided into two phases—reception of the Word as word, and reception of the Word as flesh.
The reception of the Word as word occurs in the first part of the
Mass, and is the preliminary to his reception in the flesh, from the
Offertory to the Communion.

The first part is common to both the Old and the New Testament, for the Word of God was already present in the Old in the
form of the word, but his object there was to promise his own
coming in the flesh, and to prepare men's hearts for that event.
In the New Testament this promise starts out from a fulfilment
already achieved and proceeds to a new fulfilment, but both together make up the whole promise of something to be fulfilled,
finally, for eternity. The dialogue with the angel that once took
place at Nazareth is continuously reenacted with the Church as a
whole—God, the Trinity, already present in the word spoken by
the angel, promises himself in the flesh, announces his coming,
seeks the consent of the virgin, who is to become mother, and
completes his revelation by the descent of the Holy Spirit, who
brings the Father's Son into the heart of the believer.

The important thing for us here is the act of contemplation contained in the liturgy. The word of God is spoken to the Church, and officially mediated by her to those who pray, in order to be understood. We have only to consider the origin of the word—how it was proclaimed to the people by the prophets in those highly dramatic settings in which the people understood only too well what was meant and what was demanded of them, but so often did not want to understand; or how the epistles of St. Paul were read to the communities with the imperative claim to be understood and followed in their entirety; or how, from the beginning, the psalms were used in prayer; or how the letters in the apocalypse were sent to particular Churches, to be received by them and observed with scrupulous accuracy—we have only to consider these to realise what is really meant and what we should expect in the Church's liturgy. The reading of the Epistle and Gospel is no mere recalling to memory of a word that was once effective, any more than the Eucharist that follows is a mere commemoration of a former real sacrifice. The Word speaks to the Church as he spoke formerly to the seven communities of the Apocalypse. In the Mass, then, contemplation forms an essential part, and the sermon, which should have no other aim than to explain and bring home the true nature and content of the word of God just presented, transforms the assembled community into a Church which hears the word : the Church contemplative. It has a double significance, being (together with the confession of sins in the *Confiteor*) a preparation for the Communion to be received, and, at the same time, itself a Communion, a real, interior reception of God's word in the soul made ready for it by faith.

This is still more evident when we recall the chief function of the Mass : to be a memorial of the Lord, not only of his passion and death, but, in association with them, of his whole being and life. "Do this in memory of me", he said—without restriction. The Church follows his injunction to remember him in the bread and wine so precisely, in her solemn prayer of the Canon, that she carries over the commandment given at the end of the recital of the institution into the subsequent prayer : "Wherefore, O Lord, we thy servants, as also thy holy people, mindful alike of the same Christ, thy Son, our Lord, of his blessed passion, his resurrection from hell, his glorious ascension into heaven". This moving remembrance in gratitude was, in former times, the entire content of the Canon—before, that is, the numerous prayers of offering and intercession were added—and still, in most of the Eastern liturgies, forms its principal part. There it flows uninterruptedly from the beginning of the Preface, and commemorates the entire redeeming action of God, thus giving it a new, spiritual and actual presence in the consciousness of the Church. We are to see it all as much more than a mere recalling of a past event in history; for, while the acts of God have a definite place in history, they are not limited in their effect, like other events subject to the laws of time, whose effect gradually fades. Heaven and earth may pass away, but these remain and retain their special place in the Church's faith, which keeps them perpetually alive by a commemoration constantly renewed. Indeed, the Church is herself a spiritual womb which, by what it holds and preserves, becomes fruitful, and, in the enactment of the Mass, approaches ever closer to her true nature, to the unity wrought by the Holy Spirit and indicated by the "in unitate Spiritus Sancti", at the end of the Canon—both in the eating of One Bread as participation of the Body of Christ (1 Cor. X. 17), and in the one remembrance and recalling of the redemption reenacted in the present.

That is our "reasonable service", on which the primitive liturgy laid such stress, setting it in triumphant contrast with all the material offerings and sacrifices both of Jews and pagans (cf. Heb. XIII. 9-15). The liturgy of St. Basil, for example, still uses, at the beginning of the Preface, the significant expression, "spiritual service of sacrifice"—the Roman Canon used the word "rationabilis" (cf. Rom. XII. 1)—making that the starting-point of the remembrance and praise of God the Father, of the Trinity, of the world of heaven resounding with the threefold *Sanctus,* of his condescension to the world of men; recalling too the seven days of creation, the state of paradise, the fall of man, the ordinances of the Old Testament; all leading up to the remembrance of the supreme act of the Father for mankind. Here is the passage :

"When the fulness of time was come, thou spoke to us in thy only-begotten Son, through whom thou created the ages. Since he is the splendour of thy glory and the image of thy substance, and bears up all things through the word of thy power, he thought it not robbery to be equal to thee, God and Father. But, eternal God though he is, he appeared on earth, associated with men, took flesh from a virgin, emptied himself ... to pass judgment on sin in his flesh through being himself subject to the law, so that they who die in Adam might live again in this thy Christ. . . . To fill all things with his being, he went down from the cross into the kingdom of death and tasted himself the pangs of death. On the third day he rose, and opened up in his flesh the way to resurrection from the dead. . . . To be our forerunner in all things, he returned up to heaven, and took his seat on the right hand of thy majesty on high. As a memorial of his saving passion he left us that which we have now offered according to his commandment. For, when he decided to go to his voluntary, ever-memorable and vivifying death, on the night when he gave himself for the salvation of the world he took bread into his holy and immaculate hands, offered it to thee, God and Father, gave thanks, blessed, sanctified and broke it, gave it to his holy disciples and apostles with the words : 'Take and eat, this is my body. . . '."

The epiclesis of the eastern liturgies rounds off the commemorative survey which takes in the entire indivisible history of salvation by recalling the descent of the Holy Spirit, whose work it is to keep the Church's memory alive, to fill it with heavenly truth and reality, and finally to realise the sacramental aspect of the sacrificial offering, just as he was the author of the incarnation of the Logos. No doubt, it was justifiable to suppress the epiclesis when it was looked upon as the actual formula of transubstantiation; still, we may regard the Roman rite as the poorer for omitting to recall Pentecost and the work of fulfilment effected by the

Spirit in the Church and sacraments, and the contemplative recollection of the whole course of redemption. For it is the Spirit
who dominates the Mass between the consecration and the communion. He makes the Word newly present, spiritually as well
as sacramentally; he is the Pax which the community, on becoming a communion, receives and interchanges among its members;
indeed, he is that communion which is the essence of the Church.
Finally, it is he who empowers the Church to offer herself in her
eucharistic commemoration, while offering the Son to the Father,
in a single offering, whose indivisibility derives solely from the
unity of feeling wrought by the Spirit, unity of "spirit" with
Christ. Only then can we understand that the Mass is, in the inmost heart of the Church, a free spiritual act supported by grace,
an act of reason remembering, that is of contemplation. Then we
shall realise, that, by the very nature of the Church, contemplation
and the sacrament form an indissoluble unity.

Those who find that the practical ordering of the Mass fails to
meet their needs, and that they cannot respond adequately to its
demands or desire the full benefit it offers, must fill the gap with
their private contemplation, and do so by joining in the spirit of
the Church's liturgy. As a member of the congregation at Mass,
the individual can seldom attain a fully satisfying contact with the
word. For the people as a whole and their power of comprehension
has to be considered, and perhaps the preacher does not give him
what he personally needs. He may find the language difficult, or
the words pass too quickly to take root in the soul. Yet the act of
hearing fully and submissively is essential, not only in itself, but
as a preparation and a purification for Holy Communion ("You
are clean by reason of the word I have spoken to you"—John
XV. 3; "Per evangelica dicta deleantur nostra delicta"). It is a
liturgical act, that is to say an act of divine service on the part
of the whole Church. It is not a sacramental act, but a purely personal one, preparing for the sacramental act of Communion; we
cannot attribute to it any kind of efficacy *ex opere operato*, which
it does not possess nor is intended to. No, the Church, who in

Mary as archetype encountered the Word of God, retains always this personal encounter; it is of her very being, and must be constantly actualised in all the members of the mystical body, the bride. St. Ignatius's prayer, for example, clearly indicates the liturgical and personal character of contemplation; "Ask grace that all my intentions, actions and conduct may be ordered purely to the service and the glory of his divine Majesty" (Exercises, No. 46). And there are too the great prayer-scenes of the Apocalypse, which describe a heavenly and eternal liturgy, the adoration and glorification of the Word and the Lamb seated on the throne : solitude and community are conjoined, but the sacramental eating and drinking of flesh and blood are also presented as taken up into the "communion of the Word" now fully accomplished. There is no longer a temple, "for the Lord God Almighty is the temple thereof, and the Lamb" (Apoc. XXI. 22). "The throne of God and of the Lamb shall be in it, and his servants shall serve him, and they shall see his face, and his name shall be on their foreheads" (XXII. 3-4).

We may draw from this an important lesson for the practice of contemplative prayer, namely it neither can nor should be self-contemplation, but a reverent regard and listening to what is characterised in its inmost being as the Not-me, namely the word of God. "What *no* eye has seen, no ear heard, what has never ascended into the heart of man"—that is what God has revealed to us by his Spirit. If contemplation is liturgy, then it must of necessity lead away from the self, and have God as its end directly, not just mediately.

It is not a question of turning first into oneself, as if that were the main thing, so as afterwards to transcend oneself and reach God. It may well happen, in fact it cannot be otherwise, that in meditating on what God says, the person himself stands out in relief and takes on a pronounced reality. But that happens, not through reflecting on himself, but through hearing God's word, in which he sees as in a mirror what he really and truly is. It is wrong to imagine that the inner or higher or deeper self is our true reality, and that we must escape from the distractions of the world, and turn our minds "inward" so as to renew this power to the word in us, as though it derived from our "better self". The reverse is true; all the power of our better self comes from the power of God, who keeps it in readiness for us and imparts it in his word. The person who fixes his gaze on himself in order to know himself better, and so, perhaps, effects a moral improvement, will certainly not encounter God. If he desires to find God's will for him, he must set about this task differently. But whoever seriously seeks God's will in his word will find himself incidentally, and in so far as is necessary. In striving after the transcendental self, man blunts his sense for the word of God and his sense of adoration; we see this in the German Idealist philosophers. But in applying our deepest self to hearing and adoring, we are sure of being taken up into the transcendence that really matters.

Contemplation is a part of the liturgy, taken in its fullest sense. The liturgy performed in public worship can, in practice, bring a hearing of only a small part of the word of God in Scripture. Even the liturgical Office of monks and priests cannot, in the annual cycle, go through the whole of Scripture. Consequently, the liturgy points beyond itself to personal contemplation of the word. There must be, within the Church, those who hear and pray, if the word not contained in the official missal and breviary is to be given proper scope. The purpose of the word is, of course, not attained by those who read the Bible out of curiosity or study it scientifically. Theology and exegesis may border on prayer, but their pursuit is not necessarily prayer; or, at any rate, not explicitly. They can and should be accompanied with a disposition to worship in the depths of the soul, just as all the acts of the Christian life, both spiritual and otherwise, should have this general basis. Indeed, the reader and student of Scripture may well—like St. Anselm and many other theologians who were also saints— enshrine and penetrate his reading and reflection with habitual adoration, and, in this way, bring a liturgical attitude to bear upon the work of his mind. He should always remember, however, that adoration of the word is an end in itself, and that prayer is not to be lowered from that plane to serve as a means to a better understanding. Many, such as Evagrius Ponticus and perhaps, at times, Hugh of St. Victor, deliberately practised contemplation of the word so as to reach higher states and illuminations, more subtle theological insights, or simply to learn the inner laws of contemplation, and so, from their own experience, to be able to help others. They prayed and worshipped *in recto,* and, at the same time, observed themselves *in obliquo,* as it were photographing their own ascent. The execution of this second act makes it impossible for the spirit to rise above its own self, and the danger is that the liturgy of the word should be brought down into the immanence of the finite spirit seeking to understand itself.

The layman who devotes some time each day to contemplative prayer may well, in spite of his ordinary occupations, maintain a truly liturgical outlook and a genuine transcendence of self. This will come easier to him the more conscious he is of the close connection between contemplation and the liturgy. Even if he cannot hear Mass each day, he can still relate this part of the Christian liturgy, as performed in the spirit of the Church, to his contemplation as an active element of the Church's own living spirit, as a spiritual communion with Christ, the Word of God. For spiritual communion is not merely an act of desire to receive the Lord under the sacramental form; in its most exact sense, it is an act of prayer proceeding from a living faith and understanding, which communicates with Christ, the eternal and living truth, and enters into a living communication and communion with him. This communion occurs of course, within the context of the New Testament, not of the Old Testament or divorced from the Incarnation of the Word. It is a real encounter, in the word, with the whole Christ, inasmuch as contact with the word in the Church's liturgy (as, for that matter, was the relation of the disciples to Christ at the beginning) is the way of access to the sacramental mystery. There is the same unbroken continuity here as in the Gospel of St. John, where Christ's discourse goes, without any abrupt transition, from his reception as bread in faith ("that everyone who seeth the Son and believeth in him, may have life everlasting, and I will raise him up at the last day"—VI. 40) to the eucharistic bread ("If any man eat of this bread, he shall live for ever; and the bread which I will give is my flesh, for the life of the world"—VI. 52).

The Fathers of the Church always saw and stressed this connection (cf. the passages in the Office for the octave of Corpus Christi). Sacramental reception of the Eucharist is vain, unless it is accompanied with living faith and love, and so becomes an efficacious supernatural sign of the spiritual communion effected. Whoever is brought, by the Sacrament, into a more vital relation with the Son of God, proclaims his decision to make Christ's own laws of living his own, to adopt Christ's ways of thinking and feeling so as to live accordingly. But this does not happen automatically, it demands personal effort; and the personal side of this mystery of the word consists in the living faith of the individual, that is in the spirit of obedience that makes him receptive, consenting and docile. Each aspect of the mystery demands the other, and both are conjoined in the unity of Christ and the Church. The sacramental presence of the Lord is not an island in the life of the individual Christian that arises and disappears, any more than it is for the Church, where the Lord is always present sacramentally, though this does not prevent the renewal of his presence every time Mass is celebrated. The mystery cannot be elucidated rationally; in fact, it would be an entirely false interpretation, were we to restrict or suppress the continuing efficacy of what took place yesterday and the day before, in order to make room for the sacramental act just repeated. So the Christian will derive the effectiveness of his contemplation to-day from the continuing action of his Communion of yesterday—my Lord and my God, the same who was pleased to come to me, is pleased now to speak his word to me, and I am able to hear, understand and adore him as present within me, whose life in me wills to become deep rooted in my spirit. "The life was the light of men, and the light shines in the darkness."

Some laypeople, with a view to taking a more sustained part in the liturgy of the Church, follow, to some extent, the manner of life and prayer of priests and monks, and say the daily Office either in whole or in part. But, in general, they have less understanding and spiritual freedom than those who, in the less formalised practice of contemplative prayer, allow God's life that is in them to illuminate their way. The former practice may be recommended in exceptional cases, but, for most people, it is a mistaken one. Contact with the word of God through contemplation is, for those who are capable of it, the normal way to develop the resources of the sacramental life; above all, it enables them to derive more fruit from the sacrament as time goes on. Everyone knows that the *opus operatum* of the sacraments is effected or frustrated, is more or less fruitful, according to the dispositions of the individual; it is precisely his living faith which disposes him aright, and this, in turn, is simply a docility in accepting the word of God in his own life, as well as the truth and enlightenment given by the sacrament. These the believer is alert to obey and to them he joyfully submits. The word "disposition" means being set out in order, part against part. What it stands for is something personal and actual, and so is ordered to the divinely personal and actual element in the sacraments and the liturgy. It is related, that is, to the word here and now, to light in actual living, to revelation as containing the demands grace makes of us. There is no such thing as a disposition for grace in general or the sacraments in particular which can be considered apart from the individual; for that reason, all reception of grace within the Church includes some hearing of the word—of the word, that is, contained in the sacrament of the Eucharist, none other, indeed, than the total and indivisible One Word of the Father, which is Christ.

In contemplation is found the link which binds together the two parts of the Christian life—the "work of God" in the Church and the work of man in the outside world. Contemplation unites the two in a single liturgy, at once sacred and secular, ecclesiastical and cosmic. Without contemplation it would hardly be possible to bring the two into unison, if only for practical and psychological reasons; the impression wrought by the liturgy grows faint in the course of daily life, and the secular world is, mostly, too remote from it to be linked in a living spiritual unity without some intermediary. In contemplation, however, the liturgy takes on a spiritual form, which, in turn, can become incarnate in ordinary life. This, of course, is what happens implicitly in all real Christian living. Whoever hears Mass with devotion and receives Communion in full awareness of what he is doing is bound to attend to the spiritual meaning of it all and to the necessity of informing his daily life with the Christian spirit. But the more this "attention" is made conscious and definite, the better the two parts are interlinked, the supernatural form, whose source is in eternity, and the matter, which is daily life in the world. If, on the other hand, the attempt is made to conjoin the two without contemplation, one of two results follows. Either the sacramental principle is pushed to extremes and has a quasi-magical power attributed to it; or else mundane activities are held exaggeratedly sacred, and a kind of theology of the things of earth set up which ascribes to business, technology, material well-being, the State and secular culture, an overriding place among the factors which build up and further the kingdom of God—this view is currently held nowadays precisely where contemplation is undervalued. Those, however, who approach their daily occupations with minds formed in the school of Christ's law will take as sober a view of them as does Scripture itself, while, at the same time, fully conscious that the world and its work are directly bound up with the work of heaven. A liturgical movement unaccompanied by a contemplative movement is a kind of romanticism, an escape from time, and inevitably calls up, by opposition, the counter-romanticism of a false conception of the sacred character of secular activity.

Those who work to assimilate the divine word contained in the liturgy, in their prayer and contemplation, are labouring to attain a full spiritual personality founded upon the Church and sacraments as they actually are. It is to this end that Church and

Sacraments are ordained, and such men, armed with the "sword of the spirit", are capable of going forth to do the work of Christ in the world. They realise that the "being" of the Church in time is twofold—it is an irruption of *eternity* into time, and really into *time*; something other-worldly, then, eschatological, yet not drawing the contemplative away into flight from the world, but instructing him how to live on earth according to the spirit and design of heaven. When he leaves his prayer and comes to his work in the world, he is not blinded by the splendour from above, or unable to find his way about, and only too glad to hasten back to the delightful regions of contemplation. He comes as one sent, who has received unawares, in contemplation, the full equipment for his task as a Christian, the power as well as the aptitude, and, also the taste for it.

Since he regards contemplation as part of the Church's liturgy, he does not indulge in any pleasurable absorption in it, imagining he has a foretaste of the joys of heaven. Even in his indescribable commerce with God, he is calm and humble, a servant of the Lord, presenting the same attitude of mind in which he assists at a sacred action, formed, as he is, and possessed by the sense of the Church. This attitude, received from the Church in his prayer, becomes part of the structure of his interior life, and remains intact when he goes forth to his daily occupations. Seen from the outside, it is the same kind of attitude, cheerful and frank, matter-of-fact and unromantic, in which the ordinary, respectable citizen approaches the unexciting and dull business of the day. But the Christian receives a growing strength from a higher source, which, on occasion, when God so wills and sees fit, makes its activity suddenly felt and brings special illumination. Generally, the Christian has no need to concern himself with such occurrences, or to advertise himself, by the way he acts, as one who practises contemplation. It is only rarely that he can turn what he gains in contemplation to direct account in ordinary life, but he has no need for anxiety on that score. Love alone, which is the content of Church, sacraments, and of all God's utterances and laws, is

what must always flow directly from his prayer into his action—
the one, indivisible love for God and man, indeed for the entire
creation. In any case, contemplative prayer radiates of itself into
spheres unknown to the contemplative, ever unknown to him in
this life; occasionally too into spheres where he can observe its
effect, though that knowledge is only given him as a little en-
couragement, so that he may believe more firmly in the latent
power of contemplative prayer.

The person sent, who goes to his work sustained by the word,
is a person purified. The Word himself said : "Now you are clean,
by reason of the word I have spoken to you" (John XV. 3). It is
no automatic cleansing that is meant here, but that brought about
by the word in those who hear it. If anyone opens himself to the
light, it pours into him; and his darkness is brought into the light
of day and changed into light. "All things that are reproved are
made manifest by the light, for all that is made manifest is light"
(Eph. V. 13). And this too is closely connected with the liturgy—
for contemplation is closely related to Confession.

In the sacrament of Penance we submit ourselves to the judgment of God's word. We confess, not only that God is righteous
and ourselves unrighteous, but also our sinfulness in the light of the
word addressed to us, the word that judges, and, in judging, justifies and sanctifies. This acknowledgment of God's right over the
individual is an element in all contemplation—thou art just, thou
art my justice, and, when I fail to submit to this justice, I am unjust. But if he is to say this, the penitent needs an initial insight
into the nature and content of God's justice; to acknowledge it,
he must know it. It is not enough for him simply to ascertain God's
law; but he must, at the very least, have his conscience enlightened
by the grace of God revealing himself. But, as a Christian, he
possesses a conscience to whose formation the historical word of
God has contributed decisively, one trained to be an organ of
hearing the word. He knows, through his conscience, if only in
an implicit and logically undeveloped fashion, quite simply this :
God is the truth, and he has spoken it to me in his Son; further-

more, the truth of the Son has, by the Son himself, been entrusted to the Church. In confessing his sins to the Church, the believer submits himself to the truth of Christ. It is the truth for him—now, since he acknowledges his wrong, and for the future, since he submits his life to it anew. In deciding to do so, he cannot do otherwise than contemplate the truth. He must fix his gaze on it clearly in order to centre his life on the precise point where the light meets it, on the exact point assigned to it by the truth. He must look towards the truth of God, not only to gain some understanding of his sins and to confess them, but equally in order to take the right kind of resolution for the future. Furthermore, he must relate himself to the entire kingdom of God, in its concrete reality, so as to see exactly where he stands himself. And then he confesses his guilt before the whole of heaven, before "the blessed Mary, ever-virgin, blessed Michael the archangel, blessed John the Baptist, the holy apostles Peter and Paul, all the saints and you, Father".

The sinner turns his gaze to the whole of heaven, in order to recognize and confess his "grievous fault" : that is part of the Church's liturgy, both in the Mass and in Confession. But it also forms part of contemplation, which (as we shall see more in detail later) is a meeting with the word of God, the word that, in judging, condemns and justifies. For this reason, a person who regularly practises contemplation is always, to a great extent, prepared for Confession; he is accustomed to look into the mirror which shows him to himself as God sees him. Certainly, there is the danger, as in all that pertains to the Church, of what is most excellent being misused by sinful man, of a help being turned into a hindrance, of the light becoming ultimately darkness to one who does not expose himself to it with simplicity and courage—"everyone that doth evil hateth the light, and cometh not to the light, that his works may not be reproved" (John III. 20). Or else he receives the pure light of God as if it were some human or Old Testament kind of law, and not the total love of the Father, which sacrificed itself to man in the crucified Son. It may be, too, that, by the mere repetition of this truth, man gradually comes to see, in what is so wonderful as to surpass understanding, an ultimate law of the universe and nothing more. Perhaps he genuinely and fully acknowledges the authority of God's word over his life, but, owing to a kind of paralysis of the spirit, is incapable of drawing the consequences.

In spite of all these dangers, the simple law still holds good, that, by contemplating divine truth, we become purified, justified and sanctified; it is a law capable of bringing health of soul to all who sincerely desire it. Of course, the free gift of God's grace justifying us is what turns us to him and opens our eyes to his truth : so long as we turn away from him, we cannot be justified. Yet although grace first turns him towards God, man must play his part, and, acknowledging the truth of grace, admit his own guilt. In confessing grace (confiteri Domino), he, by a necessary consequence, confesses his fault (confiteri peccatum). All this is, perhaps, so secret and simple, that it can hardly be expressed in words—"Thy light, my darkness! Thy sweetness, my bitterness!" But it is contemplation, in its mature state, that gives depth and permanence to this simple disposition; the "dark night of the soul", the contemplative way of purification, is but the practised repetition, the branding more and more deeply and painfully in the soul, of this contemplative experience of Confession. So it is that the nights of the soul also belong to the liturgy; they are, in the existential order, Confessions in which, on account of the intense darkness, the broad expanses of the Church and the heavenly court are scarcely visible, but which are ever accompanied with the silent presence and prayer of the Communion of saints on earth and in heaven.

The Christian who gives himself to contemplation has to know all this. It should prevent him seeing his life in the world, placed as it is under the law of the word he contemplates, as a constant danger, a source of fresh impurities, and make him conscious of being sustained and upheld by the word of God, which never ceases to feed him as bread from heaven, and continuously purifies and absolves him as the word of absolution. He has need of this, for he is always falling short of the demands made on him. It is for God to complete and round off the essential work; to support our defects, discouragement and backsliding, to look at our inadequacies in the light of the perfect work of his Son. That is the situation of redeemed man in this world; it should stir him up, not to subtleties of dialectic, but to simple gratitude to the Saviour. His life consists in serving the God of grace, a *leiturgia*, a fully personal and responsible service performed as part of the community of the saints. This it is which gives his service value in the sight of God.

3. Freedom.

Up to now we have been describing the contemplative's place in the Christian cosmos, his situation in its scheme which comprises the word, the history of salvation and the function of the Church. Now we have to consider how the individual should set about ordering and shaping his own contemplation, and this is best done under the heading of freedom. For, while the slave is subject to law, the child of God is free, free to speak with the Father as his heart prompts him. He may receive advice from others, he may benefit from the experience of those who enjoy greater freedom in prayer; but he always remains free. The Spirit of God is in his heart, prays in him, witnesses to him of the Father's love in the Son; and this Spirit is himself the outflowing love of God. The Spirit is freedom, and nothing should be allowed to dim, imperil or weaken in us the consciousness of our Christian freedom. God's word before which man kneels in reverence is God's word to him; he is called and summoned to go forward, the word belongs to him, he can take hold of it with his two hands and press it to himself, and feel God's mysterious heart-beat within. No alien rule, imposed from outside, may restrain his intercourse with the Beloved. Only he is often at a loss, like someone unexpectedly come into a great fortune, who, not knowing what to do with it, listens to suggestions from this or that person who surely knows better than he.

The counsels that might be given to those starting on the way of contemplation are numerous, but can be stated briefly. Seen in the right light, they consist of the advice that might be given to anyone who loves; and that in itself is an important indication of the true nature of contemplation. Nothing is so free as love, and there is no freedom apart from love. Anyone who begins to love feels himself breaking out of his own private world; but he has to take care that after attaining freedom he does not fall back into a fresh servitude. For instance, he can once again become self-seeking in his love, without being aware of it—aim at his own enjoyment, using his partner as a means to this, or at his own advantage, appropriating the material and spiritual goods and privileges of the other person, till the day comes when he realises that his love is extinct, because he has always, secretly, been seeking himself. Warning-signs, then, simple enough but often ignored, are placed on the ways of love, to remind us that love makes us free if it is selfless; and it is selfless if we are able, for the sake of those we love, to renounce enjoyment, privilege and the absence of bonds. Since no earthly love is perfect at the outset, it must always undergo this kind of purification. Periods, long or short, must be expected, when love is tested by renunciation, when we are made to see if the enthusiasm of the first stage was love at all, when the immature love, if it was present then, is purified and deepened in the fire of renunciation.

For this reason, the first group of counsels simply urge the need for loving. Love is the content and aim of contemplation, and so, from the outset, should be directly sought and realised. Love desires the presence of the beloved, and so the person praying places himself in God's presence; or rather he realises in his spirit the truth that God has long since placed him in his own presence in a special manner. Nothing stands between him and the eternal love; there is no need of a mediator in the case of a single being (Gal. III. 20). All that occurs in contemplation is contained in the framework of this presence. All that I hear of God's word, the insights and joys I find in it by God's grace, the praise of God and what I gain from it, all derives meaning from love, and is the fruit of mutual presence and immanence.

Love desires to have the beloved before its eyes. For that reason, the person contemplating will use the faculties of the "inner senses" and imagination to call up the image of the Incarnate Word—Jesus, as he appeared in the body on earth, as he spoke, the tone of his voice, his intercourse with men, his appearance at prayer, in an upper room, at his Passion. The image is not intended as a photographic reproduction, but as an image of the love to which nothing matters but love, the love of the Father, therefore, which manifests itself here in the Son and in all the circumstances of his life on earth. That is why the person praying tries to represent to himself the human form of Christ on earth—not to provide support for a weakness which prevents him, for the time being, from rising to the purely spiritual, but to seek God's love, see, hear and touch it in the humble form in which it willed to proclaim itself to men. But since man in prayer seeks love, seeks the divine love through the earthly image (which he can never do without), he is always led beyond the Jesus of history to Christ dead and descended into hell, risen and ascended into heaven, present eucharistically in the Church, and hoped for in his return to glory. This alone is the whole, living Christ, over whom death has no more dominion, the "Christ of faith", who gives himself up and reveals himself to those who pray with love, making them partakers in his eternal and glorified life (Rom. VI; 2 Cor. V. 15 ff.). Him love seeks in his earthly form.

Love desires to rest peacefully in the company of the beloved. Hence, the further counsel not to look feverishly for new thoughts, fresh aspects, as though contemplation required one to deal with a definite quality of matter instead of quite simply and lovingly considering each aspect as it presents itself. Each word of Scripture leads directly right into the depths of the Godhead, to the centre of fulness and unity where the outwardly separate words meet together. Indeed, the Son of God is this fulness. He alone is the bread of life for which the soul hungers, and which it may not pass by in search of some other food, an illusory spiritual satisfaction. He suffices for the soul. All that takes place must be in the truth, so that the person praying rests, not in his own feelings, but in the Lord; not in the insignificant thoughts he may chance upon, in unconscious and complacent self-reflection, but in the sublime truth of the Lord continually unfolding before him. If he loves, he is capable of this, and learns it better as he practises it; only by loving does one learn to love better.

There is in love, too, a burning desire to learn to know the beloved, and so it considers him closely, looks at him from every angle, and keeps him always in mind. That is one reason why the Word of God was made flesh; he wished, out of love for the Father, to let himself be seen and handled in human form. Contemplation then is never idle; it has no wish to "sleep" in the presence of the beloved, it is ever on the alert to feed on "every word that proceeds from the mouth of God". Yet it is never curious or insatiable, but knows how to prize and be content with the word and the food of the moment. This is what is given him to be tasted here and now; and the soul is gladdened by it and draws strength for the next stage of the journey to Mount Horeb. As time goes on, it learns to do with less and less matter in contemplation—it comes to see and grasp in each detail all its depth of meaning. The "prayer of quiet" once attained with the help of grace, extension is replaced by intensity; the roving discourse of the mind is replaced by a kind of intuition which, in a single glance, comprehends more than the multiple considerations of the beginner.

Finally, love resolves to imitate the beloved. When the model is at once God and man, any mere mechanical reproduction is out of the question. What is possible is precisely what Christian love empowers us to do—a following of Christ as practised by his disciples and the holy women of the Gospel, in humble and simple obedience, together with a reproduction of his image in that Holy Spirit, implants in our hearts the sentiments of the Son of God and carries them through into the conduct of life. The Lord is not niggardly in sharing his own life; and it is one of the most astounding things in the Gospel that, even before his Passion, he spoke so freely of the cross that all who desired to follow him had to take up daily (Luke IX. 23). It almost seems as if he were sanctioning the misuse Christians would make of the words "following" and "cross" by daring to link the petty vexations of life with the tremendous mystery of redemption. The grace of Christ, however, allows us to direct our lives by the law of his life, and so, by loving contemplation of his life, to bring ours into relation with it, to be transformed in that light, even as to the most ordinary practical decisions. For the most part, we are not concerned with complicated matters, but with the simplest of all, which is love. What is complex we generally understand better than what is simple, since the latter, by its very simplicity, makes such demands on us. Just as there is, for the understanding, a "prayer of simplicity", so there is one too for the will and the practical resolve; for the beginner must dwell on the details of his daily life and of his inner disposition, which he has to correct on the model of Christ—hence the necessity for him of a control, of the particular examen—whereas the more experienced may dwell preferably on the general attitude of Christ and try to reproduce it in his own life. In this way, he grows in simplicity and liberty, which indeed have their root and being in love; and, with constancy in prayer, he steadily emerges from the world of law, of the Old Testament and the promise of love, into the New Testament, the manifestation of pure love whose existence and effect embraces all laws, and is not itself "under" the law.

The second group of counsels concerns the way the time of contemplation is to be apportioned. And the first thing to be observed is that the supreme law here is the liberty of the children of God. No sort of division may be imposed as necessary or even as specially suitable; at the most, a few suggestions may be made, and even these are to be adopted only so long as they do not hinder the real law of contemplation in its workings which is the free spirit of God leading the individual along the path of freedom. St. Ignatius's method of prayer never claimed to serve any other purpose. The three points, into which the matter is divided, are only intended to facilitate understanding of the passage; the person is not to be overpowered by its wealth of meaning, but to find something to help him along. When he has this, and some aspect invites him to dwell on it, St. Ignatius himself allows the scaffolding to be removed, and gives the law of freedom precedence over all else. We must never aim at carrying out a prescribed programme in prayer; as soon as God's word makes its impact, we must leave all the rest and follow it. Once we have grown wings and rise from the ground, the laws of the air and the spirit come into play. We lose nothing in receiving God's fulness in the fulness of the word.

Still less should we rigidly adhere to the scheme of the Ignatian "contemplatio" (Exercises, No. 106 ff.)—first "seeing" the Gospel scene and the persons in it, then "hearing", then considering their "actions". Or that of the "meditatio", given more from the contemplative's point of view—first bringing the "memory" to bear on what took place, then discovering its significance through the "understanding", and lastly embracing what is thus disclosed with the "will" and "affections", appropriating it and incorporating it into our own life. It is, no doubt, easy to give such schemes a certain universal validity on psychological and theological grounds—*memoria, intellectus, voluntas,* according to St. Augustine, make up the threefold essence of the created spirit, the image of the eternal Trinity, and so, in observing this order, we ultimately obey the basic law of our own being, and this precisely in so far as it is turned to God and opened up to his action. Something of the sort may be said of the other schemes as well, since in the sequence of acts, seeing, hearing, doing, the progressive embodiment of the divine revelation made available to the person at prayer receives its expression.

These various procedures, then, are much less formal than they at first appear. Still, as a means of apportioning the period of contemplation—for example, a quarter of an hour to "seeing", another to "hearing", and the rest to considering "action"—they are quite provisional and subservient to liberty. This liberty is not an extreme and exceptional case, but the normal thing. St. Paul's whole teaching on liberty has to be applied to prayer (Gal. V; Rom. VIII). Love knows no other law than itself, provided that it is genuine love, and not a pretext to "give a foothold to corrupt nature". But precisely for that reason liberty will not be inordinately coveted, but will humbly and gladly make use of every reasonable help that is available, if it really helps, and so long as it furthers freedom. It is normal, for beginners especially, to start with some suitable method, and later to discard it and venture into personal intercourse and inquiry, returning to the method the moment one's own *élan* weakens, fatigue sets in, and emptiness supervenes. Then is the time to ask, Where did I start from? What was the succession of ideas? Yet contemplation quite often has no need to return to its point of departure, but, like a rocket, leaves the earth's gravitational field and soars up into space.

The methods also point to something that brings us back to the first group of recommendations, namely, that the curve of contemplation corresponds to the curve of love. Contemplation must not be confined to the intellect, to distinguishing aspects, probing hidden meanings, for "knowledge puffs up, but charity edifies". "Seeing" and "hearing" must lead to "touching" (1 John I. 2), to "contact" with God (Exercises, No. 108). Certainly, the flame of love will normally spring from the wood of knowledge, and often more strongly, the deeper and more actual the knowledge. But this should not serve as a pretext for dwelling on the intellectual plane so long that love is put to one side and even the basic attitude of worship disappears in the vain subtleties of mere knowledge.

A third group of counsels emphasises the ordinary virtues that proceed from love. The supreme moments of blissful intercourse are not many in the life of lovers; they spend the greater part of their lives separate, in their respective duties and work. It is here that love must prove its strength; it becomes loyalty, patience and humble service. In the thought of his wife and children many a man bears with the emptiness and crushing monotony of an occupation which has for long been an affliction to him. For love of her husband the wife endures weeks of loneliness at home, while he is travelling; indeed, it may be that, with the passage of years, she learns to bear, for love of him as a person, his bodily contact without ever letting it be noticed how irksome she finds his demands. Similarly, contemplation, after a few months or years of the first enthusiasm, enters on a stage in which fidelity is put to the test. Is it true that we have seriously ordered our life according to God's word, and desire to make it our daily food as the worldly make the things of the earth theirs? Do we really do so in homage to the divine love, and not out of spiritual egoism, for our own enrichment or spiritual delight? Have we, in fact, entered with the word into a new and eternal covenant, within which alone are possible the interchange of love and life that was the meaning of the agreement made and the fidelity undertaken? Or is it the case that we, who in the civil sphere cannot condemn the evil of divorce sufficiently, act, in the spiritual sphere, as if the bond with God were valid only as long as the pleasure lasted? Are we still as children who have not yet faced a choice of life which binds them once and for all? We need to be very clear that the essence of Christianity consists in fidelity given freely and finally, persisting through all the difficulties of daily life, aridity of spirit and even the seeming remoteness of God.

Wherever we find an unhindered mutual love and its richness revealed in those who forego everything for each other's sake, there is always a protective force surrounding it, a firm, unshakeable framework. In God this third factor is the Holy Spirit, the witness and warrant of the love between Father and Son, the objectivity of this love and its unity—for the Spirit proceeds from Father and Son. This unity is not identical with the two loving Persons, but is their fruit and their rapture, and drives them to a constantly renewed intimacy; it encloses and seals their love, keeping it for ever inviolable and true to its own nature. In God's covenant with Adam, Noah, Abraham and the people at Sinai, the mystery of the Trinity was given to them outwardly : the Covenant is the expression of the love between God and the man he loves, and it is only in its setting that a real life of love is possible. In the New Covenant the mystery receives its final form; and so we have the firm framework of the Church, and the still closer bond which is the structure of the Christian life : a definite choice, the irrevocable gift of oneself to God either in marriage or life according to the evangelical counsels; that framework protects the mystery of the marriage between God and man in all its splendour, a mystery daily reenacted. Contemplation has its own place within it, and should form a part of this Trinitarian structure. It does so when seen as a love not merely indulged occasionally, in dilettante fashion, at times when it gives pleasure, but pursued with that fidelity which characterises the Church and her archetype, the Mother of the Lord. The relation between inner "spirit" and outward "form" is the most intimate conceivable (in the light of faith); they are both one, each presupposes the other, they sustain one another and grow in conjunction. The "framework" *is* the fidelity of love, and fidelity is what makes the life of love possible and keeps it vigorous. A breach of fidelity is the sign that love no longer exists, and in the Old Testament a breach of the covenant was regarded as adultery.

The life of contemplation is perforce an everyday life, of small fidelities and services performed in the spirit of love, which lightens our tasks and gives to them its warmth. The sun may at times, perhaps often, be shrouded in mist, but that is no reason for giving up work. What St. Paul says applies here—"He that will not work, neither let him eat" (2 Thess. III.10). Contemplative prayer is work, work done out of love for him who "in all created things strives and toils for my sake" (Exercises 236), who recoils from no drudgery, endured even the cross, to bring me his love. Contemplation is work that continues even when imperceptible to the person contemplating; just as a woman puts her love into her handiwork, even though her work may pass unnoticed. It is a conversation in which we try not to be tedious, not to say and think the same thing day after day, but use our gifts of imagination or reason to offer God the little we can draw from our own resources. In this effort God sees a token of love, some response to the love of the Holy Spirit, a love that opens our eyes to ever-new aspects of God. Contemplation should be performed with becoming sobriety, like all activities within the Church; indeed this should characterise the whole life of the Church; and is one of the virtues most frequently emphasised in the New Testament. But there must be nothing hard and repellent about it. The sobriety of the saints goes with a kind of serenity and joy, expressive of the tenderness and docility of heart in which all things should be done. The Holy Spirit acts gently, sweetly, makes himself known to those who seek him, not in perfervid dispute with God, but in the slightest and lowliest of signs indicative of his love. The heart too must so act if it is to gain some sight of the hidden light disclosed by the Spirit.

"Dryness", then, should not be accepted in principle as a penance or trial imposed on us, but as a normal, everyday aspect of love, which generally begins by exhibiting some exceptional feature, before attaining its normal state. For that reason, there is nothing alarming about dryness in contemplation; on the contrary, it is reassuring. Love does not succumb to the routine of daily work, but makes use of a hundred imaginative ways to transfigure and revivify it, and the man of prayer goes daily into the presence of God whose eternal youth is the source at which he can renew his inner senses. Fatigue, satiety, discouragement and distaste, come solely from man and, as God holds in readiness all that is needed to give him fresh vigour and life under his burden, he has no cause for complaint. His part is to bestir himself and shake off what weighs and drags him down, and, having got rid of it, start once again.

The self-discipline of a faith true to itself and its own inner logic constitutes the real element of penance, intended as such by

God, in prayer. For we can never take up love and its laws against the grain and in a spirit of penitence; and everything in us that hinders the practice of love must be overcome in and through penance, and so eliminated. Indeed love impels us so strongly to do so, that the penance itself seems a gift and a secret source of joy. The penance is a preparation; it clears the way to love and is conjoined in advance with the penance entrusted to us by, and proceeding from, love, the penance we perform, consciously or unconsciously, through love, for the purpose and needs of love. God, in his plan of salvation, makes use of faith unfelt, surrender without prospect, and a blind hope that seems only to grasp the void. To whom then should he turn, if not, above all, to contemplatives? After all, it is they who, as it were *ex officio,* practise and present these acts to the Word of God. God may even make contemplative love dark and troubling, so that it seems almost beyond our strength. Normally, we should not attribute these qualities to God, but ascribe them, in the first place, to our own lukewarmness; and they are best pointed out to our confessor and left to him to judge. Only when we submit our state to his control, can we, without danger, know ourselves to be called to the way of spiritual darkness. The night of the soul has its own safeguards; if a man "stumbles" in it he will not fall, for he is upheld by God, who brought him to this state; but the protective shield thus formed round the contemplative, created by the night itself, should normally be explicitly discussed with a priest. Because the Holy Spirit leads him in a special manner, the contemplative needs the guidance of the Church. In the mystery of the night the covenanted love of God is more exposed than ever, and the Lord of the Covenant watches jealously over it, and nearly always places his accredited watchman at the gate.

No one can rush into these ways on his own initiative; they depend on vocation and a special mission. The ways of the "purgation" of love are open and indispensable for everyone but they do not necessarily take the form of the night of the cross. God can purify the hope of a believer from self-seeking, without making it pass through renunciation of all hope, through the "amour pur" of the crucified soul that seeks nothing for itself. There is, too, the slow gentle way of ordinary life, the "little way" of St. Teresa of Lisieux. Who can say if this way is less, or equally, exacting? Its characteristic is always the "smile", and where contemplative prayer is concerned, that means the presupposition of love on the part of the man of prayer. It means alertness in going to meet the word of God, whether we feel eager or listless; bringing to it the same interest and attentiveness, the same joy, whatever our momentary disposition—in fact not treating our mood as an inherent feature of prayer. At times when our own source of joy runs low we have to supplement it from the reserves faith maintains and from the store of joy present in God and the Church. Where this joy comes from is unimportant; it need not come from our personal intercourse with God—just as it is immaterial to a guest where the food set before him is bought.

All this is what is implied in St. Teresa's idea of the "smile". It is akin to the "good manners", "deportment", of former times; and perhaps it is being worked out explicitly in the Church because it is losing ground in ordinary social intercourse. The aristocracy and upper classes instinctively adopted that form of behaviour; it was looked on as a matter of propriety, of correctness, rather than of virtue. It was the way one treated guests, a friendly, pleasant manner, without letting them see one's own moods or discontents; making conversation in spite of one's disinclination or the unresponsiveness of the other person; showing interest, not just making a pretence of it, even when one's own inclination at the moment led elsewhere. Of course, like everything valuable and estimable on the human plane, it was liable to become formal and lifeless; but it is not so on the spiritual plane, for there we learn the right way of intercourse with God under the tuition and direction of the Holy Spirit, the Spirit of love. In human relationships it often, though not necessarily, curtailed freedom, as in elaborate Court-ceremonial, but, in those of the Spirit, it is conducive to freedom; for they are rules showing us how, in the seeming monotony of ordinary life and the apparently restrictive framework of fidelity to contemplation—and nowhere else—the fulness of God's word comes to pervade our life, leading us out of our bondage to the things of earth into the broad spaces of God's immensity.

4. The end of time.

When contemplation becomes a reality, it belongs to a present moment of history, which both determines its nature and is determined by it. It is specifically contemplation in the *time* of the Church, or, as it is called in Scripture, the "last days" : contemplation betwen the two comings of the Lord, in an appropriate time ordained to it. Nowhere in Scripture do we find the idea of the proximate second coming linked to the idea that the Christian should devote the remaining time of the Church to action on the widest possible front. The injunction, "work while it is day", refers to our life-time; not to historical time but to the time of grace, which is not indefinitely at our disposal but is always "today" (2 Cor. VI. 2 ; Heb. IV. 7). The Church's being is emphatically contemplative, for it belongs to the time of waiting for the *parousia*, "abiding" after the bridegroom's departure, as St. John is fond of saying; a time, indeed, of waiting in the desert, exposed to the unceasing assaults of the dragon, who is all the more active, "knowing that he hath but a short time" (Apoc. XII. 12 ff.). The Christian is active because he (and the world) has yet to attain the state accessible to him in principle through Christ's redemption. But he can only be active (always moving from the Old Testament to the New), in virtue of the grace of the New Testament he has received, and so in virtue of contemplation.

In the "end of time" in which the Church lives, nothing "new" in the history of salvation can any longer happen, for everything is "consummated", and the conqueror "till his enemies are made his footstool; for by one oblation he hath perfected for ever them that are sanctified" (Heb. X. 13-14). The Holy Spirit, who leads

us into the fulness of Christ and continues to unfold it till the end
of the world, draws from a source that, historically speaking, lies
in the past. The contemplative, too, cannot do otherwise than
turn his gaze to the past. Consequently, the Christian always goes
counter to the forward rush of time, and this tendency is bound
to be a scandal to those who are wholly taken up in the cycle of
history.

From this point of view the Church can be seen to have an
affinity with the last phase of the Old Testament. Then the people
in exile gained a deeper insight into the past history of salvation;
they were compelled to contemplate it as from a distance. And in
fact after the exile nothing basically new in the history of salvation
originated. That was the period in which "theology" took its rise,
the period of the sapiential books which, themselves part of Scripture, inaugurated the contemplation of the history of the
Covenant. The books of Moses only received their final form when
the past was understood as part of the history of salvation. The
tremendous event of the Covenant then found expression in an
appropriate language and imagery; and the oral traditions and
individual sources united in a single whole, under the inspiration
of the Holy Spirit. Revelation, too, came at last to contemplate
itself in the sapiential books, which stressed the connections, disclosed the foundations, drew out the lessons and applications,
turning the whole to the praise of God and the profit of the faithful.

Contemplation, indeed, set forth that glorious history, invested
it with a new warmth and humanity, so that the splendour of it
almost blinded the beholder. Yet this very circumstance involved
a special danger, that of resting complacently in contemplative
wisdom and in understanding the people's role in preparing and
awaiting what was to come. The journey through the desert,
Mount Sinai, the conquest of the Promised Land, the time of the
Judges, of the Kings and the great prophets, were all deliberately
ordained to what was to come; it was a present duty imposed for
the sake of a future. The danger of this contemplation lay in its

finality, in the temptation to replace the true messianic relationship by a more and more pronounced "mysticism" of an apocalyptic type, in the temptation to erect an occult system of supraterrestrial mysteries, based, indeed, on the prophecies, but becoming more and more remote from them and borrowing extraneous elements of cosmology and psychology. In Israel the hearing of the word gave place to vain speculation on religion, a decadent form of contemplation, and in conjunction with pharisaic moralism, this prevented acceptance of the prophetic message of the Baptist and the eschatological teaching of Christ.

Contemplation in the Church is in an analogous situation, and has to beware of a similar danger, that of dissolving the eschatological element in a "mysticism" of its own creation. This, indeed, has a certain validity in the New Testament, but not in the Old. For now the good things of salvation are really, though in a hidden manner, present. Christ is risen from the dead, and lives, in his glorified state, above and within his Church. St. Paul and St. John, each in his own way, emphasise that those who believe are baptised and nourished with his flesh and blood, have died and risen with Christ. In this light, contemplation might seem the way in which the truth accepted in faith might, in some degree, be seen in itself and perhaps even experienced directly; in fact, a foretaste of the heaven to which the believer—in Platonist language—already belongs in "spirit", while he remains bound up with the old aeon only secondarily, through the body. The Church then is seen (as Origen, for instance, saw it) as the splendour of Christ in time, the reflection of the Lord of heaven upon earth; in the Church, Christ contemplates himself, and contemplation within the Church is a participation, given by grace, in Christ's own glorified and eternal self-knowledge.

There have always been attempts to treat a mystical element of this kind as absolute. They have menaced the true character of contemplation in the Church from the very beginning. We see it in extreme Origenism and in the later Palamatism of the West—both on the borderline of orthodoxy—and also in the one-sided teaching of monastic writers on contemplation in the Middle Ages, and the undisguised agnosticism of a later date (from Boehme to Schelling). The aim of one and all is to reduce the historical character of Christianity to the general, pre-historical relationship between God and man, between a time which passes and an eternity always latent in it and above it. A further characteristic of this attitude is that the transition from the Old to the New Covenant, from the promise to its fulfilment, is made relatively insignificant by being given a mystical and spiritualised interpretation. On this view, the Old Testament mystics themselves belong to the New Testament; on Sinai and Horeb they beheld God in a luminous darkness; in the Canticle of Canticles they experienced the mystical marriage; and only the common people, strangers to contemplation, needed the coming of the Word in the flesh.

Certainly, the Old Testament is to be interpreted in the light of the New; but not so as to eliminate or minimise the difference and the historical cleavage underlined so strikingly and terribly in the rejection of the Jews and the election of the Gentiles. The hidden presence of the New in the Old can only really be discerned in relation to the historical sequence leading from the one to the other. This sequence is an expression of the life of the believer on earth; and even the New Testament, with all the changes it brings in fulfilling the Old, cannot eliminate the twofold relationship between them. The central point of time is Christ's life on earth, from his conception to his death. The Old Testament leads up to this point and the "time" of the Church looks back to it, a reflected image of the Old Testament. But the Old Testament derives from a past event, the creation, whereas the New looks towards a future one, the second coming of Christ. For the Old Testament the appearance of the Messias is "the day of the Lord", with its judgment on the peoples, the salvation of Israel, and entrance on the sabbath of the Lord, which corresponds to the creation and is the fulfilment of its promise. For the New Testament the retrospective contemplation of Christ is one with the contemplation of his expected coming in glory; then the hidden judgment accomplished on the cross will be manifested at the last judgment, and the day of the Lord, which began with the coming of the Messias, will receive its fulfilment. Thus the Old and the New Testaments flow in opposite directions towards Christ, and meet in him as the centre; he is seen as what gives them unity and coherence. For this reason, and no other, the eschatological horizons close up around the same centre. The sabbath of God, the day of rest at the beginning corresponds to the sabbath of the end; the work of creation "finished from the foundation of the world" in the repose of God corresponds to the final sabbath, to which the Jews did not attain and the new "people of God" make their way, the people to whom "there remaineth a day of rest" (Heb. IV. 3-9).

"Let us fear, therefore, lest the promise being left of entering into his rest, any of you should be thought to be wanting. For unto us also it hath been declared in like manner as unto them" (Heb. IV. 1-2). Christ takes over the command given to the Jews, and applies it with a new emphasis to his followers. They are to "watch" throughout the night, and he means, not just a physical watchfulness, but an inner readiness and preparedness for an event sure to happen, but whose time no mystical knowledge can suffice to tell. "Take ye heed, watch and pray, for you know not when the time is" (Mark XIII. 33). *Videte, vigilate, orate.* The "seeing" required during the time of waiting has, as a principal element, the quality of attentiveness to what the future is to bring; this derives from man's inevitable ignorance. Such is contemplation according to the New Testament dispensation—a counterpart to that of the Old Testament. Watching is a form of "praying", an openness of the heart towards God, who may come at any moment, and everything will then depend upon that disposition. Those who have served him in thus watching he accepts and serves; while those who slept, who took no pains to recognise him, remain with the door closed before them, for he refuses to know them. It is "watching" which is a prayer (*vigilate itaque omni tempore orantes*—Luke XXI. 36), so much so that prayer apart from watching, prayer which does not look to the future coming of the

Lord, is not Christian prayer at all. That means prayer that does not dissolve eschatology in mysticism, that does not translate the vigilance of the Church on earth into a foretaste of the blessedness enjoyed by the Church in heaven; though the Lord of the whole Church may give the waiting Church certain intimations, assurances or anticipations of what for her is to come, for heaven is always present.

These gifts she may not reject (as is done by a "consistent eschatology" that abhors mysticism), but she must not cling to them or regard them as the exclusive, normal end of Christian contemplation, an end sought for itself. She should desire to abide with the Son (Mark XIII. 32), in that state of unknowing which befits her earthly existence and is better for her, better because only those who do not know can practise a constant readiness of heart at every instant of time. If men "knew"—otherwise than through being momentarily raised up into heaven—they would certainly occupy the interval of time with other matters. "Watching" implies an element of decision, which must not be eliminated from the idea of Christian contemplation. God it is true has made his own decision once and for all, but man living in time must continually renew that decision and preserve its freshness. Watching the whole night through is a struggle against sleep, a constant effort to take hold of and redirect oneself, a withstanding of the physical and human forces of weariness, custom and convention. Why should we watch, when "all" sleep? Why should we be always on the look-out, when there is never any sign of Christ's return? The inner tension which summons the Christian to unceasing renewal of his decision for the Lord who was once a part of history and will return at the end of history, is incomprehensible to those outside. It is the hallmark of the historical character of the Christian faith.

All this throws a new light on what we said earlier about the service in love freely given by the contemplative. Our individual service rendered to the word of God, shown in our daily life as diligence, fidelity, sobriety, is now seen to have a complete theological foundation. The total service, as understood by the Church in her liturgy—which means service performed—has always comprised three temporal dimensions; it means serving the mystery of the Son who came in the flesh (*vigilate mecum*—Mt. XXVI. 38); serving the mystery of the Word ever present, though hidden in the Church and coming to man; and serving the deeply concealed mystery of the Word's second coming at the end of time. The fire kindled in the hearts of the disciples by their companion on the way to Emmaus came from a talk about the history of salvation in the past; but a history explained by the Lord present with them, and so, in turn, enflaming them with desire for the future sight, unveiled, of the Lord now departed from them.

Thus the eschatological element in Christian contemplation by its very nature promotes contemplation in the Church. The opposition to contemplation which is from time to time formulated on the basis of eschatology, is due to a misconception. It may be justified as a corrective to the undue emphasis placed on mystical contemplation as something timeless, in which we lose ourselves in the eternal present. For contemplation of this kind soon leads to the loss of a sense of God's word and the "hearing" of it, to a loss in fact of the sense of faith, which is replaced by "vision", whether open or hidden. It is only when we are aware that the Word of God will come at the end of time that we are continually alive to the fact that he came, historically, at the centre of time, and comes each day anew for the whole Church and each person praying—a coming whose significance is not to be lessened by any kind of vision or knowledge. The Church will only rise to the full demands of her active mission in the world if she is conscious of the Word as having come in the past, as coming in the future, and as present now. Her work is not to be hurried, as though the Word had not already fulfilled all; any more than she may neglect her work as though it were already possible to rest on Mount Thabor. By drawing on the fulness of what the Lord has done, she can wait and work for his coming; and sustained by the promised peace of eternity of which she has already received an earnest she utters her cry of longing in union with the Spirit: "Come".

The church is able to preserve and develop the great contemplative tradition of the Christian East, and so give scope to a great good that risks being wholly lost in modern Asia. But she must not regard contemplation as a technique of self-absorption in the Absolute to be clothed in Christian raiment. There is a form of contemplation native to her, whereby she looks out, from the summit of the world, to the promised eternity. The danger of perversion will, doubtless, continue to beset Christian contemplation to the end; but it has the power to renew itself from the resources of faith, and perhaps even to grow, in the course of time, into its own true nature, and to realise to the full all its various potentialities. The present forms of contemplation in the Church often reflect the ecclesiological and redemptive aspects of Christianity more fully than those of the past. In addition, the theological aspects emphasised respectively in the life of the different religious Orders are coming more and more to be seen as a single whole. The eschatological aspect is one that is not easy to incorporate into the spirituality of contemplation; but the whole situation of the Church brings it out more and more clearly, and shows it to be a necessary element in contemplation.

PART II

THE OBJECT OF CONTEMPLATION

CHAPTER I

THE WORD MADE FLESH

THE OBJECT of contemplation is God. We listen to the word, only because it is the word of God. We contemplate the life of Jesus, only because it is the life of the Son of God. We listen to something that forms part of the history of salvation —to creation and its utterance, to the Old Testament prophets, the apostles and the Church, her saints and her prayers, her teachings and sacraments—only because it is through them that God's salvation comes to us. We cannot contemplate God apart from the ways leading to him, that reveal him to us, by which he reveals himself and gives us access to him. We shall never see God, even in the "open vision" of eternity, otherwise than in his unutterably free revelation of himself, and so in a self-giving, a stepping forth from his inaccessible abyss of being, in his bridging over the infinite gulf separating us from him. For a creature can be all things, save only God. Right to the roots of its being it remains different from him, for ever. And the closer it comes to him by will and understanding, the more profoundly it experiences the gulf that distinguishes it from him who "is all" (Ecclus. XLIII. 29) and who knows no distinction in himself (non-aliud). But that there should be something outside the All, beyond the sea of being, something which is a "not-all", almost nothing, that exists somehow or other, to which existence is not necessary but "happens" (*esse accidens*)—that indeed invites question, arouses our sense of wonder and is really incomprehensible—it drives us constantly to interrogate Being and to search for the meaning of this scarcely-existent thing. The creature is a continuous interrogation of God.

As a spiritual being exercising its act of being, it can do no other than differentiate and distinguish itself—and thus relate itself.

God is the absolutely other, fundamentally and in every conceivable way, and he is therefore the solution to the question that I am. Only in looking on him is there any final hope of salvation. Whoever desires to know what this means should read and pray the psalms : "The Lord is my light and my salvation; whom shall I fear?" "My heart hath said to thee; my face hath sought thee. Thy face, O Lord, will I still seek. Set me, O Lord, a law in thy way, and guide me in the right path. I believe to see the good things of the Lord in the land of the living. . . ." Our every sense of existence turns our gaze toward God and becomes a word spoken to him, a recollection of him; every situation is clarified when seen in relation to him. It is the wretchedness and nobility, the lowliness and dignity of man to be obliged and permitted to relate himself in this way; to be only through God, without ever being God; to be able to affirm himself, not to speak of the whole world around him, only if this great Yes and No, built into the very foundations of his being, are uttered together—No, I am not God; Yes, I need God as my beginning and my end. No being is Being itself, but none is apart from Being, and each exists only as relative and pointing to Being.

That is why the contemplative thinkers and sages of the past have at all times attempted to see partial being in relation to Being. Often enough, we find them designating Being as the world in its totality, though that is, in fact, a faulty expression of their intention, which was to define Being as the all-embracing foundation of individual beings. They failed to observe that the totality cannot be qualitatively different from its parts. Often enough, too, they were able to distinguish the nature of the ascent from the quality of beings to the wholly other quality of Being, and then their whole endeavour, their contemplation itself, consisted in attempting to effect that spiritual ascent. They, therefore, thought that by turning away from finite being, with its limitations and its whole mode of existence, and from the corresponding experience and way of thinking, they could perceive something of the Being which is the ground of all being. Their contemplation might take various forms, aesthetic, ethical, intellectual, or even religious, according to the predominance of one or other faculty, one or other objective aspect, in the attempted ascent. Yet there was never any real hope that any of these roads would lead beyond their one intuition— that no being is Being; it directs us to Being, but does not exhibit it; in dying, it can only testify to the life that is not itself.

There was only one way out of this situation, which was that the infinite and eternal Being should express himself in a particular being, and so take on a presence and manifestation, an epiphany and a *parousia*. Then we should be able to hear the infinite word in a finite word and behold the eternal, imageless archetype in a finite image. Thus our contemplation is a groping approach to the mystery of the hypostatic union, in which two natures are united in the divine Person of the Son. This union is not brought about simply to effect a communion of will and life, but is expressly a self-manifestation, an exterior utterance, an explicitation and a presentation of the eternal Being to beings in time. Hearing, seeing and touching an earthly form, we are meant to remain in continual communication with the eternal "Word of life", who is with God and is God.

There is, certainly, also the way of simple faith, which embraces the mystery of the Incarnation in a single sentence, a plain formula, and is humbly content to do so. But that is not contemplation, which only begins at the point where the mystery begins to reveal itself to the believer, and to enlighten him in his depths. That does not mean that he starts to doubt, or weakens his hold on the firm doctrinal formulas, but that he experiences a feeling of awe right in the very ground of his being. We must never overlook the fact that the mystery of Jesus Christ is something far removed from any experience of God on the part of natural man, of man in his actual, historical setting; even beyond the experience of God in the Old Testament, deeply impregnated, as it was, with the mystical sense of awe, in which the natural knowledge of God finally issues. The men of the Old Testament are deeply aware of the distance between God and creature, between whom, certainly, when God so willed, conversation might be possible, an alliance and fidelity, but never community of being—as if the true God could become an earthly figure, one of the idols which it belonged to his very being as God to destroy in the day of his coming, the day of his wrath.

One who has never experienced a deep sense of awe before the being of God—not merely before the "mysteries of existence" and the profundities of the world—is not yet prepared for the contemplation of Jesus Christ. He ought at least to let himself be educated to this sense of fear and terror through the Old Testament; otherwise he is in danger of coming to Christ like someone deaf and blind, seeing in him only an example of human perfection, and contemplating in him, not God, but man, that is to say himself. That the absolute Being of God should have decided to present itself in a human life, and should be able to carry out his will should be a perpetual source of wonder to anyone contemplating the life of Jesus, should seem a thing impossible and utterly bewildering. He ought to feel his mind reeling at the idea, feel as if the ground were giving way under his feet, and experience the same "ecstasy" of incomprehension which seized Christ's contemporaries.[1] For they were beside themselves with astonishment, stupefied, overwhelmed, literally sent out of their minds; and this, not once, but repeatedly;[2] just as, they were "astonished at his wisdom" (Luke II. 47), to the point of declaring him out of his mind, out of his senses (*hoti exeste*—Mark III. 21). But although the astonishment of the crowd was no doubt often a shallow emotion provoked at the sight of the miracles wrought the contemplative has to let himself be moved far more profoundly at the sight of the Truth himself. The Gospel foresees no instance when anyone who really met Christ did not either adore him or revile him.

[1] *Hoste existasthai pantas*—Mark, II, 12; *exestesan ekstasei megalo*—Mark, V, 40; *lian en heautois existante*—Mark VI, 51.

[2] cf. Mt., VII, 28; XII, 24; XIII, 54; Luke, II, 48; IV, 32; VIII, 56; IX, 43, etc.

In the Old Testament, the appearance of God was always accompanied by signs threatening the end of the world. All the phenomena of nature—lightning, thunder, earthquakes, fire, darkness, smoke and vapour—that threaten to undermine the accustomed order, were so many means of indicating the presence of the absolute Lord (cf. Apoc. II. 19-20; Heb. XII. 18-21). There is an unbroken logical development leading from the language of prophecy to that of the apocalyptic visions in the Old and New Testaments, and Jesus himself made use of this language. Not only was its imagery familiar to him, not only did he adapt himself to the capacity of his hearers, but he adopted it as a form of expression suitable to his message, so that the entire Gospel is interwoven with a new form of apocalyptic utterance, presented as the truth of the earlier message. In his own prophecies of the future he makes use of the traditional forms of expression, but gives them a new accent, peculiar to himself. His death—when the true, though secret, judgment is passed on the sinful world—is accompanied by all the traditional signs with which the day of the Lord is to be proclaimed. But his whole life, too, his sayings and actions, pulsate with the violence of the spiritual tempest that sweeps through them, and he is himself that tempest. He came to cast fire on the earth, and he is himself the fire. Every word that issues from his mouth is a consuming flame; they are very often openly provocative, and it is not surprising that the flames should leap forth. And yet that is not the fire he desired, the fire he wished to see burning in the souls of men. That is why he invariably tried to put out the flames, though it was in vain that he forbade the spread of sensational news (Mark I. 43; VII. 21; VIII. 26, 30; IX. 9, 30). What he wanted was the true fire, adoration in spirit and truth, acknowledgment that he was the Son of the living God, the Holy One of God, and that he had the words of eternal life. He is sparing of his miracles, so as to work them not for unbelief, but for belief. Yet he always stirs up the fire. He veils the love that he came to bring in words of judgment and threats of perdition; and he speaks more often than his disciples of the flames of Gehenna, and eternal wrath. "He looked round about him in anger, being grieved for the blindness of their hearts" (Mark III. 5).

All this is even more strongly stressed in the narrative of St. John. There we find love in its most provocative form; whoever does not eat his flesh and drink his blood has no part in him and no access to the Father. "This saying is hard, who can hear it?", but the hardness of the words gives way before love, their sovereign power breaks down before his powerlessness, their light sinks into darkness. It is openly proclaimed that what love here says and does originates, not just in a higher "world", but in what is more than a world, in the place where the Father dwells. "I speak what I have seen of my Father" (John VIII. 38). "I am from above" (VIII. 23). "No man hath ascended into heaven, but he that descended from heaven, the Son of man who is in heaven" (III. 13). The harshness in St. John is so powerfully stressed in order that, contemplating the Son, receiving his word, and wondering at his deeds, we should, at all costs, experience the *quality* of the divine—even though we stumble against it blindly, more blindly than an animal against the world of the human spirit, as blindly as a sinner against the quality of the absolute, consuming purity of the all-holy God.

There is no question of our ever being "equal" to receiving the impact of the Absolute, or of exercising ourselves to be "better" capable of it, or orientating our contemplation with a view to gaining a further "experience" concerning it. The feeling of helplessness which overwhelms us when God makes his appearance in Christ is something that comes only from an ever-deepening humility and renunciation, a more complete simplicity, nudity and poverty. This is the poverty of heart and spirit that is declared blessed in the first sentence of the Sermon on the Mount. Everything that helps to empty man of self helps him to see what is to be shown him, and is the condition for his being able to see in Jesus Being among other beings, the essence of Being itself, giving itself to us as absolute love. A love, then, as we are warned by St. John, that is not our love, which comes from below, but a quite different love whose quality it is given us to experience in looking with faith on the Son as he expends himself for our sake.

It is at this point that contemplation begins. What the Son is and what he does is, in one respect, human; and therefore understandable. Psychologically, we can understand how a man could be so filled with a sense of his mission as to think of nothing else, staking all on one throw and in the end letting himself be crucified for his ideas. If we were unable to "understand" the human side, the incomprehensible element would not strike us with such force, and there would be no starting-point for contemplation of the divine aspect. But our very understanding of the human element is steeped in what is beyond our powers of conceiving. The quality of the human element itself distinguishes and differentiates it from anything else on the human plane. None the less, the humanity of the Son of God is truly human, neither disfigured nor distorted. It bears within it the quality of the divine like iron the capacity for incandescence, and the divine reveals its sovereignty through that intact humanity. For if magnitudes of the same order were involved, the greater would inevitably imperil the less. A tree planted in a flower-pot breaks it; but God can make his appearance in a creature without destroying it. Through faith we are able to contemplate the divine in what is created. "Philip, who sees me sees the Father". Faith can see the absolute Being, which no idea can compass, expressing and sinking it in the particular and finite being chosen to be its vessel; and, through contemplation, faith can develop, no longer confusing the Absolute with the finite, until finally it reaches a pitch of intensity expressed in continuous adoration, drawing from it further sustenance, till adoration becomes its whole life.

Starting with the words and deeds of Christ that point, beyond question, to his being the Son of the Father, the contemplative will gradually be able to see Christ's whole life as the revelation and word of the eternal God, so as to embrace the features which reveal him as no different from us, and even the long years of obscurity of which nothing is recorded. For under the impulse and sanction of faith, contemplation penetrates into all parts of the building, even the innermost, which harbour the Son's sentiments of love and obedience to the Father, indeed his vision of the Father. The contemplative can never understand everything, but basically nothing will be entirely closed to his view. He takes his stand before the mystery of the hypostatic union, so as to behold all that is human opening out into the divine, and, at the same time, all that is divine entering into the human. For that reason, Christ's words and acts will not be segregated into those deriving from his divinity, and those deriving from the "man". Everything he does, says and is will be seen as the manifestation of the being of God in a human form. Manifestation however does not mean identity. When Christ suffers on the cross, the divinity does not suffer. But Christ's passion, abandonment by God, death and descent into hell are the revelation of the divine mystery, the language in which God chooses to make himself and his love comprehensible to us. His love is not a "general" love, which the human mind could understand in some other way, and which only happened to be expressed in one of a thousand equally good ways. It is a love addressed to me, elected by it, in a specially chosen language, a word specially coined for me, a word in which I am to recognise the unique utterance of the one God as he turns, here and now, to me, to the Church, and to all mankind. This word, this utterance, is Jesus Christ; not selections made from what he said and did, but himself, whole and entire, who, as an individual, is also Being itself, and so can claim the great abstractions which indicate Being itself—"I am the way, the truth and the light". And equally all those designations which reveal him as the transition, the point of change, the door to the new life : "I am the way", "the door", "the resurrection".

The contemplative, then, has to see each concrete episode of Christ's human life in the context of that "opening" or door which is given to us in the mystery of the two natures and their union, so that it tells us something of the inner life of God. In that way, the concrete event is endowed with universal validity and necessity, qualities which, otherwise, belong, as far as this world is concerned, only to abstract laws and rules. It becomes a word and a law of God valid for all times and places, without, on that account, foregoing its concreteness, the stamp of an actual historical occurrence. There is nothing that is abstract or detached about it; indeed, there is no such thing as an abstraction in theology, no "teaching" separable from the event and universally valid apart from it, no purely spiritual "content" that retains its validity apart from the sensible form presented in the Gospel. The sudden broadening out of the event into an apparent abstraction (no longer *a* true thing, but *the* truth) is simply a sign that, for the person contemplating, the divine Concrete in all its fulness has replaced the concrete fact of history.

For this reason, the contemplative must avoid taking up a kind of detached attitude to the object of his contemplation. The Word has become flesh, and is the historical person who acts, teaches and urges men to follow him. We cannot behave as detached onlookers; the only possible attitude is to respond to his word. His "flesh" touches ours, in him God becomes our neighbour. The contemplative must therefore be present "with all his senses", though he is not to understand anything "carnally", in a wordly fashion, so as to rule out the divine. He should, in thought and imagination, put himself in the place and situation where God's word sounds audibly and impinges on the senses, and, taking his stand there, let a real, concrete meeting with God build itself up by degrees. The fact that it is God who is manifested in it amply assures to each particular historical occurrence a validity for all time, for an unlimited future. This validity is not based on an abstraction—as if Peter or Mary Magdalen were simply a "case" illustrating some general teaching—but on a presence : the eternal Concrete Being in the flesh in a situation which effectively communicates him to us.

All this justifies the designation of Christ as the central "sacrament", and makes us see the place of the Church in this connection. I am able to put myself in the place of the disciples or of the crowd at the sermon on the mount, joining in their travels, listening with them, only because the Church was already in existence. With the incarnation of the Word a reality was brought into being, in which the individual, through becoming part of it, is able to perform the act of contemplation that is at once adoration, obedience and insight through faith. The fact of the Church was given in principle by the appearance of the Absolute in the midst of human history, and so linked to mankind through his conception, birth, life and death; he is thereby linked to all generations, and they are stamped *a priori* by the entrance of God into them. The Church, then, understood in the radical sense of the community of the redeemed with Christ, belongs to the object of contemplation. The Church is not God, it cannot share the adoration due to the Son. But the Son must not be isolated from his brethren; the way opening on to heaven—and he is the way—cuts through the whole of mankind, and that rent, that breach, is the Church. Thanks to the reality of the Church I can enter by contemplation and imitation into the reality of Christ. It is, for me, the place where God is manifested to men in Christ. But the fact of the Church is a direct reminder to me that contemplation is only complete when accompanied by imitation. Even the somewhat detached attitude of the sapiential books is no longer permissible. All things form a kind of cone narrowing to the point where the Word becomes flesh, to the narrow gate of simple obedience, only to broaden out again at once and without pause, into what has absolute validity. From now on, only he who "does" will "know" (John VIII. 31); whoever fails to do, proves clearly that he does not know (Titus I. 16; 1 John IV. 8).

The following of Christ, however, has the most wonderful promises attached to it—"Come and see"; "greater things will you see ... you will see the heavens open" (John I. 39, 50-51). The life of the Son on earth is God's free revelation; whoever places himself in the path of this light has his own activity and understanding illumined by it. He does not himself become the light (John I. 8), but "walks in the light" (John XII. 35), so that he becomes for others a witness of the light, receives the power of enlightening (Mt. V. 15; Phil. II. 15), becomes a child of the light (Eph. V.8; 1 Thess. V. 5). His contemplation of the divine mysteries of love in Christ is perforce a participation in the mystery of Christ's being, light, that is, from light, and so able to illuminate others.

Yet this "becoming light in the Lord" (Eph. V. 8) means an impoverishment of man, at least in appearance, since something (the best part of him) is at once borne away by the *élan* of adoration into that opening of the finite being to Being itself which is contemplation. No doubt the believer contemplates in his own spirit and, correspondingly, is illuminated, strengthened and enriched in his mind and will, in his life as a Christian. Still, he is aware that his contemplation has its ultimate truth in God rather than himself, that the acts he clumsily and unsuccessfully attempts to produce have to look elsewhere for their full completion; that is where his faith and he himself are both surpassed, where they rest in God and are laid up against the day when what is hidden "will appear together with Christ" (Col. III. 4). For that reason, following Christ means, ultimately, renunciation of a final knowledge and casting all my knowledge into the knowledge which God has of me. "If any man love God, the same is known by him" (1 Cor. VIII. 3). "Now . . . you have known God, or rather are known by him" (Gal. IV. 9). "I follow after, if I may by any means apprehend, wherein I am also apprehended by Christ Jesus" (Phil. III. 12). "Then I shall know even as I am known" (1 Cor. XIII. 12). That is why the Christian never really has the characteristics of a "sage", that unmistakeable type of man we come across in all philosophies of life, who rouses admiration by his wisdom and enlightenment, and, in the long run, becomes slightly irritating. It may be part of the function of a particular Christian to know and say much about God and the things of God; but, for the most part, Christians, including the true contemplatives, the saints, remain modest and reticent about what they know, and, whenever they have to make something known, they do so in such a way that the message sounds as if coming through them, from a distant source, and as if they were not wholly accountable for the meaning and effect of their utterance. In that consists the simplicity of their discipleship, in which, as it were in advance, the surplus fruit of their contemplation is taken away and used for the purposes of God and the benefit of the communion of saints. The "sage" has a kind of controlling view and spiritual equipoise over all actual and possible knowledge, which is not shared by the Christian, because his wisdom resides in God rather than in himself. In some sense or other, his head is already in heaven, while his earthly being, dying daily and rising to new life, continues in the following of Christ; for "everyone shall be salted with fire" (Mark IX. 40).

The impoverishment of the contemplative, finally, should be seen in relation to the mystery of the hypostatic union, for he is a member of the mystical body of Christ. As such, he contemplates his Head, which he, as a member, is not, but from which he receives his mode of being and law as a member. His own truth and wisdom are not to be found in him, but in the Head, who thinks, beholds, speaks and looks upwards to heaven for the whole body. What the member—himself, of course, a spiritual person—executes in the way of such acts (which, in the natural order, come primarily from the head) has, in the supernatural relationship between Christ and the Church, its primary source in Christ, the Head. Christian faith is a participation in his vision. Christian hope is an insertion into his confidence and assurance. Christian love is an outflow of his love. What we said earlier about the *analogia personalitatis* in regard to the God-creature relationship in general and the indwelling of the Holy Ghost in the souls of the just, is seen now in concrete form, christological and ecclesial. The contemplative act of the member derives indeed from the Head, but its transcendence is ultimately based, not on a simple relation between member and Head but on the singularity of the Head himself, who, in the hypostatic union, is *the* transcendence. Christ's human nature has its being in the divine Person, and so— without prejudice to its fully human integrity and its own finality

—beyond itself; it is the perfect instrument of divine revelation and redemption. And the transcendence of Christ's human nature towards God reveals the transcendence of the Person of the Son in relation to the Father within the Godhead, and thereby the trinitarian form of the eternal divine love.

Thus the contemplative within the Church already participates ontologically, not only in the mysteries of the objects, but also in the mystery of the act, of divine revelation. It is given to him to understand, not merely by exterior vision, but by inner experience, that the Father's revelation in the Son through his coming down in the flesh takes the form of a sacrifice of love, of total self-impoverishment (2 Cor. VIII. 9), and that this revelation, in the complete giving of himself by the Son, points unmistakably to the origin and nature of the divine love which glorifies itself in this way.

That is why the contemplative's gaze always turns back to the humanity of Jesus. That is the infinitely precious treasure entrusted us by the Father, a treasure of which he has, in a real sense, deprived himself (John III, 16), and to which he constantly draws our minds—"ipsum audite" (Mt. XVII. 50). The Son is no emanation from the air above, but the fruit of this earth and its history; he originates from Mary (the representative of the Old Testament and of all mankind) as well as from the Father. He is the grace that ascends as well as descends, the supreme response of creation to the Father equally with the Father's Word to creation. He is no God in disguise simply coming to give us an example of how to live, like a teacher writing on the blackboard the solution to a problem which presents no difficulty to him, since he has no part in the laborious efforts of his pupils. Christ is the summit of the world which strives upwards to the Father, and he clears the way by becoming the spear-head of all its endeavours. He can do this, and actually does so, only by becoming "in all things like as we are, without sin", the bearer of our burdens, the scape-goat (Heb. XIII. 11 ff.), "the Lamb which was slain from the beginning of the world" (Apoc. XIII. 8, vulg.), standing at the summit of heaven and earth.

It is of equal moment that all "know" him as the son of Joseph and Mary, that he himself accepts this recognition, as that all are mistaken about him and fail to see his origin from above. The Messias the Jews expect is one that appears out of the air—"when he comes, no man knows whence he is" (John VII. 27); in their eyes, Christ's human origin tells against his mission. The Christian, on the contrary, makes it the object of his contemplation. Here is the man without sin, because he has given himself to the will of the Father with all the strength of his love. Here is a man whose inner life is perfectly free in the insignificant and oppressive circumstances of life, a freedom which is the fruit of prayer as we know from the sovereign self-assurance, so strikingly evident in contrast with his disciples and, even more so, his enemies. Here is the man whose love is perfect, although he often imposes on others the same inflexibly rigorous demands he makes on himself. Here is the complete man, not by any means one who accommodates himself to all and sundry, but a finely etched personality, far more memorable than any other, whose words have an absolutely unique stamp, whose conduct is without parallel, whose influence on history has been enormous. He is one who fulfilled the roles of friend and leader of men perfectly, who, in spite of his intense application, was never overwrought; marvellously self-possessed and with the simplicity of a child; a stranger to any show of quasi-adult sophistication, but a lover of children (most significantly) and commending them as a model to the supercilious. His reactions are never conventional or foreseeable, they are always original and spirited. In fact, the Gospels, the entire New Testament, abound with vitality in the literary, as well as the philosophical and religious sense; how barren, how relatively void of originality, the sayings of Buddha and the Koran are by comparison—once launched on their lines, we could very well continue them unaided!

No doubt, all these epithets are false or at least inadequate; and they have often been used by Liberal exegetes to express a frank admiration for the Gospel, but with the intention of going no further. The believer, however, for whom Christ is the Son of God, often tends, unconsciously, to overlook or dispense with them, so as to attain the divine aspect more readily, or else (a still greater mistake) he tends to intensify them to such a degree that they are no longer human excellencies, but a kind of pseudo-divine hybrid (the monophysite error). The human aspect of the Lord in the Gospels must not be left aside, even in contemplative prayer; that would be to belittle the Incarnation, and would undermine any real historical influence of the Gospel on our time. Even as man, the Lord wills to be loved and taken in full seriousness, to excite men's enthusiasm, and—why not?—to be followed deliriously. There is always time to purify the flame, to mellow the young disciples; an easier thing by far than to turn a jejune and soured religiosity into genuine Christian faith. Real holiness in the Church and the influence she has exercised on history is bound up, and always has been, with a simple and sincere acceptance of the humanity of Christ, whereas affection in Christian life and art derives from a failure to do so. How can we take the sacraments seriously—for they are after all something human—and pay but slight regard to the human side of Christ, to the human quality of his love and commandment of love, for example, to its obvious literal interpretation, on which the spread of Christianity, both in the past and the future, depends? "I have given you an example, that as I have done to you, so you do also. By this shall all—all!—men know that you are my disciples, if you have love one for another". Nowhere is the assurance given to the disciples that the keys of Peter and the institutional side of the Church would convince men and convert them. Love, however, can convert them and has always done so when taken literally. The saints who loved made even the power of the keys seem lovable, and reconciled the mistrustful to it; they are keys to love, and must be used and administered with love.

Only when we accept the importance of the human element have we the right to call the Church the total sacrament of salvation. For in the sacrament the sensible sign, as rite, matter, sanctifying word, is indispensable. But this is only the case, because Christ, considered in his totality and in all that he laid down and bequeathed to posterity, possesses a real, undiminished humanity. This human perfection of his is the efficacious sign of the Father's revelation, the language used by the divine Word in the hypostatic union to unfold the world of God before men. In addition, this perfection, taken in its entirety, points to an even greater truth, one eternal and absolute. What an inexpressible dignity conferred on our nature! What a source of joy for us, even in the dull daily round! Christianity is not only the truth from heaven communicated through a human channel of speech; it is the truth of man. It is not just a hypothesis expressed in mere rites and commands that are acknowledged to be valid in some special context or other remote from real life, but not in the prosaic reality of every day. It is the daily round itself, as God views it and as he gives it to us.

Certainly, since Christ brought redemption, not through victory in the worldly sense, but through death in helplessness and abandonment, the following of him must be a way of renunciation, a way of the cross. This by no means goes against what we have just said, but, in fact, confirms it. The Passion does not mean that the man, Christ, was more and more emptied and reduced to nothingness so as to make place, increasingly, for God. It means, primarily, that those human liabilities, which men fear, abhor, and keep silent about, are seen in their true value; that we can still achieve something when our positive and active powers fail. Heroism, even of a purely human kind, includes in its concept something of suffering—holding out in spite of danger and pain, and ultimately, in the face of weakness and death. Christ went far beyond the frontiers of heroism; about his heroism there can be no question. Only when this is recognised, can the "accomplishment" of Christ in remaining obedient and faithful in weakness, anguish and abandonment be seen as the greatest manifestation of divine in human love; only then can the Son's obedience unto death be seen as the act in which the old man was judged, condemned and buried, to make place for the new. But he who accomplished this is himself the new Adam, and what he achieved was, indeed, what St. John calls glorification—that, namely, of God in a human love carried to such lengths.

Since Christ is perfectly human, the following of Christ is possible to man. It is possible in the human community set up between the Lord and those who encounter him, those who, like Mary and Joseph, formed a human community with him from the beginning, or those who, like the apostles, come to him so as to be formed in the fashion of his humanity. It is here that contemplation exerts a powerful effect on living, here that its serious pursuit is seen to be indispensable. It is my life that is meant, not my speculations, imaginations, religious and theological phantasies, but my actual way of living. The life in question is life in faith, and so in obscurity rather than vision. Whoever contemplates the gospel, or the history of salvation in general, is constantly surprised by this obscurity. It seems as if God cared little, in his revelation, about any sort of well-rounded system. How much there is of Jesus that we do not know! How often we have to turn to the rules of literary composition to gain a better idea of his message, his Person. The same and similar passages are placed by the different evangelists in various contexts, the same events are related differently. It is as if the Holy Spirit, the author of Scripture, had spread a veil over the mystery of the Lord's earthly life. He himself is there present, testified to beyond all doubt by descriptions no one could have invented. His portrait stands out in clear relief, but he himself escapes confinement in any network of concepts—*transiens per medium illorum, ibat* (Luke IV. 30). The contemplative comes to love this mystery. It is part of the hiddenness of Jesus, of his will to be flesh and not spirit, son of man and not sage, ascetic, mystic, or theologian; his will to be taken for son of Joseph. There is much in Christianity susceptible of exact analysis, but it is ultimately shrouded in the silence of the divine mysteries. What is ultimate in Jesus is turned, not to men, but to the Father; it is itself contemplation, and, through contemplation, action.

CHAPTER II

THE LIFE OF THE TRINITY

WE CONTEMPLATE Christ, his world and his truth, in order to encounter God and to "see" him; to see him truly and objectively with the eye of faith, with our mind and our senses that is, but inwardly illumined by the indwelling Spirit. We have already spoken of our capacity to do this, and now we are to treat of the object of contemplation. This we said was God. All the rest, creation, man, the history of salvation, are contemplated in relation to God, and in order to find him; to find him in a spiritual and personal encounter of which we become conscious, through faith in the life God gives to the believer objectively as grace—a participation in the divine nature and the life of mutual love within the Trinity. That participation implies an encounter. God's inner life is not merely ontological and objective, but spiritual and personal. A purely objective participation, unaccompanied by the revelation of the word which informs the creature of the grace received, and enables him to deepen his knowledge of it, would be self-contradictory.

Christ, the Incarnate Word of the Father, is both of these. He is the centre of the sacraments, the flesh and blood given to us for our food and drink, which alone communicate the life of God. He is the centre of that spiritual revelation, for in giving himself, he unfolds its meaning—"Know you what I have done to you?" (John XIII. 13). Thus the Lord presents what he has done, brings it to the notice of men, and then requires them to understand it. "What I do thou knowest not now, but thou shalt know hereafter" (John XIII. 7). The same thing is repeated in the words:

"Whither I go thou canst not follow me now, but thou shalt follow hereafter" (John XIII. 36). What comes first is the Lord's action, one exclusive to himself, which counts on our accepting it as taking place in us, and, when this acceptance is not given explicity, assumes it as implicit. *Only* then can the second thing follow : the inward illumination of what we were participants in from the outset. And what the Lord made us share with him, from the very beginning, despite our disobedience, was his loving obedience to the Father, the divine mystery of their mutual life, a mystery which bears the name of the one Spirit common to both.

We can, therefore, say that we would never attain to a knowledge of the life of the Trinity in Christ, even in virtue of our "objective" elevation given by the "state of grace" (assuming that such a state were possible in a purely objective sense), unless we had also been made participators, from the outset, in the subjective relationship of the Son made man to his heavenly Father in the Holy Spirit. If, then, grace is the gift of all three Persons in their unity, it is essentially a participation in their trinity, into which we are introduced—in faith, not in sight—through our encounter in faith and communion with the Son on earth. For this reason, it can be said, in a strictly theological sense, that our "seeing, hearing and touching" of Jesus Christ as the "Word of life" imparts to us a knowledge of the trinitarian life of God, veiled indeed, but absolutely true and objective. Grace is in us a participation in this life, and so it imparts to us the subjective organ enabling us to perceive, with the certainty of faith, the trinitarian element in Christ as he is shown to us, as the object of our contemplation. Further, it is an essential, or rather the distinctive, activity of Christian contemplation to develop this implicit knowledge of faith into a continuous seeking and finding, to promote and invigorate the "seeing, hearing and touching" of faith in the sphere in which the Incarnate Son of the Father stands before the Father in the Holy Spirit. In this way alone can the purpose of the Incarnation be attained, for its object was to disclose and entrust to us God's own inner being and life, to make us experience the meaning of "God is love" in our inmost being, with all our faculties of sense and spirit.

Here we would make some observations by way of parenthesis. Liberal Christian thought, not to mention non-Christian and Jewish, always deplores the narrowness of the New Testament idea of divine contemplation. To them it seems not only an impoverishment but an error to claim that heaven stands revealed in Jesus Christ, and that the Father should point to him as the one we have to hear, giving his revelation an exclusiveness previously unknown, so that the breadth and variety of earlier revelations ("in sundry times and in divers manners"—Heb. I. 1) both within and outside Israel, in history and in nature (cf. the psalms and the sapiential books and their strong attachment to the contemplation of nature), should "at the end of time" contract to a single point, and focus on the only Son, the "appointed heir of all things". Nor can a Christian dispose of this view by a simple negation. The tremendous assertion of the Christian faith must, indeed, include a negation, as light involves shadow—"whosoever denieth the Son, the same hath not the Father" (1 John II. 23); "he who honoureth not the Son honoureth not the Father" (John V. 23); "no man cometh to the Father, but by me" (John XIV. 6); "he that hath not the Son hath not life" (1 John V. 12); "neither me do you know, nor my Father. If you did know me, perhaps you would know my Father also" (John VIII. 19). But the narrowing down to the One on earth, sacramentally representing the One in heaven for us all, is no impoverishment of the relation to God, provided that this single point is the indispensable condition for opening the inner life of God to us, and if this could not be attained in any other way; provided, also, that the outpouring of the Spirit on all flesh be the crowning of the history of the incarnation of the only-begotten Son.

Christianity owes it to the world to present its witness to the one Redeemer, in whose name it "brings every intellect into captivity into the obedience of Christ" (2 Cor. X. 5), as clearly related to the witness of the Holy Spirit, in whom all the world awakes to a religious freedom and universality otherwise unattainable and, indeed, unthinkable. So it was that Christ preached his own mission; so, too, the apostles, especially after the resurrection and Pentecost, sought to gain men for Christ. If the world fails to hear, see and touch in Christ the trinitarian "Word of life", if the preaching, the life and the institutions of the Catholic Church do not offer men the divine life now opened and made accessible to them, the world may well stigmatise the dogmatic captivity of man's religious contemplation, imprisoned in obedience to Christ, as something deplorable, indeed as the greatest catastrophe in man's religious history. This defines the duty of a trinitarian contemplation : what Jesus shows us of himself and enjoins us to imitate must be the irruption within us of the inner life of God.

The liberal attitude, whether Jewish or pagan, is invested with a halo of broadmindedness, by contrast with Christianity (and, for that matter, with strict Judaism). In its religious ideas and intimations it sees the world as a whole; from whatever point man sets out, it is possible for him to enter into a relationship with God, and, since all such points are fundamentally equally essential, each of them includes all the others. In this consists the liberal catholicity of truth. In contrast with it, the Christian conception is a monstrous paradox in that, *although* God chose a single people and, within it, willed a single individual to be his only-begotten Son, *in spite* of and precisely *on account* of this, he intended to save all peoples and all men through him. The fact is, however, that the oneness of God can only be perfectly represented in the world through the oneness of the mediator, the particular man, Jesus Christ (1 Tim. II. 5). But the Messias would be the most deceitful of prophets, if he had merely introduced a new "teaching" about God and a new religious "institution", and if he had not, in "giving himself up for *all*", revealed the will of his Father "that all men should be saved" (1 Tim. II. 4-5), and, through this revelation in his life and death, proclaimed the very being of God as Love in Trinity.

This is proved, for instance, by the fact that the tremendous novelty of Christianity, namely the universality of the salvation freely decided on by God for the world, which St. Paul was able to designate as a mystery hitherto concealed (Eph. III. 2; Rom. XVI. 25), is still, after so many centuries of official Christianity, an unheard-of novelty—literally not heard. It is, indeed, incredible if separated from the figure of Jesus Christ, and in his historical uniqueness it is just as astonishing now as it was at first. Only when the truth is seen as trinitarian does the statement that God is love—love that burns, consumes, judges and redeems—become visible to the world in general; and the truth becomes trinitarian only when one of the Trinity becomes man and shows us in human form the love which is eternal.

The crucial point is that Christ constantly speaks to a Father and refers to a God with whom he stands in a dialectical relation, who is therefore a Person other than he, but with whom he is, at the same time, one in essence. It is this that is indicated by all the expressions of "being one in the other" (John X. 38; XIV. 11), the assertion simply of their "oneness" (John X. 30), the statement that "all my things are thine, and thine are mine" (John XVII. 20). No doubt, there are in the Old Testament certain remote analogies to such a relationship with God; but once it appears in its perfect form it seems something so extravagant, so far beyond the natural religious consciousness of a normal man, that we are not in the least surprised that it is presented as quite different from any other. Jesus never prays in common with the apostles; he cannot, for his relationship with the Father is not the same as theirs. He himself points to the earlier stages of Judaism in order to distinguish himself sharply from them (John X. 34 ff.). His object was not to keep men at a distance and to confine his discourses to enlightening them about his heavenly Father, with whom he, and he alone, lives in community of being; if this were so, there would have been no need for him to draw attention constantly to himself, to point to himself and his external manifestations as inexplicable except on a basis of faith in the Trinity. Once his hearers accept him on this basis, acknowledging that "I am he"

(John VIII. 26), they become participators in the truth, for the Father is "true" and "faithful" in giving his Son, the promised Messias, for the world, and the Son is "true" in that he speaks and does nothing but what the Father says to him (John VIII. 26). Both together form the one divine truth revealed to the world in Christ. Both together form a double testimony having legal force as the testimony of two persons, yet wholly given in the single witness of Christ, by reason of the mutual indwelling of Father and Son (John VIII. 13-18). To do justice to the external facts one must interpret them in a trinitarian sense.

The necessity of faith follows logically; the facts admit of no other interpretation. This man is neither a mere man, nor is he "God", understood as the Jews understood him as the Father who created the world, chose the people of Israel and promised the Messias. He is a man, but not one like them; he is "of God", without being "*the* God" (*ho theos*). At the same time, he is someone unique, not, like the prophets, an ordinary man "charged", for the time being, with the word of God and made an organ of God. But he is, equally, not "a God" temporarily disguised as a man. On the contrary, this human personality who goes about among men is a Person pertaining to God, one who, in his mission, not only speaks of the Father, but represents him; reveals him too in every conceivable way, active as well as passive, in strength and in weakness, in his utterance and in silence, in what he discloses as in what he conceals from view. This relationship is the inexhaustible theme, the limitless field, of Christian contemplation.

Although it is the Son alone who became man, and not the Father and the Spirit, yet in his human form his relation to the Father and the Spirit is also, of necessity, made manifest.

In his "coming down" into the flesh, the Son reveals, first of all, himself : his self-abasing, humble and obedient love. In the acts of the Lord from his birth and lowly childhood, his "going about doing good" (Acts X. 38), to his final abasement in the washing of the feet, the Eucharist, Passion and death, wherein he gave up his spirit, what is manifested to anyone who surrenders, unprejudiced, to the actual events (and that means, directly, to assent in faith to the facts) is not only a sublime parable of the eternal love but this love itself, whose presence in this man proclaims what its own essence is, expresses it in visible form. For, although the acts and sufferings of this man remain on the human plane, their meaning is seen only when they are viewed and interpreted as expressing the nature of the love which is in God. Otherwise, we would have to agree with those liberal thinkers who see these acts as a doubtless well-intentioned, yet a monstrous mistake which in the disillusioned cry of the dying man on the cross, redounds to his honour indeed, but also attests their own perspicacity. For at that moment, in their opinion, the sufferer in his tragic destiny was, however heroic, in fact utterly foolish.

The Son, by humiliating himself, intended to express, not a kind of neutral "essence" of God, but, as he repeatedly said, the particular "essence", the inmost nature and disposition of the Father who sent him. From the Father there came into the visible world his divine image, his "Word", who, like him, is a Person, his Son. In all that the Son is and does the Father expresses himself. The Son's love in its totality is a representation of the Father's; his acceptance of death on the cross, his sense of utter abandonment by God, all this was to make visible how the Father "so loved the world as to give his only-begotten Son". So that the Father really and not just fictitiously, passes over his Son's dead body to reach a stranger, an enemy, namely man, and draw him to himself. The Son's passive, suffering love is at once the direct and reversed image of the love of the Father.

In addition, we are shown the relations which bind the Person of the Son to that of the Father, relations which become incarnate in those of the creature to the Creator and bring them to fulfilment, with the result that we obtain a supreme archetype of our relationship to God, and are given a concrete understanding of how all is founded and subsists in the Word and Son, how he is the beginning of all creation and its inaccessible archetype, or, ex-

pressed more comprehensively, how the eternal trinitarian relations between Son and Father in the Spirit are the condition of the
possibility of creation *ad extra*. As we contemplate the attitude
of the Incarnate Son to the Father, we come to a knowledge of
the archetypal image within the Godhead. Within this image
creation is such as it ought to be according to the Father's eternal
vision of it, and this, certainly, it can never be in its own proper
nature as a creature, but only in being elevated by the Son into
his own relation with the Father. This relation is, admittedly,
divine, and so inaccessible to the creature. The unity in which the
dialogue between Father and Son is embedded differs from the
unity capable of being established between creature and Creator.
The Son pointed to a food of which we know nothing (John
IV. 32), spoke of a "vision" proper to him alone (V. 19; VI. 46;
VIII. 38), likewise of a "hearing of the Father" (VIII. 26, 40)
and a "knowing" of him (VII. 29; VIII. 55). At the same time,
he makes himself our food and thereby brings the mystery of the
divine communication between the Persons into his Incarnation,
in order to introduce us into that mystery—"I in them and thou in
me, that they may be consummated in one" (John XVII. 23).
Then seeing the Son is all that is needed to see the Father, whom
no man can see (VI. 46 and XIV. 7, 9; XII. 44), to hear him
(VI. 45; VIII. 47), indeed, to be of him (VIII. 47) and in him
(1 John IV. 16). What seems in the Son to be inaccessible to men
(John VII. 34), even incomprehensible (VII. 36), becomes, for
those to whom the Son is the "way", accessible to a degree wholly
unexpected. In disappearing from sight and beyond our reach,
he prepares us a place and returns to take us with him, "that where
I am you also may be"; in fact, he gives the believer previous
knowledge both of the way and where it leads (XIV. 2-4).

Consequently, in the descent of the Son and his return to the
Father, we come to know the relation, now become manifest, between the Son and the Father. We know it as the way we have
to follow to reach the Father through the Son. It is the way of
renunciation of our own willing and thinking, surrendering them

to loving obedience in faith, not, indeed, as our own work but the "work" of the Father in us (John VI. 28-29). It is, thus, a taking up by the Father and Son of their "abode" in us (XIV. 23), an expression which signifies that our dwelling is with God and prepared in him.

There is yet another, a quite different, dimension in God that is manifested through the Incarnation of the Son. It is a new one, by no means a repetition or appendage of the Father-Son relationship. The way, too, in which it is manifested is different. The Son always prays to the Father through and in the Spirit; we never see him praying directly to the Holy Spirit. Yet the Spirit is clearly present in his prayer. It may be that the dullness of our perception by faith could not discover the Spirit in the Son, did not Scripture so expressly direct our attention to him. The Son is the archetype of those who are "led by the Spirit" (Rom. VIII. 14); and this Spirit, who in visible form comes down from the Father on the Son at his baptism, and so is the Spirit of the Father, who inwardly impels the Son to speech and action of a most personal stamp, and so is the Spirit of the Son, shows in the Son's visible life on earth a sovereign freedom that clearly reveals to the believer his own divine personality. The obedience with which the Son does the Father's will is not that of a "slave" who carries out with literal exactness the orders of a master; that would be wholly alien to the Son's freedom. Nor, however, is he free in the sense of acting arbitrarily according to his own estimate of the conduct to pursue. He possesses a freedom of a kind not to be found in the world; it clearly derives from God himself, subsists in heaven as a relation between the Father and the Son, and, even if we knew nothing of a third divine Person, could only be represented as proceeding simultaneously from the "Spirit of the Father" and the "spirit of the Son", as the unity of them both.

This is something glimpsed by reverent contemplation as an impenetrable mystery, and is hardly expressible in human language. It is an indwelling in the inmost being of the Son that neither infringes, nor violates, nor overwhelms him in his personal will, but leads his own being to its full realisation, in such fashion, though, that the Son, in his openness to the Spirit, listening to him, following his intimations, is brought to entrust and surrender to him entirely all that he has and is. It is only because there is a Spirit that the Son can do his work as a man fully real, limited, indeed weak and failing, a work that, *as human,* can, in consequence, be no more than a man's work seemingly lost in the immensity of human history, and, from the earthly point of view, doomed to collapse in suffering and death. He can *allow it to be so,* without being perturbed, without falling into despair or incomprehension in view of the enormity of the task he has "yet" to do. He knows this; that the words he speaks are "spirit and life" and that "it is the Spirit that gives life" (John VI. 63), the Spirit that makes the words, works, prayers and sufferings transcend the limits of what is humanly possible and, breathing where he will, scatters their seed abroad. It is in the Spirit that Jesus keeps his human equilibrium intact; in view of the prodigious nature of what he says and does, he could not do this of himself without the Spirit. Inasmuch as he surrenders to the Spirit, he obeys the Father, for the Spirit is that of the Father; he draws the Father's will spiritually into the Son, imbeds it in him, pours it into him. But, in thus obeying, the Son also obeys his own will, a will indeed which, issuing from his own inmost being, transcends him, drives him out of himself and makes him as one "inspired". So it is a will that both dominates his (being the will of the Father) and liberates him (being his own rational and personal will), and, through the sovereignty of the Person of the Holy Spirit, conveys to him all that the apostle calls the fruits of the Spirit, the mysterious inner flowering and outpouring within the Godhead itself—"charity, joy, peace, patience, benignity, mildness, faith, modesty, continence, chastity" (Gal. V. 22-23). It is an outpouring from inmost being which hides, too, an eternal surprise, as the child is the surprise of the love between parents, the fruit the surprise of growth and flowering.

The Son knows this mysterious source, he has it in himself

(John VII. 37; XIV. 20), and promises it to all who will to live together with him in the Holy Spirit (VII. 37; IV. 14). Thus baptism in the flowing waters of the Jordan is not only an efficacious sign of the washing away of sins, but also an initiation into the spiritual element that surpasses our understanding. In the beginning, this element moved over the waters of the abyss, and was communicated to the earth "consisting out of water and through water" (2 Peter III. 5); the element that is "more active than all active things, and reacheth everywhere by reason of her purity", that is "pure emanation of the glory of God" (Wisdom VII. 24-25); it is the Spirit which entered, through the Incarnation of the Son, into the water of creation. The visible and the invisible element together make possible the new birth, are the origin of the sacraments of the Son who, at his death, gave both of them with his heart's blood, both Spirit and water (1 John V. 6-8). This Spirit who is in the visible Son and becomes visible with him, "gives testimony" that the Son is God, and does so in union with water and blood (1 John V. 6-8). But he is only visible to those whose faith opens them to the same Spirit and to whom he is promised by the Son, the bearer of the Spirit. After his resurrection—again a thing perceptible to the senses—he is breathed upon them, and finally, at Pentecost, poured out upon them from heaven in the eschatological (2 Peter III. 7, 10), and now visible, element of fire.

Fire is the second element of the Spirit, and, like the first, always linked with the Son made visible. In contrast to baptism with water—which belongs to the ancient world—Christ's baptism is "with the Holy Ghost and with fire" (Luke III. 16), in connection with which there occurs the reference to "unquenchable fire" (III. 17). Fire is one of the most frequent images for the action of God in the Old Testament. The judging, searing, consuming, but also purifying, element reaches its ultimate significance in the Incarnate Word—God's word of fire (Ps. XIII. 31) will itself "cast fire on the earth" (Luke XII. 49) and is the first to burn with it in the baptism of fire (Luke XII. 50) and to be salted, as a sacrifice, in the fire (Mark IX. 48). And the last form in which the Son appears is as one aglow in the fire of the Spirit, the Son of man from whose eyes the Spirit blazes out (Apoc. I. 14; II. 18; XIX. 2).

The third element that makes the Spirit visible does so too in close connection with the Son. For he breathes forth his spirit back to the Father (John XIX. 30), and, risen from the dead, when he has taken up his spiritualised humanity into the one divine source of spiration, he breathes the Holy Spirit into his Church in a visible manner (John XX. 22). Now the Spirit, "which bloweth in every country" (Baruch VI. 60), whose freedom it is to "breathe where he will" (John III. 8), becomes a "mighty wind" in the house of the Church (Acts II. 2) and henceforth breathes visibly and irresistibly through its members, working the great things the Lord foretold (John XIV. 12). Those who believe will "know him, because he shall abide with them and be in them" (XIV. 17). He will endow them with eyes of fire, the eyes of contemplation, which will enable them to understand from within all that the Word of God has spoken to them exteriorly. So the contemplative who beholds in Christ the trinitarian revelation comes, finally, to contemplate contemplation itself; not as man's own work or his own inmost being, but as the incomprehensible medium—water, fire, wind of God—in which the inscrutable depths of God open out to him. "For the Spirit searcheth all things, yea, the deep things of God. . . . We have received the Spirit that is of God, that we may know the things that are given us from God" (1 Cor. II. 10-12). Through the Spirit we look upon the Son, and are enabled to know him by our participation in his Spirit. Through the Son we are brought within the Father's Spirit, who forms a single Spirit with that of the Son—a single Spirit, who bears the likeness of the Father and the Son, who, indeed, brings to clear view their inmost personal being, and yet is himself personal and inimitable, because himself imitating no one—for he is *the* freedom of God.

All this revolves, in a mysterious manner, round the Son and extends back into the Old Testament history of salvation, that of Noah and Abraham, David and the prophets; forward too into the history of the Church, of the apostles and their successors, the saints and believers of all times. It is full of mystery, and becomes to those who contemplate it deeply a mystery ever more profound, at once more and more clear and obscure, more luminous and more veiled. The uninformed see only the surface, but to the contemplative is disclosed a third dimension, one of relief, of life. Certain insights admit of being co-ordinated, but a general, systematic view of all the aspects is out of the question. Whoever contemplates simply, lovingly and willing to obey the word, may be confident of being taken into the greater "system" of divine truth. He is known exhaustively and has no need, for his part, to be anxious to gain an exhaustive knowledge. The sphere in which he lives, in which he moves by his growth in knowledge, is that of the eternal trinitarian truth—for the time being, in faith, "through a glass, darkly" and "in part"; only later will he be granted to know perfectly, "even as I am known" (1 Cor. XIII. 12-13).

The object of contemplation is God, and God is trinitarian life; but for us he is life in the incarnation of the Son, from which we may never withdraw our gaze in contemplating God. If we try to contemplate God's life in the Trinity in itself, we only find a vacuum, unreality, mathematical concepts or vague speculations. We can no more make the Trinity in itself an "object" of contemplation than the pagan mystics and Christian ascetics of old could "objectify" the superessential unity of God by abstraction from all created multiplicity.

God, in linking our contemplation to his Son's humanity, makes his gift to us not less, but greater. He presents us with a concrete vision of the life of the Trinity, a vision contained in full measure in the grace and the earnest following of Christ. The vision in question is simply the interior illumination of obedience in faith practised with Christ towards the Father in the Spirit. The archetype of such contemplation of the Trinity is Mary, who was directly addressed by God (through the angel as bearer of his word) in a trinitarian form (Luke I. 26-38). It is significant that the three words of the angel, of which the first manifests the Father, the second the Son, the third the Holy Spirit, provoke three corresponding reactions on the part of Mary, none of which is mere speculation about God, but each the outcome of her reflection on the right way of answering the message and the responsibility entailed. The revelation of the Father provokes a feeling of fear (as must be the case with any creature placed directly before God) and prompts her to reflect on the meaning of the salutation—on what answer it required and what demand it made. Her second reaction, following on the revelation of the Son whom she is to bear, and who is both God's Son and David's son and heir, is the still more concrete question : how is she to conduct herself in face of the obedience expected of her? The third, after the revelation of the Spirit who is to overshadow her, is her accord with God's Word that is to come in her, rule in her, and take flesh of her. Each step in the revelation of the Trinity is a divine response to a question prompted by obedience. Mary's reflection on the Father's message, "The Lord is with thee", is a prelude to the sending of the Son; and when she asks how this can be possible, she prepares the way for the Holy Spirit's answer. The revelation of the Trinity in the New Testament is not only bound up with the incarnation of the Son and inseparable from it, but inseparable from the obedience of the contemplative in faith; it cannot form an object of contemplation in itself.

Furthermore, contemplation of the Incarnation need not be explicitly trinitarian; the trinitarian dimension is revealed from above, while Mary is at once wholly taken up with bearing God. In doing so she realises that her Son is God, and that the Holy Spirit is to bring her the Father's seed. From then on, in nurturing her Son and following him, keeping all his words in her heart and reflecting on them, she penetrates more and more deeply into the understanding of the Trinity—of the Father, whose daughter she is, of the Son, whose mother and mystical bride she is, of the Spirit, of whom she is the vessel. That is precisely what the Church as a whole is, and Mary is thus her archetype. She does not indulge in speculative thought, but adores and obeys; she opens her breast to the Spirit, and bears the Son, his members, his brethren to the end of the world. She is the woman in whom the life of the Trinity is fulfilled, the woman who, through her existence, compels the divine mystery of the three countenances to shine forth and be manifest. The obedience of Christians is, too, and in contemplation especially, the medium in which God reveals himself as three in one.

The same situation recurs on Mt. Thabor when the institutional Church is introduced to contemplation of the mystery of the Trinity. The three "pillars of the Church", Peter, John and James (the latter as representative of the later bearer of the same name), who symbolise its trinitarian structure, are "taken up" on to a high place, where the Son in his "form of God" (Phil. II. 6), as the "second man from heaven" (2 Cor. XV. 47), and as the "eternal Gospel" (Apoc. XIV. 6), in his discourse with Moses and Elias, the Law and the Prophet, presents the trinitarian form of the divine revelation of salvation. But while his conversation is "horizontal" on one plane, it is at the same time the exposition of the supreme "vertical" discourse; the Father's Word is heard above the incarnate Word while the *schechina* of the Spirit completes the theophany. As long as Jesus is conversing with the representatives of the Old Covenant, a splendour shines from his own countenance bright as the sun, and from his garments of dazzling whiteness. But, when the revelation comes to a close, and the Son is no longer seen as the fulfilment of the promise of salvation, but as the one fulfilled, accredited, and glorified by the Father, the splendour becomes a bright overshadowing cloud, a revealing veil, a "darkness" (Luke IX. 34) that is supremely bright. And it is the simple human form of the Son, "Jesus alone", emerging from the cloud, who finally compels the disciples to fall down in fear and adoration before a sublime, though oblique, revelation of the divine Trinity. It is this human figure that turns towards Jerusalem and goes towards his Passion, when, in obscurity he will be "assumed" (Luke IX. 51), "raised up" (John VIII. 28; XII. 32) and "glorified" (John XII. 3, 28; XIII. 31-32). It is significant that the conversation with Moses and Elias concerns "the decease he should accomplish in Jerusalem" (Luke IX. 31), and Peter "knew not what he said" when he proposed to set up tents of contemplation on the mountain at the very moment when Moses and Elias "departed"; for the conversation had finished and the reality of what had been said was on the point of beginning. The whole scene is shown to the Church, so that she may go forward with the Son to the fulfilment of the Passion, and so that the same fruitful cloud, the Holy Spirit that "overshadowed" Mary (Luke II. 35) might overshadow the institutional Church and make it fertile (Luke IX. 34)—even though the institutional element in the Church is filled with dread at the thought of its betrothal to the Trinity. But that the fruit has started to grow and is not, as with the unbelieving people, doomed to wither, is shown by the observance of the command to keep silence (Mark IX. 9—the command; Luke IX. 36—its observance). The mystery of the Trinity contemplated by the Church and kept in her heart, is not for idle speculation, but bears fruit in the following of Christ in his Passion.

CHAPTER III

WORD AND TRANSFORMATION

T HE WORD sent to be our ransom and our brother entered the world of space and time, the world of change and transformation. Space and time, with the changes they involve, are the quantitative media, the surface on which the qualitative riches of life are spread out in all their fulness and made manifest. Our faculties perceive change and are involved in it, and change itself leads us through the adumbrations and images of unity to the perception of its full reality. Little by little, first in one thing, then in another, we come to descry the unity of which they form part.

There are three ways or media through which we are shown the entrance of God's Word, through the Incarnation, into this world of change. The first is that of a normal human existence extending from birth to death, a field where the tension is so dramatic, and the forces at work so tremendous, that it seems "as though made" to exhibit a more than human drama, a spiritual power and life that is divine. And, in fact, that is the real purpose of its existence. The life of Jesus is the ideal drama in which the contemplative man can see the meaning of life unfolded, scene by scene, episode by episode—the meaning, that is, which it possesses in the mind of God, and that he desires man to discern.

There we see the Word of God in his humanity, whose manhood coincides so intimately with our own, though coming from God and returning to God (John XVI. 27), not of course by revoking his Incarnation, but by his resurrection from the dead. And that is the second transformation, striking down vertically into the first, which God the Father accomplished in his dead Son; and its cause ("for which cause"—Phil. II. 9) is the Son's obedience unto death, and ultimately the power given by the Father to the Son of having life in himself, the power of renouncing it and taking it up again (John X. 18). It is the transformation from death to resurrection, from abandonment by God to sitting at the Father's right hand, from extreme helplessness to absolute omnipotence. In it is spread out before the contemplative the full range of the Lord's dominion—"He that descended is the same also that ascended above all the heavens, that he might fill all things" (Eph. IV. 10).

Both these transformations open on to a third, in which the fulness of Christ's transformation is "distributed" from heaven through the Holy Spirit in history, and poured out profusely into the Church. It is a medium devised to present and unfold the fulness of Christ through all ages down to the end of the world (Eph. III. 10). It is "his body and the fulness of him who is filled all in all" (Eph. I. 23), so that all his members "may be filled unto all the fulness of God" (Eph. III. 19).

The three dimensions are interconnected. Each presupposes the others and points from within itself to them, showing such a variety of senses, each reflecting the other as if in a hall of mirrors, that the object of contemplation becomes infinitely extended. Man in prayer experiences what Origen did in reading the epistles of St. Paul "St. Paul seems to me to speak like a trusted and wise servant brought by his master, a great king, into the royal treasure-store, and shown numerous and vast rooms with countless ways of access to them . . . these treasures are only shown through half-open doors and are only glimpsed momentarily, so that, while he gains some idea of his royal master's treasures and riches, he cannot see them in detail or examine them at length. At one time he goes in at one door and out by another, at another he goes in by a different one and passes quickly into the next room, so that, if you wait at the door he entered, you fail to see him come out" (*Commentary on the Epistle to the Romans* V. 1).

But so great a variety does not confuse the contemplative; he is always able to orientate himself by the main lines of the building, clear as they are to the simplest intelligence. A single movement of the mind is enough to reduce the most subtle refinements to the statement that God has manifested himself to us as love, that he gave his life for us and invites us to give our own lives for him and the brethren. That is the glory of the eternal love that glorifies itself in resurrection from the dead to eternal life, not for its own sake only but for the world and in the world.

The first dimension in which the one, unchangeable love moves and is delineated before our eyes is that of human life. Here contemplation is easiest. The contemplative only needs to let himself be led from image to image, and to see the human aspect of each as a revelation of the eternal love of the Trinity. In the first place, all that is simply human : the child with his natural characteristics, the boy, the youth with his, the grown man; each stage of life, each condition; waking and sleeping, alertness and fatigue, solitude and human intercourse, the events of morning, midday and evening, work and rest, eating and fasting, enjoyment and abstinence, human affections and absence of all feeling, days of festivity and of grey routine—each of these human conditions was conceived and formed by God the Creator, and now, in the fulness of time, he has sent his Son to share in them, in order to try them himself and to make of them "experiences" of God in human nature, assume them on his own account, to crown them as a work fulfilled, to carry over their truth, their quintessence, into eternity. Henceforth, the relation between the human life and the divine life is no longer a vague "similarity in a still greater dissimilarity"; there is communion, and the transitory becomes the vessel of the eternal, filled to the brim and overflowing with signs manifesting the divine love. The child's resting in his mother's arms, fed by her and sleeping on her lap; his first smile, first steps; the first words learnt from his mother, the first things made with the guidance and help of Joseph, comradeship with its joys and disappointments, school, religious practices, solitary walks and prayer—all these begin to speak of what "was kept secret from eternity and now is manifest" (Rom. XVI. 25), namely, eternal love. His humanity is the flesh of the Word of God, the expression of the eternally True, but not of a truth which, once known, is universally accepted (as a secret, once divulged, is no longer a secret, a crossword puzzle, once solved, is no longer of interest); it translates the temporal into the eternal and vice versa, but only here and now and in this particular individual. It is *his* translation, one stamped by *his* personality and inseparable from it. It must always be studied in him; and, if it is partially visible in others, in his mother and foster-father, his cousin Elizabeth and her son John, in his predecessors and followers, that is because of him.

Everything human is sacramental, a transparent symbol, containing and manifesting God's love effectively, and through Christ this symbolism becomes a twofold obligation of faith in Christ and imitation of him. Not every mother who nurses her child is an image of heavenly love in the same sense as Mary. But she can, with Jesus and Mary in mind, actively share in the likeness, and the contemplative who believes can bring the example to life. For God took upon himself an individual life in order to give value to the whole human world. He did not do so for his own sake (for how could the Creator not know the work he himself conceived and executed? How could he "that planted the ear not hear, or he that formed the eye not consider?—Ps. XCIII. 9). But he did so for the sake of his creature, to give him security and a home with himself, to endow this transient life with an abiding, eternal, divine meaning.

Our task in contemplation, is not to flank each particular feature of our Lord's life with a mystical sense. Parallels of this kind are impossible, if only because each feature points to the infinite and inexhaustible riches of God. They may be experienced by the same person at different times, or by different persons, in different ways, without prejudice to the meaning borne by a particular word or act of Christ in his teaching. They are impossible, too, because our human imitation of the divine is freely carried out in the person of the Word; it cannot be incorporated in a system independent of this freedom. That is what makes the personal encounter of the individual with the Lord in each new act of contemplation so dramatic and fruitful : one can never foresee how the Eternal will offer himself in terms of the temporal, what aspect will predominate, whether these already known will be more deeply scrutinised, or those still unknown will be brought into the open, whether they will be brilliantly illuminated, or left in partial obscurity. Each human life is unique, and each individual will see the life of the Lord in a different way. Furthermore, the special love of God for each individual makes use of Christ's life in contemplation as an instrument from which to draw an incomparable and original melody. The instrument's keys are limited, as are the words of Scripture; but the possible variations on the theme of self-giving, divine love and of initiation into the depths of divine meaning are endless.

Anyone who is, in some degree, versed in contemplation has certainly experienced this. Each scene of the Gospel presents itself every time in a new light, and is in no danger of becoming staled, blunted or meaningless. On the contrary, the same miracle is constantly repeated, and the Gospel, alone among historical realities, rises superior to the laws of history. "Heaven and earth shall pass away, but my words shall not pass away."

The words of the Gospel, though a part of history, are the pillars of heaven and earth and of all that passes : the word as *Arche* (John VIII. 25), the God-Word that "upholds all things by the word of his power" (Heb. I. 3), within which, therefore, the events of my life unroll themselves; words that are true archetypes, only they are not in me, but I in them. Among these events there are, indeed, many evident miracles, which attest in sensible fashion the irruption of eternity into time. But the Lord's discourses are no less wonderful, indeed for the contemplative they are even more so, and in the Lord's own view, they have precedence as proofs of the truth of his mission over the "works", which are intended more as auxiliary evidence for those who find understanding difficult (John X. 36-38). The miracle of the word consists in its power in history, the authority with which the eternal word continues to show its power in the very changes and transformations of history, and in its own transformations shows itself to be the unique word, ever the same, yet able to submit to temporal variations, and even to those arising from weakness, helplessness and death, without forfeiting its divine supremacy.

The second change is that from the old to the new eon, from the death of the old man on the cross to the resurrection of the new at Easter—change so radical indeed that the subject of it cannot achieve it himself by dominating it from some particular point, but can only let it be accomplished in him by the Father almighty. The change which followed on the words of consecration spoken by himself, from the historical to the eucharistic mode of existence is one which he performs; but he is not the author of this transformation which took place when he went from the kingdom of death to sit at the right hand of the Father : for at this point he allows the Father's power to show itself, so that it may be manifest how prodigious is the turning of mankind from sin to redemption, from unbelief to faith. Words fail St. Paul when he speaks of this supreme power of God : "That you may know what the hope is of his calling and what are the riches of the glory of his inheritance in the saints; and what is the exceeding greatness of his power towards us who believe, according to the operation of the might of his power which he wrought in Christ, raising him up from the dead and setting him on his right hand in heavenly places, above all principality and power and virtue and dominion . . . ." (Eph. I. 18-21).

The contemplative is free to reflect on this change, the foundation of all subsequent changes within the Church. He can compare the Word of God in his human form as portrayed in the Gospel, with his glorified form and with his testimony to himself in heaven through the Holy Spirit. But wherever we look we perceive the same humility, the same humiliation bearing the same fruit in the same glory. And this becomes doubly vivid, so that it breaks into our contemplation and pulls us up short, as we look into the abyss of Christ's death and descent into hell. All that is of sense is swallowed up in the abyss; the life, the hopes, the intentions of the old man are engulfed—and then our life and hopes revive again, unforeseeably and unexpectedly, so fresh and so new that they seem to have neither beginning nor end. Over the abyss of death and hell hangs the sign of reconciliation, of the "everlasting covenant that was made between God and every living soul of all flesh which is upon the earth" (Gen. IX. 16). The contemplative thus comes to see how vital it is that Jesus through his word of promise should have linked together the old life and the new, and thus have conferred on every bodily event, however short-lived, an eternal significance and effect.

Our capacity to contemplate the earthly and heavenly Christ simultaneously also has a representational value and we are spared actual experience of the descent into hell, for it is symbolically accomplished in baptism, once and for all (Rom. VI. 3 ff). On this account Holy Saturday may itself be taken as a subject of contemplation and applied to the Church : the Church "survives" her Lord and, in virtue of a power derived in anticipation from his resurrection, throws across the abyss between the old life and the new the bridge of faith, hope and love. But then she comes, through contemplation, to understand better and better that the outcome of this grace must be a participation, not only sacramental but spiritual and contemplative, in Christ's death and descent into hell; and that the faith, hope and charity of the Church—not of the institutional Church (which is not here affected), but of the individuals who make up the Church—must pass through death and darkness to imitate Christ and so to know him; "Whither I go thou canst not follow me now, but thou shalt follow hereafter" (John XIII. 16). "Follow thou me" (John XXI. 19).

Thus, in Christ's own life and in the faith of the contemplative some shadow of the absolute change of the old into the new eon—a shadow not quite corresponding to the original—is cast upon earthly life and contemplation. The persecution and the fatigue, the failure and betrayal, the steadily growing, inconceivable hatred focussed upon the Lord and his disciples, are all a forewarning of the coming storm, and charged with meaning for salvation. The finality of the cross gathers up into itself the accumulating tensions of the previous years. The Lord too has, and prescribes for his followers, a cross of everyday life ("Let him take up his cross daily" —Luke IX. 23), and a daily dying of the old and a fresh beginning of the new man (2 Cor. IV. 16; cf. Eph. IV. 22-24; Col III. 9-10). This gradual dying, however, should not make the contemplative disregard the other aspect, the "once and for all" (Rom IV. 10; Heb. VIII. 27 and *passim*), the irrevocable (Rom. XI. 29; Heb.VI. 17) which is a new stage charged with grace, in the understanding of the atonement. It is, in a way, a slow-motion picture of those elements which can and should be understood by the man who follows Christ; while he must all along remain aware that the greater elements of the cross and particularly of the descent into hell always remain hidden in the mystery of God's love that judges and redeems. Following Christ, therefore, implies that the person for whom he suffered and died, who is therefore spared the main experience, has also to leave to the Beloved the inner, experimental knowledge of what was accomplished—out of love—and take no part in it himself.

The gradual process of dying continues till it reaches into the Lord's passion and death. These too are still on the human plane, though experienced with human powers that grow steadily weaker; and seem almost to succumb as the inner darkness becomes thicker and understanding ceases. Admittedly, the different scenes of the passion disclose only in a very indirect way these inner states of the Lord, which are what really matter. What they show, almost exclusively, is the conduct of the sinful participants— Christians, Jews, pagans—with Christ like a passive plaything in their hands. The result is that the contemplative is placed by the sacred text before the door behind which takes place the dialogue between God's justice and mercy. Nevertheless the dry, formal, official account of the passion offers so many points of approach, so many intimations for faith to take hold of, that the sinner receives far more than he merits. The texts which admit to us the mystery are reticent enough to turn away those not disposed for it. Indeed, this point must be insisted upon if the mystery of the passion is not to be profanated by the effusions of the pious press and the repository trade. At the same time, the texts tell us enough to show us that the grace of participation in the passion is given to the Church for the individual understanding to grasp. Anyone who has felt humiliated finds the points where his experience can be integrated into the humiliation of the Son of man; and those who no longer understand the ways of God may at least understand that the Son of God himself did not understand why he was abandoned by the Father.

Those whose function in the Church is to contemplate the death and resurrection of the Lord must be prepared for trials and transformations. There is indeed a kind of contemplation where, through a special, in a way "institutional", grace, the person focusses his gaze simultaneously on both extremes from a kind of neutral standpoint, and is able to describe them in their relationship. This is part of the Church's preaching-function, to which her theological function is ordained and subordinated. But the great danger for those entrusted with this function is to tone down the great drama of the end of the world and the beginning of heaven, making it into a picture, an event within our human compass to grasp. For that reason, there exists the quite different continuity between the two extremes which consists in imitation, and living experience, with all the interior anguish and violent oscillations of mood it involves.

These completely elude human calculation and estimation, and any theory of mystical contemplation. The contemplative (and in him the Church) has to let himself be as clay in the potter's hands, and be moulded in the course of his contemplation, content not to know the law of his transformation, only sensing it in advance from the potter's hands acting fiercely or gently, roughly or softly. Both forms of contemplation are found alongside in the Church, just as doctrine and life, theology and spirituality, belong together.

It is only the third form of God's word that opens all the doors of contemplation. This is the form in which God's truth in Christ becomes valid, understandable and obligatory for the Church and, through the Church, for the whole world : the unique truth of Christ's existence is conveyed to mankind through the Holy Spirit—not derivatively, but from the outset—in forms and channels which give it a universal, catholic significance. Believer and contemplative receive the truth which saves them through those channels and none other. It is therefore not only impossible, but contrary to the faith to search behind these forms for a deeper-lying truth concerning the "Christ of history" (e.g. through biblical criticism), that does not accord with the Church's vision and teaching about the Lord. One would have thought this was self-evident to anyone acquainted with the nature of faith; but a false notion of science has confused the minds of many Christians and Catholics, and discredited the medium of the Church so essential for all genuine theology and contemplation—to the great loss of both. "He who has the bride is the bridegroom". There is no historical truth about Christ, intended, not for the Church, but for others who regard it as purely historical matter and not binding upon all. This does not exclude the posibility of reasoned argument between believer and non-believer, for the latter may well be drawn by grace, may already be inchoatively sharing the truth mediated by the Church.

Where the medium through which the Holy Spirit transmits the truth of Christ is the Church, it also may be looked on as three-fold; and its three aspects interpenetrate. It is the medium of being, of knowledge and of love.

First the Church is the guardian and administrator of the sacraments in which the earthly life of the Father's Word (wherein the life of the Trinity is transmitted to us) is communicated to others as the form of Christian living and the power to realise it. Thus, Confession is a cross-section of the life of Christ starting from the sermon on the mount, passing through the numerous miracles of purification and healing, the various occasions of individual absolution and dialogues of repentance, and ending with the cross, where the Son made his total confession of sin, and Easter, where the Father gave his total absolution. The Christian is integrated effectively and significantly by the sacrament into this christological reality, made up of a concrete, personal life. The same may be said of the other sacraments.

The Holy Spirit, acting in the Church, brings home the meaning of the reconciliation of the world with God through the medium of knowledge : that is, through all forms of teaching dogmatic formulation, preaching, instruction, theology, as well as individual inspiration and spiritual experience in prayer, contemplation and life. Here, just as in the sacraments, the Spirit may lead us to knowledge of revealed truth at a level that the letter of Scripture touches only very indirectly or by implication. The countless books which, as Scripture tells us, could have been written about Christ and still would never have exhausted his truth and reality (John XXI. 25) cannot be altogether lost to the Church. All truth belonging to the grace of the Incarnation was intended for her and will not be withheld. It is the Spirit who leads both the Church as a whole and the millions of Christians at prayer "into all truth" (John XVI. 13). In this respect too, the Church is "the body of Christ and the fulness of him who is filled all in all" (Eph. I. 23). Just as the oil of the widow of Sarephta was poured out till it filled the empty vessels, which then all attested the fulness of the original vessel, so the meditation of Christians attests "at the treasure of wisdom and knowledge hidden in Christ" (Col. II. 3). Some individuals in the Church are placed closer to this fulness than others and overwhelmed by all that pours into them so abundantly. They are individuals within the mystical body, who are destined to be quasi-sacramental sources for the illumination of the many. St. Paul is one example; "as you reading may understand my knowledge of the mystery of Christ" (Eph. III. 4), and so too were the teachers and religious founders whose "infused" and "acquired" contemplation was to be a wellspring for future generations.

Each receives his own gift of grace in contemplation, and the interchange of knowledge in the Church is as fruitful and intense as that of love. "Let the word of Christ dwell in you abundantly, in all wisdom teaching and admonishing one another" (Col. III. 16). The Church, indeed, is no collection of solitaries praying and contemplating in isolation, and at the most entering into relation with one another in the external spheres of life. It is the "Communion of saints"; though its sacramental aspect is familiar to us, its individual, personal aspect is much more remote to us "Church Christians" than to the sects. The essential and necessary complement of preaching, by which the word of God is expounded, is the spiritual exchange of ideas, where different Christians communicate the insights obtained in prayer, to their mutual profit. This should be done in a spirit of humility and simplicity, and with discretion too, but at the same time in a spirit of communion in the Church, whereby "the members are mutually careful one for another" (1 Cor. XII, 25). For the Church grows from the stage of "children tossed to and fro and carried about with every wind of doctrine" to that of the "perfect man, unto the measure of the age of the fulness of Christ", through the interaction of the charismatic functions and the insights of individual members (Eph. IV. 13-14).

We should also try to preserve a corresponding relationship with those who have been honoured with special contemplative graces. Everyone should make part of the contemplative tradition his own, and get to know some of the works of the great masters of prayer directly or from a study of their lives and influence. The Church's treasury of contemplation is "ours" in virtue of the Communion of saints, but it is not an object of contemplation —whose primary object is always God in Christ—so much as a means of clarifying and interpreting its object and furthering our insight into it. St. Francis of Assisi is not really an object of contemplation, but we may learn from him how to contemplate, drawing on his contemplation to our own profit, and, in his company, joined in the same love, adore Christ in the manger and on the cross.

If this rule be observed, there will be no danger in bringing Christ's truth to bear on one's life in the Church, no risk of so distorting the basic relations of the various parts of revelation that they are hardly recognisable. In such contemplation, some particular detail may occupy the foreground, and this may well be due to illumination by the Holy Spirit, who gives it an emphasis it does not possess in the literal sense of Scripture (or at least is not discernable at first sight). But the intention of the Spirit is that this prominence given to details should serve the better understanding of the whole. Thus, the attention given to Mariology in these days brings a deeper insight both into Christology (of which it forms a part) and of ecclesiology (Mary's privileges exemplify the Church, prophesy the Church at the end of time, and are a prototype of the living community of the saints). The person contemplating must apply the details to the whole picture as it appears in the living interchange between Scripture as expounded by the Church and in the Church's exegesis and tradition as controlled by Scripture.

The third way in which the Holy Spirit explains the life of Christ to us is through brotherly love. It is the last and most important transformation which the Word undergoes. As the Son of the Virgin (and not of any individual man), the Lamb of God who has borne the experience of sin common to all his brethren as flesh and blood poured out in the Eucharist into all men, Christ's presence is what makes them truly brothers and "neighbours". That is why our brother is a sacrament of Christ, not Christ in disguise—the sign that Christ is infallibly present in a form in which we can encounter and discover him. Owing to the variety of human situations these may be regarded by the believer as transformations of the word—always new and always original forms of encounter with Christ. The demand expressed by these situations indicates the meaning of Christ's word. The man who "does" that word has understood it, and those who do it often are the more practised in understanding it. To love is to know; he "knows God, for God is love", whereas those who do not love do not "know". Whoever loves is "born of God" (1 John IV. 7-8), engendered of the Father together with the only Son. He is an expression of the Father's feelings, and they are in him, not as in some neutral disinterested container, but in the same way as the child contains the life given to it by its Father.

Christian love sees others solely in the light of faith and of the insight given by contemplation, and the light that shines in that love reveals the supernatural aspect of its object, our neighbour. A sinner, some antipathetic and insignificant individual, enemy of the Church and of Christ, is in reality my brother, whose guilt, like my own, was borne by Christ (so that it is not for us to reproach one another). His defects are a burden he drags along consciously and unconsciously, related, in some way I cannot see, to the total burden laid on the shoulders of Christ himself.

Christian love as we see it in the Lord is an active love which the disciples receive. And since the love freely given them by Christ is one of pure humility—whether in the washing of the feet, or in the form of instruction or in whether he reproaches them, makes no difference—the necessity of receiving it is, for them, the appropriate way of accepting the example of humility. But in his teaching the Lord describes Christian love as something active. The Christian who loves should always take the initiative: he should, when he has sinned, even before praying, go and be reconciled to his brother (Mt. V. 23 ff), but if his brother has sinned against him he must also go to him, speak alone with him, and only when this is of no effect call on witnesses or appeal to the Church (Mt. XVIII. 15 ff). He should raise up his wounded brother, and take care of him (Luke. X. 25 ff "Go thou and do in like manner"), and accomplish all the works of mercy (Mt.

XXV. 35 ff.). This love does not wait for its cue, but acts and creates the situation of its own accord, acts from the truth (which is God's forgiveness of sins), and once again produces the right situation; pursuing reconciliation whenever possible ("thou hast gained thy brother"—Mt. XVIII. 15), or, if he is willing, furthering the reconciliation without more ado. Christian love always establishes truth between two or more persons, and that truth is ultimately Christ who dwells in the midst of those gathered together in his name (Mt. XVIII. 20). Love is thus seen to be the ground, the medium and the end of all the sacraments and all that the Church does to lead men into the truth; for sacraments and teaching are both an initiation into the reality consisting of man's participation in God's love, which has all the qualities enumerated by St. Paul in his hymn to charity (1 Cor. XIII).

For this reason contemplation is the source of fraternal love. It is essential to have gazed deeply into the features and conduct of incarnate and crucified love in order to make its law a firm support to our own wavering love when a decisive situation arises —the law which bids us bear all things, hope all things, believe all things, and to be patient (1 Cor. XIII). That love is the flowering of contemplation in the truth of human life, the test by which we can know if it is genuinely Christian and whether we have obeyed the word and allowed God's truth and love ascendancy over our untruth and egoism. It is an act of adoration in spirit and truth, the renunciation of complete knowledge in favour of total love. For knowledge passes away, but charity remains (1 Cor. XIII. 8); and so the "love which surpasses all understanding" can be "known" (Eph. III. 19) only in an act beyond knowing, which is the act of loving—loving with God and from God, as God's truth itself is one with his life of love flowing between the three Persons.

To those who reflect upon it, the inexhaustible variety of the situations in which men are brought together and given occasion to practise mutual love is a lesson in Christian truth. In every situation, understood in a Christian sense, whether as loving or loved or even as witnesses, we experience an event in which the truth is present and manifests itself. The experience of that love brings the sudden illumination : *"That* was what was meant !"— something marvellous that seems almost easy even in the most heroic instances, because it harmonises with our nature though we should never have found it by ourselves; something liberating, though it humbles and judges us, purifying and searing—that is the inmost essence of all reality ! There we have, not only the essence of Christianity with its dogmas and teachings, but the essence of God himself, who gave his Son for us and poured into our hearts his Spirit, a Spirit of love.

Brotherly love makes contemplation absorbing and fruitful. A man will suddenly become aware that he is beginning to know himself in new surroundings. He has made the experience we have been speaking about all the time. He is filled with joy at discovering that he has no need of "higher studies", of straining after the higher reaches of contemplation; he only has to plunge into the element of love and strike out boldly. The person who loves never abandons contemplation; on the contrary, he alone thirsts for it in the right spirit. God gives himself to him in prayer, and the more he loves others the better he can understand. Being filled with God, he is capable of a new love for the brethren, a joyful and self-forgetting love. Love brings contemplation itself into the mystery of change. It is no longer a neutral point from which the transformations of love are beheld; it is carried away in the flood of the love which is ever the same and ever new, for ever changing.

The three ways in which the Word is transformed : in Christ's human life, in his death and resurrection, and in the forms of the Church's life—as sacrament, instruction and love—together form a single stream in which God's love is opened and made accessible to us. They are the doors through which we can enter, media in which its inner fulness can be spread out so as to be intelligible and imitable by us. Each dimension gives the others new depth and force of attraction. The Gospel narratives by themselves might come to seem flat and banal, did we not know that they become present in the sacraments of the Church as gifts of divine grace. The sacraments and fraternal love, through repetition, would ulimately seem matters of routine, did we not see in them all the varied colours of the life of the Gospels, a life set vividly before us ever anew in contemplation as the manifestation and presence of the divine life among us for our sakes.

CHAPTER IV

THE WORD AS JUDGMENT
AND SALVATION

WHAT GOD says to us is his truth, not ours; it becomes ours only when he utters and gives it us, and we conform to it. For that reason it becomes a judgment on us in so far as we do not submit to God but rebel against him. We can only penetrate the truth of the Word as persons judged, recognising the condemnation of their state as "outside the word". This act of judgment follows ineluctably and its necessity cannot be evaded or denied, "once" (ἅπαξ) God pronounces his verdict upon sin, and on the old sinful world, which happened preeminently on the cross. All particular judgments are applications of that central judgment emanating from the Cross —whether on individuals entering the Church or on a section of their life on earth (in confession, for example), or on the entire life of the believer after death, when it is judged in a final comprehensive view (in the "particular" judgment).

The Christian confronted by the word of God finds himself inwardly divided, and this shows the self-contradictory character of sin. As a baptised person, he has passed through the judgment of God's word; in principle he has abjured the dominion to which he was once subjected and, in place of Satan's lies, acknowledged God's truth to be his own truth as a Christian. But he has not kept his baptismal promises unbroken. He falls into venial or mortal sin, not only through inadvertence or physical weakness, but also (otherwise there could be no question of moral fault) by setting himself spiritually in opposition to the truth of the word. If, in a grave matter, quite freely and consciously, he sets his own word against the word of God, he commits a grave sin. If he does so in a grave matter, but not in a fully free or conscious manner, or else in a light matter (known as such), so that he does not deny the basic authority of the word in his life, then he commits venial sin. But he thereby introduces contradiction into his life. Indeed he contradicts his own word, by which he proclaimed himself to be a Christian, and, in fact, solemnly vowed it in Baptism. And, since no one is without sin, and whoever says he is deceives himself and stands outside the truth of God (1 John I, 8), the word of God, through which every man receives grace, has, throughout man's life, the aspect of judgment.

In contemplation—before the word of God—this becomes inescapably obvious. In ordinary life one can exclude the contradiction from one's consciousness or postpone its resolution to a more convenient time. In contemplation nothing of the sort is possible : one has to look the word in the face, feel God's gaze fixed upon one, and, in acknowledging him to be right, condemn oneself. That is one of the main reasons why people so persistently avoid contemplative prayer, and, though admitting its necessity in principle, evade any personal encounter with the word.

It is quite impossible to contemplate the word if one does not seriously intend to let it influence one's conduct. For it calls for love of God and neighbour so imperiously that it would be meaningless to face the demand without the will to comply with it. It calls for prayer, continual prayer; and it would be mere stupidity to occupy oneself theoretically with this demand without giving it some authority over one's own life. A theological interest in the word divorced from the will to repent simply intensifies the contradiction. Many Christians are well aware of this, and, if they are resolved not to effect any definite improvement in their lives, leave contemplation severely alone, only acknowledging its existence with a perfunctory gesture.

"Whoever comes near me comes near fire", the Lord is made to say in the apocrypha, and the beloved disciple saw him, the Logos, "as one like to the Son of man", "with eyes as a flame of fire, and his feet like unto fine brass as in a burning furnace . . . and from his mouth came out a sharp two-edged sword" (Apoc. I. 16). This image is that of a judge who prepares to judge his people by his word. On seeing him, the apostle fell at his feet as dead; but the Logos laid his hand on him and countered death with death. "I was dead, and behold I am living for ever, and have the keys of death and of hell" (I. 17-20).

Any one who practices contemplation must have the courage to face the word, the sharpness of the sword and the burning fire. At first sight, the Old Testament truth would appear to be repeated: no one can see God and live. To see God's word as it really is, undistorted and undimmed by the veil of sin and habit is to fall down "as dead". The full light of truth is harder to bear as we appreciate it, more exacting and severe; for if "a man like us" (Phil. II. 7) could, before our eyes, fill the full measure of love, what excuse can we find to make to him and to his love? If God's love abased itself to the point of becoming man and the friend of all, has it not, as St. Augustine so often insists, become the implacable enemy of the sinner in his obstinate refusal to love? "I will fight against them with the sword of my mouth" (Apoc. II. 16). And as John says of the Logos going forth to battle: His eyes were as a flame of fire, he was clothed with a garment sprinkled with blood, and out of his mouth came a sharp two-edged sword to strike the nations; he will rule them with a rod of iron, and tread the wine-press of the fierceness of the wrath of God the almighty (Apoc. XIX. 12-15). No man of prayer can say that this image of the Word does not concern him, and choose instead the gentle form of Jesus the Saviour. No one who declines to let the sharpness of the Word act on him will ever encounter anything but an imaginary redeemer, and those who do not, will never experience the judging quality of divine grace when they place themselves before the judgment of Christ in contemplation. Crucified love is something that sears and consumes, and its two aspects—redemption and judgment—are inseparable and indistinguishable. It is almost a matter of indifference which word of Scripture one chooses for contemplation; the fire he exposes himself to, provided he surrenders to it and does not elude it, will continue till it reaches his inmost being. "For the word of God is living and effectual and more piercing than any two-edged sword and reaching unto the division of the soul and the spirit, of the joints also and the marrow, and is a discerner of the thoughts and intents of the heart. Neither is there any creature invisible in his sight, but all things are naked and open to his eyes, to whom our speech is" (Heb. IV. 12-13). This tremendous utterance is not only relevant to a few isolated words, or certain of the Lord's attitudes; it expresses the essence of the word. The whole of revelation, each word of the Old Testament, of the Gospels, the epistles and the apocalypse plainly bears the same stamp. To lay oneself open to the word is to experience this. Contemplation, then, is an anticipation of the fire of the judgment, of the final, inescapable confrontation of the word with all who have evaded it.

The sacrament of Penance, being a sort of foretaste of the judgment, comprises both fear and repentance, and transforms them into an experience of grace unobtainable in any other way. In the same way, if the contemplative genuinely exposes himself to the fire of the word, not just for the sake of appearances, or to obtain an esthetic thrill, he will see it transformed into what he long desired, a real source of beatitude. In contact with the purity of the word he will learn to know his own impurity and burn with the desire to be rid of it. He will throw himself, of his own accord, into the flame, so that it may enlighten him, and also consume and enflame him.

For that it is necessary for him to receive the word "not as the word of men, but, as it is indeed, the word of God" (1 Thess. II. 13); so that he does not dwell on the preliminary work of the mind, the philological and historical aspects, or adopt a scholarly attitude so objective, critical and superior as to make it practically impossible for him, in contemplation, to submit to the plain judgment of the word. The philologist and the historian develop habits of mental reserve that can be detrimental to contemplation. One who has dissected a text like an anatomist an organism runs the danger of overlooking the vital principle which forms it and is irreducible. Great theologians and spiritual masters like Origen keep an attitude of loving prayer and a consciousness of the divine character of the word through all their philological investigations. They even carry out their dissection of the word out of reverence and love for the Logos become man and written word. That is the only objective philosophical attitude, for it alone does justice to the uniqueness of the object.

Those who desire a deeper understanding of the word to which they pay homage, in order to place themselves unreservedly at its disposition will, therefore, only make use of exegetical works which, despite an alleged "exactitude" of research, do not neglect the most important kind of exactitude, in which thought is always orientated towards prayer and judging the word includes being judged by the word. The word of God is simple and clear; and its profundity is never confused or obscure, or comprehensible only to the learned. The Jews learned in the scriptures thought otherwise, and so they "shut the kingdom of heaven against men". They failed to enter it themselves, and made it impossible for others to gain access to the judgment that brings salvation (Mt. XXIII. 13). Christ, however, wishes that children should come to him and declares the poor in spirit blessed. The "parrhesia", which means free access is, throughout the New Testament, access to God's word; and it is obvious that as with the access through the Eucharist, it is subject to the rules of the Church. But God's word is simple and clear, and no-one should let himself be turned from a direct uninhibited contact with the word, or allow his contact with it to be dimmed and dulled, by problems and mental reservations aroused by the thought that scholars interpret a text quite differently and more accurately than he can. In any case, the content of the word is not *less* than what it can and will convey to one who hears it in a docile spirit. How often, in the course of time, has a scientific exegesis been refuted and abandoned! A learned commentary only justifies itself if it shows me *more* in a text than I, a simple believer, can myself find in prayer.

The Son, as the Word, is God : the quintessence of truth, in the eternal unity of the divine nature and person, made accessible and available in human words. No creature is equal to this truth of which he can only grasp comparatively little; nor can he withstand its density which robs him of his own powers. He only hears the sound of the word, the ordinary human meaning it bears in the average frame-work of religion. What he has to try and hear is the unique meaning that cannot be reduced to general terms, a common denomination. What he must hear is what God desires to say to him—"this individual"—endowed with the hearing of faith. He may, in contemplation, turn aside to what is universal and of general application, and, indeed, find much that is useful and true in it, perhaps even something God specially intended for him. But, if he pursues this line of thought with the object of evading a genuine encounter with the word, then there is an element of disobedience in his contemplation, and he will not reap the fruit intended for him. He must come face to face with the word, the word which is Christ speaking to him not only in the Gospel but in the Old Testament and the apostolic writings. His spiritual gaze, his reflection, the stirrings of his will must never, for all the freedom God grants those who pray, stray from the axis of obedience, however painful it may become.

Here we may recall the Sermon on the Mount and the injunction to forgive one's brother before going to pray, so that the Word of God may forgive us too (Mark XI. 25; Mt. V. 23-24). "Having something against someone" is the impediment the word has to burn away before it enters truly into the soul. It may be "something" against our neighbour, an individual or one's fellow-men in general; but it can be, and often is, "something" against God himself : resentment, holding back, a refusal, a secret rebellion, which must be brought to light in contemplation through the word of God. In order to hear the word as I should, I must make contact with the word, not through acts of understanding or will, but through my conscience, with my whole self; for faith, the organ of hearing is not simply one of the soul's faculties, but the whole man. Man must, in fact, hand himself over to the divine physician, in all humility, naked and unprotected and expose himself like a sensitive photographic plate to the objective image of himself contained in the word of God. There is a method of approaching Holy Scripture—many theologians could tell us about it—which, perhaps on the basis of a sort of spiritual economy that saves and safeguards the soul, only exposes the understanding (informed by faith) to the light, and postpones a real personal contact to a future that, in fact, never arrives. But, in today's act of contemplation the "day" of the Lord has definitely arrived with all the inevitabilty set out in the epistle to the Hebrews as accompanying a true encounter with the word; its refusal is ascribed to the "unbelieving heart", the heart "hardened", "rebellious", "negligent", determined to escape the necessary operation and the knife that wounds.

Nowadays we hear much about the "ethics of the situation". How seriously it concerns us is nowhere better seen than in the contact made with God's word in contemplation. Here, however, it is not merely a question of ethical demands, though these are always present, but of a right attitude towards Christ, of proper docility and submission of mind to him who, in the form of the sacred word, is present and offers himself to us, and desires us for himself.

It is just because the very core of the personality is involved that contemplation must not get bogged down in peripheral moral considerations and resolutions. In this sphere it is always bound to end in failure, since we never rise so fully to the demands of the word that our "progress" is not marred by backslidings and failures that tempt us to despair. The word, indeed, exacts definite "resolutions", but that does not exhaust its demands on us. If that were all, it would amount to saying that the man who has achieved a definite measure of obedience in the ethical sphere would be able, relying on his own works, to set himself in a special relationship with the word of God. But what ultimately matters is not particular works, but a genuine, serious surrender of the person; the love which gives itself, that despises the calculated risk, and yet because it is so utterly in earnest, never for a moment overlooks the practical aspect. The self that prays should be conscious of having its love proved and tested, not of submitting to a kind of moral accountancy. It is only in *personal* love that man really submits to the judgment of the word; the one person is divine and sits in judgment, the other is human, a sinner and is, therefore, to be judged. The relation between the two is unique, because the persons themselves are unique, and the individual cannot therefore take refuge in the universal, the abstract, in what is generally valid. In the sphere of the universal, where man can survey God as a concept, as it were at a distance, he can reflect at his ease, reason and meditate, even object and find fault with the order of things. But all this disappears upon real contact with the word. Then it becomes clear as daylight that God's word is always right, and that it is edifying always to be in the wrong before God (*Kierkegaard*). One cannot avoid associating the idea of judgment with that of contact with God.

But this attitude of mind must be correctly envisaged. It is not an advance admission of our degradation, made in a peevish mood of weary resignation, so as to feel at peace in the future. There is a kind of recognition that God is right that goes with an attitude of revolt in practice. Mere resignation to God's overwhelming power is an Old Testament attitude (cf. Job) and unworthy of a Christian. There is too a sort of general protestation and acknowledgment of God's rightfulness which avoids going into the detail of what God wishes. There are two kinds of "sorrow", sorrow "according to God" and sorrow "of the world", and they must be sharply distinguished. The former "worketh penance, steadfast unto salvation", the other works death. A sullen resignation in the presence of the word that judges, an inert acceptance of condemnation, is near to that which "worketh death". The other is a form of love : "For behold this selfsame thing, that you were made sorrowful according to God, how great carefulness it worketh in you : yea defence, yea indignation, yea fear, yea desire, yea zeal, yea revenge" (2 Cor. VII. 9-11).

What we may call faith's antecedent assumption, namely its unexamined acceptance of the Word's judgment, is also love's assumption. That is why, in the Old Testament, it is not for the most part followed up. That only happened when God's Word to whom judgment belongs himself became man, and submitted blindly to the absolute judgment of the Father. In this Word, obedient to death in abandonment by God, we shall be judged. We are to be led in a love free from fear by this word, become our brother, and so, "without murmurings and hesitations" work out our salvation "in fear and trembling" (Phil. II. 12-14). It is those who love who are most easily convinced that they have reason to fear if they look at themselves in the pure light of the Beloved. They do not indulge in theoretical estimates of the *fiducia* contained in faith, or of God's grace outweighing in advance all their sins, and making any real fear quite superfluous. And it is love that enables man, in contemplating the cross, to see in it an exact reflection of his immeasurable guilt, and "pierced with fear" (Ps. CXVIII. 120) to deliver himself up to the severity of judgment, so as no longer to wage his own war against the truth, but to take sides with the truth against himself. "What wilt thou have me to do?" asks the man thus subdued; and the answer is a demand for love, love lived in daily life among men, but proceeding from a deep heartfelt contrition before God.

The love that has seen the inexorable character of the judgment of the cross undergone by the Son is prepared, in the antecedent assumption of faith, to admit to any degree of sinfulness, even to that which deserves damnation, when judged by the Son. *If* thou shouldst damn me, says the soul, I should know that thy verdict was just. Since I have accepted thy verdict in advance, I must accept even this extreme one, though let thy mercy avert it from me. Uncertain as I am whether I deserve favour or condemnation, am worthy of love or of hate (Ecclus. IX. 1), I agree to this judgment, not in the spirit of Kafka's characters, whose admission of guilt is extorted by exterior pressure of increasing severity, but as one to whom it is self-evident that God is truth, even if man at the time fails to understand. Is not sin necessarily a lie, and does not the lie necessarily deceive? Does not stifling the conscience, darkening the mirror, obscuring the light belong to the essence of sin? Does not the revelation of God's word involve for the sinner a complete and terrifying revision of values and particularly of his estimate of himself? It may well be, therefore, that the fact that "I have nothing of importance to reproach myself with" rests on a deep misconception, that it is an indication that my conscience judges by very rough standards, perhaps quite false ones without being aware of it, as compared with those of God's word. In view of such a possibility, surely there must arise in man a longing for the true judgment, the final, exact verdict of God's word, while, at the same time, he hopes to be able to sustain this judgment through the grace of the Lord, and no wise through his own merits.

Man longs for the truth, and so he looks towards the word of God as a mirror of the truth. In his thirst for the truth, he is unwilling to dwell indefinitely in the fog of the godless, "fleshly" judgment of the world and of himself. At the same time, he is unwilling to let the decisive event, the forgiveness of sins, take place solely in the objective sphere, the sphere of the sacraments and the Church. He knows that as he was the one who sinned, so he must play his own part, a secondary and halting part, with sorrow, conversion and expiation. With this conviction he approaches the word of God, the Gospel with the history that precedes and follows it, and experiences something altogether wonderful. He enters on a world of purity and love. It is a world with two aspects. On the one hand, it is perfectly human, not exaggerated, not even lofty or sublime in a human philosophical sense or by the standards of a "wisdom" or of religious mysticism that is "above the heads" of the simple and uninitiated. Everything about the Lord is perfectly human, his dealings with other men, with his apostles and disciples, his mother and foster-father, his friends and his enemies too. At the same time, the whole simple picture radiates the searing purity of God. This applies to each slightest part of the Gospel, and also to the world of the epistles of St. Paul and St. John; in fact, to the whole of scripture. Into this world the contemplative is drawn, in a plain human fashion; but once there, he finds himself suddenly in the scorching wind of the Holy Spirit, and all the more so the more he moves, as believer and contemplative in the world of the word.

For example, he comes upon the passage where St. Paul admonishes the Philippians to bear with one another, to renounce all strife and ambition and, at all times out of humility to deem others superior to themselves. That is the kind of thing a wise man of the world might have said. But then comes the statement that derives this attitude from that of God emptying himself even to the death of the cross, and the demand that each of us should be animated with the same feeling (Phil. II). Or perhaps he reads the passage where St. John urges us to love our brethren, and this duty of love may well be derived from man's conscience and his very nature. But the next sentence, to the effect that whoever hates his brother is like Cain a murderer, and whoever loves his brother knows God because God is love, is a tremendous assertion, a consuming fire. That is how the word takes man into the truth, opening up a world of love where he feels himself at home, which he is obliged to recognise as the most just, the most commensurate with him, the most desirable, but for which, if he is to live there, he has to purify his heart to its very roots.

The revelation given by the Father has a twofold aspect, for he sent his Word and his Son into the world. These two are one, but the "Word" of the Father came with the absolute relentlessness of one charged with a mission from on high, who can do no other than carry through to the very end, exactly and painfully, the task entrusted to him. The "Son", on the other hand, is the only-beloved of the Father, delivered up by the Father because he so loved the world. In the revelation contained in the New Testament we come into contact primarily with the Son in his human form; and in our intercourse with the man Jesus Christ he becomes for us the Word, becomes fire and sword. We are first initiated into the aspect of love, then into that of judgment.

In St. John, the Lord himself indicates this double function : "If any man hear my words and keep them not, I do not judge him; for I came not to judge the world, but to save the world. He that despiseth me and receiveth not my words hath one that judgeth him. The word that I have spoken, the same shall judge him in the last day. For I have not spoken of myself; but the Father who sent me, he gave me commandment what I should say and what I should speak" (John XII. 47-49). The Son does not judge and condemn as Saviour and Redeemer, but as the Word of the Father, who is the righteous Creator, the upholder of the world-order and of his own holiness, the avenger, too, of his Son's holiness; and no one can spurn or offend the Word without incurring judgment. Judgment is due, not to the Son, but to men's rejection of him. If they disdain his love it turns in them to judgment, not because the Son judges them, but because they are self-condemned. "For God sent not his Son into the world to judge the world, but that the world may be saved by him. He that believeth in him is not judged. But he that doth not believe is already judged, because he believeth not in the name of the only begotten Son of God. And this is the judgment : because the light is come into the world, and men loved darkness rather than the light, for their works were evil" (John III. 17-19).

In the same way whoever receives the Lord's flesh and blood without discernment "eateth and drinketh judgment to himself" because he did not submit himself to the judgment of the Lord. St. Paul goes on in the same sense to say : "But if we would judge ourselves, we should not be judged. But whilst we are judged, we are chastised by the Lord, that we be not condemned with this world" (1 Cor. XI. 29-32). In the scene of the woman taken in adultery, the word of the Lord strikes the sinners who condemned her so forcibly that they are routed and accept the word's judgment as

a punishment, so as to make room for the judgment of mercy:
"Neither do I condemn thee" (John VIII. 11 with XII. 46-48).
It is as if God left the sinner to suffer from his revolt against God's
sentence, which remains fixed in him like a goad. The more he
fights against it (Acts. XXVI. 14), the more painful it becomes;
he only drives it deeper into his flesh. The sinner carries his judgment within himself; ultimately he will himself be the one who
pronounces his condemnation in the light of God. God's light
alone will fall on him; and will continue until the contradiction is
brought out fully into the open, until the sentence passed on him is
manifest in the word of God with him. That is the meaning of
Peter's prayer: "Depart from me, for I am a sinful man, O
Lord" (Luke V. 8); and the prodigal son's; "Father, I am not
worthy to be called thy son" (Luke XV. 22).

We are not concerned for the moment with our personal judgment after death, and with the sentence passed on the sinner—
that remains the Lord's own secret—but with the contemplative
Christian in his encounter with the word that pierces and burns
him "even to the division of soul and spirit". Out of love he exposes himself to fear; and from fear of the Lord he will be led to
love. That first love is the adventure of faith, in which a man offers
his life to the Son and, like the first disciples, follows the Master
though he is as yet unknown. The second love is love purified
and chastened by the Word of the Father, the love which has
found the grace concealed in the judgment. This should make it
clear that the three classical stages of contemplation, the purgative, illuminative and unitive ways, are not successive but intermingled: the light of God's Word unifying himself with the soul is
what purifies it—although we are not to rule out a kind of
temporal succession or the predominance of one or other element.
Illumination is necessary for purification, just as the mystics teach
that the "dark nights" of the soul suppose a previous spiritual
light. And union itself really comes about, not after, but in the
course of, purification; for it is God's purifying, crucifying word

stamped on the soul that reveals itself at the end of the "night", in the "resurrection", as the Son who redeems.

In this light the assignment of judgment to the Son (John V) is clear : the evil rise to judgment, the just to life. This judgment the Redeemer is, as it were, unable to prevent; it belongs to his very being as the Father's Word : "I cannot of myself do anything. As I hear, so I judge. And my judgment is just, because I seek not my own will, but the will of him that sent me". There we have the image of the Logos, as seen by the author of the Apocalypse, inexorable and bearing the sword or the sickle. But the image of fear becomes one of hope for the living, because through the power of the Word "all will hear his voice", the voice of the Son of God, and "they that hear shall live". For the Son received the power "to have life in himself" from the Father, and so—both as Son and as Word the power to give it to others. Yet if we receive eternal life through hearing the Son's voice we are overwhelmed by the strangeness and the danger, for it means accepting "judgment", and that implies condemning ourselves in the light of the word. But, at a deeper level, and for the contemplative, it is the source of consolation, the one ground of hope, because the believer who hears the word shares in the life of the Word, in obedience, cross and resurrection. And so the Lord can say, paradoxically : "I judge not any man. And if I do judge, my judgment is true : because I am not alone, but I and the Father that sent me" (John VIII. 15-16).

The crucified love that assumes the Father's judgment in man to avoid judging us cannot however avoid becoming crucifying love, when it communicates itself and its burning mystery to others. He came, not to judge, but to save (John XII. 47) but in the end, judgment "came into the world, that they who see not may see, and they who see may become blind" (John IX. 39).

PART III

POLARITIES AND TENSIONS IN
CONTEMPLATION

INTRODUCTION

T HE ACT of contemplation, in which the believer hears the word of God and surrenders himself to it, is an act of the whole man. It cannot therefore assume a form in which man truncates his own being, whether for a short or longer time— for instance, by *systematically* training himself to turn from the outer world and attend wholly to the inner world, or turning from both the outer and inner senses (the imagination) to the pure, "naked" spirit. That kind of deliberate artificial restriction reduces man to a shadow of himself and is a misunderstanding of God's demand, namely "conversion", a turning from the manifold to the essential. Objectively, any form of restriction is a form of disobedience to the word, a refusal to give up, even in the act of hearing, some preconceived and distorted notion of man's nature, though, subjectively, in non-Christian religions, it is very often a well-intentioned mistake. Indeed, the natural man, to whom God's revelation is unknown, necessarily seeks his way to God by flying from the world. For, if God is, above all, the non-world, Unity in contrast with the variety of the material world, man has no choice but to carve a way of ascent to God through these elements in himself which seem to him to have most affinity with God, that is through the spirit unified by withdrawal from the world, the body and the interior senses. Eastern contemplation to an almost exclusive extent, and the Greek tradition, in its most characteristic forms, are dominated by this conception of contemplation which moreover exercised a powerful influence on Christian contemplative teaching in the patristic and middle ages.

The Old Testament, on the other hand, always envisages the whole man as the hearer and contemplator of the word, though it should be unnecessary to insist that it is not the animal or mineral part of man that hears God, but his spiritual soul, which comes from God and returns to him. That is why, both in the Old and the New Testaments, we see those privileged to hear God withdrawing from the crowd and seeking solitude, Moses on Mount Sinai and in the clouds, Elias in the desert and on Horeb, John the Baptist and Paul in the deserts of Transjordan and Arabia. Jesus himself entered on his external mission only after forty days of fasting and prayer in the desert. They all set about their active life after a time of contemplation in which they withdrew from ordinary life but this withdrawal was clearly seen by the people to be but the prelude to their mission in the world, and in view of which God called them first of all to his presence "out of the world". The identification of this forty days of contemplation with the Greek idea of the contemplative ascent to God was made first by Origen and his followers—a typical instance is Gregory of Nyssa's Life of Moses—but it is not an altogether happy one, especially when the Greek conception of man is introduced into the Christian idea of contemplation, the conception, that is, of a soul united with the body in a more or less extrinsic way, accidentally or by constraint and so transiently. It is the whole man who has to turn to God, retire into solitude, and listen exclusively to the word of God. And the whole man, too, including all that is most inward in him, has then to place himself at the service of God in the world and at the disposal of his brethren.

This truth can be learnt from the history of revelation and it leads us to expect to find the same basic tensions within man's nature and more especially evident in his spiritual part, determining his inmost character in the act of hearing and contemplating the word. Now this should not be regarded as the effect of an unavoidable but very regrettable defect, a weakness to be ashamed of and covered up. On the contrary, the Creator, in his wisdom and love, created us at once different from him yet in his image and likeness.

God's revelation does not take our spiritual structure into account as a doctor will a patient's sickness; nor is it enough to say —as some of the more extreme Fathers say—that some degree of compromise was necessarily involved when God lowered himself to our level, and that contemplation involves breaking through the symbolical veil. God assumes human form and adapts his word to men so that it both anticipates and develops from his Incarnation, which is in no sense superseded by his ascension or by the coming of the Holy Spirit, but eternally glorified. The tensions inherent in human nature are shared by revelation and assumed by God himself in his union with mankind.

CHAPTER I

EXISTENCE AND ESSENCE

TENSION BETWEEN existence and essence arises from the basic structure of created being. It is an unfathomable mystery, shared by man with the rest of creation, though in him it affects his spiritual being and all his spiritual acts. Created being is not, as the divine being, necessary and in it existence does not follow from what it is. If it does exist, it emerges from nothing through the mystery of the divine liberty, itself inscrutable. But the wonderful fact that the creature exists in this way is not wonderful simply in its bare "factitiousness" (existence), and as though its essence (its being such) were familiar or at least to be expected, and in no sense "wonderful". The existent being is so concrete (i.e. grown together : —*con cretum*) that the marvel of actually "being-there" and the marvel of "being such" are inseparably conjoined. An existence which was not the existence of this particular essence would have no more interest than an essence which did not possess the astonishing property of having actuality, existence, "being-there".

The mind's eye moves restlessly back and forth between these two poles. A man in love picturing the woman he loves will dwell first on her qualities. Then suddenly it will spring to his mind that all this excellence is no intellectual construction, but is bound up in the incomprehensible marvel of her existence. *She* is all this; but more than all this is the fact that she *is*, and that this "is" lies open to him, the person considering it, and is given him as his own possession! But the marvel of existence always threatens to pale into the common experience of existing, unless the inner richness of being blossoms out, and unless a man is charmed anew each day by the woman he loves being *such* and not otherwise, with these particular qualities, these hidden depths and springs of the soul which compel his love.

This tension is present both in the object and the subject; it is imprinted on the structure of what is contemplated as on that of the mind that contemplates. In the object of Christian contemplation it is intensified, in so far as the mystery of created existence in general (which depends on the divine freedom) manifests itself in Christ as the profounder, the surpassing, mystery of his will of grace. That this man, loved above all and adored, stands before me, not as a mere "thought", but a "reality" : the marvel of his existence shows me, not only that the Father willed him as an existent being—for my sake—but also that the entire intra-divine love and grace are made manifest in the wonderful fact of the actual existence of the Redeemer. In this actuality "are hid all the treasures of wisdom and knowledge", and, as the believer steeps himself by contemplation in this existence, he is introduced "unto all riches of fulness of understanding, unto the knowledge of the mystery of God the Father and of Christ Jesus" (Col. II. 2-3). It is a mystery to be known in its "length and breadth and height and depth", and by a knowledge of its essential being; and the mind returns enriched from this investigation of the divine fulness to its contact with the Person existing, in whom the unfathomable love manifests itself : "to know also the charity of Christ, which surpasseth all understanding, *that* you may be filled unto all the fulness of God" (Eph. III. 18-19).

This tension in Christ shows God's being and his love from both sides and, furthermore, the eternal identity of essence and existence in the Godhead is revealed dynamically—in so far as it can be perceived by the created mind. The effort of thought demanded by the infinity of the divine attributes and perfections is intensified when we contemplate the absolute necessity of the existence of God seen as the fundamental property emerging from all the others, and, at the same time, their source. And it is the distinction between the two poles in the creature as well as in Christ, the God-man, and the tension it engenders, which gives us access to the mystery of their identity in God.

The contemplative must inevitably fix his attention alternately on essence and existence. Each calls up the other, moves in relation to the other, reveals greater depths in the other. The dynamic relation between the two aspects results in a certain grouping of talents and tendencies though this is of minor importance. There is the kind of contemplative like St. John the evangelist whose reflections on the divine essence prepare the way for adoration and prostration before the unfathomable mystery of the divine existence. To this group belong the St. Augustine of the "Confessions", St. Francis, St. Ignatius and Newman. But there is another type of person whose primary experience is of an overwhelming encounter with the Lord, and for the rest of his life he makes despairing efforts to interpret the content of this experience, to count up, as it were, the inestimable riches poured out before him all at once. He turns these riches into verbal coinage, as did St. Paul, whose life was wholly coloured by his experience on the road to Damascus; for ever after he could only speak of the fulness of the mystery that almost overpowered him. Another example is Origen, whose *epinoiai* (essential aspects) of the divine Logos were the fruit of an original vision which is perceptible throughout his thought and speculation, Again, the rapidity and acuteness of St. Thomas Aquinas's thought is only explicable on the assumption of an original and powerful impetus derived from the reality itself.

The first type envisages the person in his existence as a unique individual and continuously returns to this aspect in all reflections about his essence. That is the fundamental contemplative type, to which we must always come back. The second type draws out all that is implied in the essence of the object, and is sometimes exposed to the danger of intellectualism and of cultivating thought for its own sake. This is the active type, which makes use of the initial knowledge given him to discharge a spiritual mission for the

Church, and gives it formal expression, but this very circumstance tempts him to lose touch with the cause of his sudden "fall to the ground" (Acts. IX. 4). That has produced a tradition of contemplation closely resembling the Greek contemplation of essences, which makes God no more than "absolute Truth, Beauty, and Goodness"; the contemplative lingers fascinated by this intellectual vision, and his perception of the seering word in time, of the God of Abraham, Isaac and Jacob, is dulled. This was not intended by God, who charged his messengers in the New Testament, as he charged the prophets in the Old, to express God's word in a form that appealed to the senses, so that the people of God, whether synagogue or Church, should be able to grasp it. Just as the prophets, obedient to their charge, always returned to the word of God, so the Christian at prayer should bend his thought to the meaning of the word (*meditatio, consideratio, contemplatio*) so as to elicit a direct, personal and existential contact with the divinity, and offer the homage of adoration.

This distinction is sharper than that indicated by the literal meaning of the terms intellectual and affective contemplation, though, often enough, these inadequate terms are used to express it. The truth is that while affections are "aroused" by the consideration of particular aspects and properties of God's essence and of his grace, the entire submission and self-giving that follows from contact with the Person as existing are more than an "affection", though feeling is not, on that account, to be wholly excluded from them.

The contrast we speak of should not be identified with the traditional contrast between more discursive, active prayer, mainly of beginners, and the "prayer of simplicity" or "affective prayer", that can dispense with a multiplicity of thoughts, and which being itself simple, can rest in the simple fulness of the object contemplated. It is true that the latter is an advance on the former, roughly corresponding to the adult's capacity to take in a page at a few glances as compared with a child spelling out each word. For all that, we must avoid the impression that discursiveness is a kind of original defect incurred by the reason (according to Greek philosophy), and that progress in contemplation is to be measured primarily by the degree in which it is overcome.

Furthermore, the distinction between what we have called essential and existential prayer must not be confused with the distinction between the Church's prayer, which is liturgical and impersonal, objective and anonymous, and the emphatically personal prayer of the individual in his private world. For the objectivity of liturgical prayer consists in participation in the mystery of the Bride of Christ, whose union with the Bridegroom is the supreme mystery of her meeting with him in his actual existence and her consequent surrender in adoration. Indeed, something of the objectivity of the Church's prayer and of the anonymity of the individual should enter into personal contemplative prayer, in order to give it wider significance and the stamp of the nuptial quality belonging to Mary and the Church. Thus, the contact of the individual with God in prayer becomes essentially, and not merely in its results, something involving the Church.

Finally, the tension which we are considering should not be regarded as synonymous with this contrast between *contemplatio* and *oratio*, or, more exactly, contemplative and vocal prayer. Although this distinction is a useful one, the two are not mutually exclusive. Vocal prayer, prayer expressed in some sensible fashion (whether audible to others or in words thoughts or images, or softly articulated), if it is to be prayer, must be accompanied by a spiritual attitude and spiritual acts which include and presuppose receptiveness to God and his word, a simple hearing of his word. A purely passive spiritual attention is quite impossible; there is always at the least an incipient response on the part of man—the whole man, body and soul. For this reason, it is a mistake to regard *oratio* as inferior to *contemplatio*, and to view vocal prayer as primarily for beginners and contemplative prayer as suitable mainly for the advanced. Each depends on the other and presupposes it, and the one should lead directly into the other. Yet the act of existential prayer has no need to be identical with vocal prayer; it can just as well, or even better, take the form of silent prostrate adoration of man's whole being before the divine Person. Contemplative prayer, in turn, (considered in contrast to vocal prayer) tends of itself to break out of the essential into the existential sphere; for in God's word that we hear, the speaker himself constantly appears in a new aspect, and it is his will to be heard and even seen (*loquere ut videam te*). He appears not only as in the Old Testament, as the speaker behind the word, but as in the New, as the Word spoken, revealed as a divine Person and, as such, making his approach to men.

It is worth while going through the Gospel of St. John from this point of view. The principal scenes are built up as a break through from contemplation into direct adoration—contemplation is viewed as a more or less provisional attitude, appropriate to what is seen abstractly, a neutral, expectant, reserved and distant attitude. The break-through occurs when the truth suddenly impinges on the person contemplating, and overwhelms him, not from without, but from within, as being itself a Person. The prologue itself describes this movement : the Word, originally with God and the ground of the world's being, "comes", moves into the world and towards men, is made flesh, and makes direct contact with us, dwelling "among us". He brings us of his fulness grace for grace, and manifests himself as the Word of the Father whom no one has seen. The first disciples accept his invitation to "come and see", and this is followed by their accompanying him, speaking with him, and being led by him to that sudden overwhelming experience in which their eyes are opened. The sequence is seen most clearly in the case of Nathaniel who came to "see", examine, and understand, when all of a sudden he has to acknowledge that he himself had long ago been seen, examined, and probed. He is the first to be overwhelmed : "Master, thou art the Son of God . . . ."

The scene at Cana, the actors in it, the dialogue between Mother and Son, the preliminary acts of the servants, are all objects of contemplation. The miracle then supervenes as something of a quite different order, which yet calls for realisation in this and no other way. "He manifested his glory and his disciples believed in him", in the sense which belief always has in St. John, that of prostrate adoration and surrender of self. The same is true of the purifying of the temple, only here faith seems to be relegated to the time after the resurrection. The conversation with Nicodemus remains in the sphere of essence; and the corresponding adoration is the humiliation of the cross. The self-effacement of the Baptist as the Bridegroom's friend, who must "decrease" while the other "increases", is the completion of the whole of the theology of the Baptist begun in the prologue : he was to point to the light that should attain mastery through its own power.

The dialogue with the Samaritan woman is the classical example of the movement from contemplation to adoration. The early phase of the dialogue proceeds in an atmosphere of incomprehension, for sin obscures sight. It is followed by confession and the woman's eyes are opened to spiritual truth. The dialogue moves on to the Messias and on to adoration in spirit and truth, still on the theoretical plane, till with the growing yearning for the truth the Person himself emerges out of the truth : "I am he who speaketh with thee". All that follows, the woman's apostolic work, is but the outcome of this adoration. The King's officer is led by the miracle of healing to adoration. The sick man at Bethseda did not at first recognise the person who cured him, and needed a second meeting with him in the temple. In the discourse on Scripture, the whole word of God, which the Jews had "searched" to find life, becomes a pointer to his Person. The multiplication of the loaves is such a clear theophany that the people seek to take hold of him. The theophany by night, on the lake, with the disciples, is hidden "in a great fear", from which he steps forth, tearing aside the veil—"It is I, fear not".

In the discourse on the bread of life, we have the tremendous appearance of the Word himself, who wills and demands to be eaten and drunk in his flesh and blood. This brings about the defection of those who are not prepared to believe to the point of unreserved adoration, whereas the apostles, through the mouth of Peter, proclaim that they "know and believe". In the disputes Christ held with the Jews, the personal nature of the truth stands out so clearly and is so much the central point that the whole conflict turns on the alternatives of faith and scandal, which means, for St. John, adoration of God or deicide. In one instance, instead of adoration, the discourse ends with the Jews taking up stones and the Lord hides himself away. The scene with the man born blind follows : first, a long exposition of the reasons for and against the miracle, a consideration of the miracle and its aspects, till at last the man healed is brought to ask the question : "Who is he, Lord, that I may believe in him?" and is ready to accept the answer; "Thou seest him. It is he who speaketh with thee"; the man at once falls down in adoration. The discourse on the Good Shepherd who gives his life for his sheep and the recognition of the Messias by his works (if not by himself) divides the crowd again into worshippers and stone-throwers; and the raising of Lazarus creates the same division. In the middle of this scene, Martha is suddenly drawn from essential contemplation of resurrection on the last day to existential acknowledgment of Jesus as "resurrection and life" (I am . . . . dost thou believe this?").

The anointing by Mary at Bethany appears to be no more than an expression of love, but is accepted and interpreted as the anointing of the Messias in view of his Passion. The last discourse in the temple contains a warning of the need for haste—"yet a little while. . . ." The light of God's truth is not always and at all times present; now is the time for it to be seen and acknowledged. Christ by his self-abasement in washing his disciples' feet certainly intended to give a lesson of love for one another; but, again, this conveys that the acts and the being of Christ are unique and unrepeatable. "Know you what I have done to you? You call me Master and Lord, and you say well, for so I am". The discourses before his departure are the Sinai of the New Testament. In the inauguration of the new ritual the Word of God—who is the New Law—pours himself out. He gives himself now as flesh and blood, engrafts those who hear him as branches in his own life, and breathes into them with his own Spirit. The final prayer petitions the Father to give eternal life to those who hear him, because they have believed in the Son and worshipped him.

In the Passion, we have, first of all, a reversed image of adoration. Judas and the soldiers fall to the ground on hearing the words, "I am he". Then comes the theme of the king whose majesty appears just here, when he is admitted by Pilate to be innocent, is adored in mockery by the soldiers and brought out scourged for the people to adore him, and finally dies under the threefold inscription of which Pilate said : "What I have written, I have written". The seamless robe is a symbol : all attempts to analyse and separate the different aspects (*epinoiai*) of the mystery and so make it more comprehensible break down before the indivisible mystery of the *persona ineffabilis*. That is the source of the Church with all its truths, rites and dogmas, which are but an emanation from the heart of the person, poured out in death and in the blood and water. No one grasped this better than Origen.

All is completed in the resurrection narratives; the Church is separated from her glorified Head by his suffering, descent into hell, resurrection and presence at the Father's side. The first effect is to enable men to see the Lord and think of him, speak with him and even obey him (as did the disciples in casting their net), without recognising him. The Lord had to proclaim himself openly in order to break through the contemplative reflection of faith to the point of adoration. We see this happen with Mary at the tomb, with Thomas, with John in his recognition of the Lord, with the disciples at the breakfast by the lake; and again at the conferring of the primacy on Peter, when, overcome with the love demanded of him he surrenders himself with tears of joy : "Lord, thou knowest all things . . . ."

Of course this movement towards adoration, so characteristic of St. John's Gospel, is implicit in the Synoptics. Nor is it absent from St. Paul, for it is not first for extrinsic reasons that his theological thought issues so frequently in a doxology, an outburst of adoration. We find the same movement again in the apocalypse, in the great liturgy of heaven. There the "contemplation" of the works and wisdom of God in his revelation and his government of the world has, as a natural conclusion, the prostration before him of the whole of heaven and their casting down their crowns, so that he, One and Unique, yet threefold, may be the All.

But it would be unduly narrowing to exclude the contrary movement depicted so clearly by St. Paul. This consists in the unfolding of the spiritual and intelligible content of revelation, its full richness, offered to our intelligence in the Word of God and his Incarnation in Christ. So Paul returned from Damascus charged with treasure which he never entirely succeeded in minting to his satisfaction, though he was always returning to it. He was entrusted with the great mystery which has been so fully interpreted and expounded in recent times and become one of the treasures of the Church and of Christianity, which every believer has the right to share.

This is set forth in every one of his epistles to the very end of his life (1 Tim. I. 12-17). The movement in question is an essential part of the active life of the Church: missionaries leave a life of silent adoration to go among the people and proclaim not only the Church's teaching, but what they experience personally; and the function of theologians and thinkers is to give conceptual form to the living faith. The dangers of this kind of thought and preaching are of two kinds. The first is that the individual tends to incorporate his own special experience, his own personal subjugation by the Word, into his message as an essential part of it, making it almost part of the content of faith. St. Paul, who so stressed his experience on the road to Damascus and his own wide spiritual knowledge, was justified in doing so, because he was the instrument of the original, objective revelation binding upon the whole Church, and was fully aware of the fact. But among those who come later with no such exceptional position, working on the basis of personal experience can in certain circumstances prove fatal. The second danger which the thinker or preacher runs as a result of his efforts to translate experience as far as possible into words and formulas is that he becomes detached from the source which is prayer, and is unwilling to return to it unreservedly, since what he has already gleamed seems enough to last for years. He is sometimes even afraid of being submerged in a flood of ideas, which would make him lose sight of his own thoughts and conceptions. As soon as he notices that his thought or sermons shows signs of crystallising in the order of essence, and is no longer nourished by love encountered existentially—for only love edifies, while knowledge inflates—he should be warned that he is in danger, and recognise a summons to go back to prayer. The idea that the task before the theologian and the religious writer is, with the assistance of the Holy Spirit, simply to elaborate what is already known, without adding anything really new or seemingly inconsistent, is entirely unchristian, and must be countered immediately by fresh recourse to prayer.

To sum up, then, there is perpetual alternation and oscillation in thought and prayer between the order of essence and the order of existence. The two poles are indispensable, for God wills to make an effectual contact with man as a partner in action and to hold intercourse with him. Mere adoration without spiritual reception and elaboration of the word would lead to servile subjection. Mere reflection and assimilation of the truth of revelation by the understanding and of the power of revelation by the will would be a misconception of God's design—of his desire to open himself to man in the highest degree possible. The constant alternation between the two poles makes contemplation an intercourse with God in which man is led through adoration to freedom of spirit, and through this to a deeper participation in adoration and in the freedom of God.

CHAPTER II

FLESH AND SPIRIT

THE TENSION between spirit and body, which is peculiar to man, introduces a profound dichotomy into the idea of contemplation. If God is pure spirit, and contemplation is a way of entering into contact with God, it seems only reasonable to assume that the contemplative must purify and raise himself to the purely spiritual sphere by a gradual withdrawal from the external world of sense. We have already suggested that this theory is not solely ascribable to the culpable *hybris* of man, who deems existence in the flesh beneath his dignity, and with the help of spiritual exercises tries to live a purely spiritual life and ascend to the sphere of the divine. On the contrary, God's radical otherness makes a movement of the sort seem in complete accordance with natural religion. For whatever God may be, any positive statement about him is infinitely difficult for the natural man to reach, indeed practically impossible; whereas negative statements, such as that he is not of this world, form a sure point of departure for religious thought and prayer. The twofold nature of religious experience must also be taken into account: man's soul has its true home with God and so strives to return to him (while the body comes from below and returns there at death), and this bodily existence of ours in guilt and mortality is remote from God. When we consider this, the conclusion drawn by natural religion is almost inevitable: from that standpoint man is, at the core of his being, a soul that originated from God; the body is the result of a "dislocation" or a fall into sin and the return and redemption of the soul has to be achieved as a movement away from the body and towards the spirit.

This conception of the spiritual life has proved universally and irresistably attractive and has dominated religious thought, though it has been sharply criticised, especially from the Protestant side, and even given a demoniacal interpretation. From the standpoint of the Incarnation this criticism certainly appears to be amply justified; but this should not conceal the fact that the criticism implied treating the chief elements of the Christian tradition of contemplative prayer as theologically inadmissable. For the Alexandrian, Cappadocian and Syrian spiritual writers of the Eastern tradition, and Augustine in the West (to name the principal streams) did not regard the revelation in Christ merely as a paradoxical reversal of the natural, human standpoint, but also, and mainly, as the freely-given fulfilment of the fundamental longing placed in the soul by the Creator, and now purified from the dross of original sin. They did not hesitate to place their Christian notion of contemplation on a neoplatonic foundation. Their virtual unanimity strengthened the middle ages in their view, and their successors down to modern times followed in the same opinion. Moreover, Scripture itself, and especially the Pauline antithesis between "flesh" (sarx) and spirit (pneuma or nous), seems to justify the adoption and baptism of Greek ideas as dating from the very earliest times. In addition, both Paul and John speak of the Father dwelling in inaccessible light, and invisible to mortal man, unless perhaps in a supreme experience such as that of St. Paul in his rapture ("whether in the body or out of the body, I know not"—2 Cor. XII. 13) or that of St. John ("I was in the spirit"—Apoc. I. 10).

Yet even the visions of the Apocalypse seem too sensible to the man who strives towards the purely spiritual. They are, to him, the external coverings that most men need for a symbolical understanding of the purely spiritual things of God. The spiritual man, who disengages the spiritual sense of God's word from its sensible wrappings, and—to use an expression dear to the Fathers—contemplates it "nakedly", will see the supreme ideal in the suprasensible, supraconceptual vision of the superessential God as granted apparently to St. Paul, though it be unattainable on earth.

In this ascent from the sensible to the spiritual, we turn from the exterior senses to the depths of the soul, and that forms an important intermediary stage. Some Christian mystics have a tendency to pantheism (Bar Sudaili, Evagrius, Ponticus) and they regard the unveiling of the purely spiritual centre of the soul—which comes from God and shines by grace with a divine splendour—as an anticipation of the vision of heaven. To Gregory of Nyssa, this self-beholding of the soul is ardently desired but calls more for the practice of resignation. The pure soul is, indeed, a mirror, a resplendent image and symbol of the eternal Spirit but only a mirror, unbreakable it is true, which does not as yet permit him to be seen face to face. St. Augustine, at the time of his conversion in Milan, adhered obstinately to the neoplatonic system of self-transcendence —as described in the celebrated vision at Ostia and the tenth book of the Confessions—in order to attain ecstasy, the end of contemplation. This was to be achieved by transcending finite being, and even his own soul. But in St. Augustine's work too resignation casts its shadow over the highest reaches of contemplation. He knows that in order to behold what is purely spiritual, he must leave the region of the soul and abandon its spiritual content; and at that point strength fails him as he turns his "trembling gaze upward"—"I could not endure the vision, and had, in my weakness, to turn away". Even the vision of God's truth dwelling in the soul is not, as St. Augustine plainly saw, the vision of his essence. Only the Areopagite's mysticism, the mysticism of the Night, could carry him further : seeing in not-seeing, the soul's eye blinded by the light of God; though the darkness and the blindness are accompanied by a falling away of the veils, a nearness to the Absolute, which is the highest point attainable in this life.

How the order of salvation in the body, as proclaimed in the Old and New Testaments, can fit in with this teaching on contemplation is plainly stated in the Christmas Preface : "In coming to know God in visible form, we may, through him, be borne up to the love of what is invisible". In the Incarnation, God, who is pure spirit, abases himself, in order to raise us to him by the same road. Christ is both man and God; and in the flesh he presents and makes effective for us, not only spiritual, but divine, reality; and by means of sensible sacraments and the message of salvation, he pours into us, in a hidden manner, the "remedy that brings immortality" (*remedium immortalitatis*). This means that in order to surrender to the inner dynamism of Christianity we must tread the road rightly indicated by pagan philosophers, though they were powerless to follow it (as St. Augustine often observed), because they were strangers to the course of loving self-surrender that is humility—the sentiment of God who became man in Christ.

This, however, involves even the most consistent of Christian Platonists in a position which cannot be reconciled with the Platonic conception of ascent from the corporeal. God has not only "come down" in the flesh that we may "ascend" from the flesh to the Spirit. The sole or principle end of the revelation of his love, of his agape, self-giving to the point of self-emptying (*kenosis*), is not to assist our natural religious *eros* to reach its goal. "In this is charity : not as though we had loved God, but because he has first loved us, and sent his Son to be a propitiation for our sins" (1 John IV. 10). In other words, since the Incarnation may not be taken solely as a means of effecting our salvation, it must not be regarded as a provisional arrangement bearing on our final "deification", something which cancels itself out and is terminated on the return of the risen Christ to the Father. The risen Christ brings his humanity, his body, to the Father, and is "the first-fruits of them that sleep". Yet is not his body a glorified body, carried up into the mode of existence of the *Pneuma,* and is it not therefore our duty to turn from our mortal bodies if we are to contemplate God? The glorified body is indeed a grace given from above to the spirit that has overcome the flesh.

Let us look deeper into the question. The whole of creation, surely, and man in particular, was brought into being and ordered in view of Christ. And since Christ is the fulfilment of the cosmos, and the plenitude of the divinity sent into the world, since, too, he fills heaven and earth and gathers them together in himself as Head, surely he is more than the redeemer from sin. It is he who was to take flesh in the middle of time—and not the discarnate Logos—who is the first born in the mind of God and "the beginning of the creation of God" (Apoc. III. 14); and it was in him and in view of him that man was brought into being, compounded of spirit and body. In this light, the Platonic myth that man's soul alone comes directly from God, while the body comes from below, from the *natura naturans,* and the two have to return to their opposed origins, becomes quite unacceptable. It is certainly God who took clay in his hands to fashion man out of it, and, when fashioned, to breathe into his nostrils the breath of life (Gen. II. 7) and it is God who gave this being, at once body and spirit, the power to hear and feel him, to hold intercourse with him and to respond to him in obedience. The consequence of this is that God's revelation to man could not be given elsewhere than in the setting of the world and its history, unless God the Redeemer were to deny and contradict the work of God the Creator.

Thus the followers of Aristotle, like St. Thomas Aquinas, are right in understanding human acts, even the highest, as a body-soul unity, corresponding to the human nature whence they proceed; and as implying a tension, fruitful in its effects, between the concrete (*conversio ad phantasma*) and the abstract, between the concretisation of the concept and the desensualising of what is perceived or imagined. The highest acts of human reason are always accompanied by those of the imagination, which make them possible by furnishing reason and will, themselves empty, with the concrete material they need to put forth their activity in all its range and depth. The platonists (whose claims St. Thomas himself admits to a great extent) emphasise the obvious disparity between the two poles. The perfect man is not an exact balance between body and soul; in him the sphere of the body is dominated and penetrated by that of the soul, and this relationship of master and servant shows that the soul is more than a mere "form" of the body, that it is ordered to the Infinite, to God, in whom there is nothing material nor any quantitative multiplicity. This brings out clearly the mysterious frontier (*confinium*, the Fathers call it) between the world and God, and man's destiny to face, Janus-like, in two directions. He has the mission, in accordance with his own body-soul nature, to order and inform the world, but while keeping his gaze fixed on the world-transcending God, whom he has to fear and love, and whose transcendence he has to reproduce in himself as Lord of creation.

The task assigned to him is a difficult one indeed, for he has to apply himself with all his senses to his work in the world, and yet not let himself be absorbed in it. He must not try to achieve an aesthetically satisfying balance between the physical world and the inmost soul in so far as each is a reflection of the other, for the depths of the soul belong to God, are directed to him, and cannot be adequately represented in terms of the sensible. Yet all real power to change the world and to bring harmony between body and soul comes through the soul lending itself to divine action. Only the Christian doctrine of the resurrection of the body yields us the vital truth that when the spirit of man turns to God, man does not turn his back on the world; but it implies a particular transcendence of the material and historical here and now, in which man really enters into contact with the world as a whole. That is the sole reason why the material cosmos can follow the soul into the kingdom of heaven when it is translated into the world of God—by virtue of the miracle of the resurrection of the body. This fulfilment could not be discovered by natural reason, and even as a revealed truth, still remains an enigma to it. For this reason, a doctrine of contemplation based on man's natural constitution cannot possibly guide his actual contemplation to the proper end of man.

The consequences of a balanced philosophy of man—not exclusively platonic or aristotelian—and of its full realisation in the mysteries of Christ's incarnation, death and resurrection are very far-reaching for Christian contemplation. A profound cleavage runs through the history of Christian spirituality. On the one hand, we have the protagonists of a platonic kind of contemplation which strives after contact with the "naked" truth, a direct "touching" of the essence of God, albeit in the night of the senses and spirit and in a simple non-conceptual awareness of God's presence; it aims at a corresponding abstraction from the sensible, first from the external senses, then from the imagination, and finally from all finite ideas bound up, as they are, with the world. On the other hand, we have the advocates of a contemplation dependent on the sensible images and concepts of the Gospel and the whole historical course of salvation. St. Bernard and St. Francis, to some extent, and St. Ignatius in particular, were opposed to the dominant traditional conception, and insisted on a concrete type of contemplation using the imagination and, indeed, the five senses. As a general rule, the Platonisers considered this kind of contemplation only useful for beginners, as they did the discursive Ignatian method employing the various faculties of the soul (representation of the object, rational consideration, application of the will and affections). They considered that the methods using sense and reason had to lead up to the "prayer of simplicity" or of "recollection" or of the "heart", in which all that is exterior and manifold in imagery and thinking becomes progressively interiorised to give place to rest in the presence of the object sought, while images and thoughts, if not wholly excluded, are relegated to the background.

Now it can be shown quite easily that St. Ignatius did not look upon the use of the senses and the discursive reason in contemplation as suited to beginners only, even though in his Spiritual Exercises he had them mainly in view. His aim in the meditations on the Gospel was not the representation of historical events, but personal contact with Incarnate Word of God, who makes himself accessible to us in history and summons those who believe to follow him.

Our knowledge of the object of contemplation, Christ, must not be an arid knowledge, but "a feeling and tasting of the things within", which must therefore engage that spiritual sense of taste which is traditionally our sense for the supernatural and the divine —*sapientia* comes from *sapere*. For this reason, St. Ignatius demands something more than an earthly kind of activity of the senses in contemplation; he wants a feeling for the reality of God made present through the ordinary power of the imagination— "to smell and savour by scent and taste the infinite perfume and sweetness of the divinity" (Exercises 124). Finally, in his mystical experiences, he has a sense of being touched by God, a contact he calls direct (without any terrestrial medium), and so exempt from any danger of deception (Exercises 330, and 336). If this be considered the highest form of the divine communications indicated by St. Ignatius (Exercises 20), an ascending scheme on the platonic model could easily be drawn from his writing. [1]

Not to lose ourselves theologically and practically among these intersecting standpoints, it is best to consider the question christologically. Christ certainly took flesh on account of our sins, but that does not exhaust the meaning of the Incarnation; nor did he, after accomplishing our redemption, cast off his human nature and return to "pure divinity". Christian contemplation must first of all envisage the actual situation in time where the Father's Word came down to our level and spoke to us—sinners, certainly —in a language we could understand. The language is that of the flesh in its humble condition, and it will do no harm to the contemplative who wishes to soar to God as pure spirit to share first in the humiliation of the Incarnate Word by contemplating it, and so learn, by this indispensable practice, what God's love has to say in this, its clearest, language. He should acknowledge himself the sinner who needs to be spoken to in this way, because he shares in Adam's fall and is shorn of the capacity for direct intercourse

[1] cf. L. Peeters, S.J., ('*Vers l'union divine*')

with the Creator that he possessed in paradise. The recognition of this fact stands, for the Christian, in place of the Platonic myth of the soul fallen and imprisoned against its will in the body. The soul has been exiled from its natural home and transferred to a lower sphere, from a world dominated by spirit to one subject to the laws of the infraspiritual—that is the core of truth in Platonism. St. Ignatius expresses this in a formula clearly suggested by the Platonic myth, though differing from it—Exercises 47 : "Consider how my soul is imprisoned in this corruptible body, and the whole man is in this earthly valley as it were exiled among irrational beasts; I mean the whole man, as composed of soul and body."

We must not ignore the fact that from our point of view the Incarnation is a concession on the part of God to our obtuseness. In the life of Christ, God speaks to us unmistakeably; and we must not turn away impatiently from the incarnate truth of the Gospel to a spiritual truth we imagine to underly it, nor abandon the literal sense in favour of one hidden behind it, spiritual, allegorical or analogical. The mistake of the great Alexandrians and their followers was not to have adhered to the literal sense in seeking to establish the spiritual. This was the result of their Platonism; they regarded sense as a prison and a disguise, rather than a means of revealing the spiritual, and they therefore believed that the sensible was of no help in perceiving and interpreting the spirit. Their philosophy could not rightly express the Biblical dialectic, for God's "self-emptying", his "becoming poor", is a direct image of his fulness and richness and the prodigality of his love; the spiritual is made known through its covering, and is brought close to us through its sensible expression.

It is true that the senses must be spiritualised if we are to grasp this, and discern what is divine and eternal in the sensible and historical event. But these "spiritual senses" (*sensus spirituales*) are stirred up in us by the grace of the Incarnation; not only through the merits of Christ's Passion and death, but through our participation in them and, indeed, in our participation with Christ in the resurrection, where the ultimate, unattainable aim of Platonism is fulfilled unexpectedly and superabundantly. For in Christ's passion the human senses and spirit were engulfed in the night which extinguished all awareness of the divine, the night in which he was abandoned by the Father, when the human faculties were lost in the void and, deprived of their natural food, succumbed. This did not occur in the realm of philosophy but in the freedom of love taking on itself the consequences of sin.

The truth of the negative theology can be seen in the cross which carried it to its furthest limit—and on the cross Christ expiated sin, as a consequence of which our centre of gravity had been displaced from the realm of spirit to the realm of flesh. His spirit endured its free yet enforced imprisonment in the body even to the point of descending into hell. In that darkness he liberated the senses and the faculties subject to sin and enabled them to apprehend God in a manner befitting their redeemed state. As believers, we are entitled to share in the resurrection of Christ; even before their resurrection our senses receive something of the spiritual quality of Christ's glorified senses, enabling them to apprehend him and, together with him, the Father, the Spirt and the world above.

As a result of his experience on the road to Damascus, St. Paul emphasises the restoration of the centre of gravity from the realm of the "flesh" to the realm of the "spirit". He uses these words to signify, not two parts of human nature, but differing states of the whole man. The meaning of the Incarnation resides in this dying and resurrection, and Christ's acts and teaching centre on that decisive point. St. Paul could therefore say that, though previously he had known (i.e. judged) Christ "according to the flesh", now he knew him so no longer (2 Cor. V. 16). In him who became man, and in his death and resurrection still remained man, St. Paul wished only to see the revelation of God in the Spirit. He desired to look on the bodily form with spiritual senses. This, indeed, is contemplation. In this he is at one with St. John who, while stressing that the form of the Word is flesh and blood, teaches that in seeing, hearing and touching this form we make contact with the eternal "Word of life" (1 John I. 2.).

The opposed movements of concretisation (*conversio ad phantasma*) and abstraction (of the spiritual, the universal from the sense-image) are now seen to be as intimately connected in theology and contemplation as in philosophy and speculative psychology. The simple fact is that, unlike St. Thomas, the follower of Aristotle, the masters of contemplation have not always brought the necessary correctives to the Platonism of the East and of St. Augustine or did not insist on them sufficiently. Since concepts without perception are empty of content, there can be no approach to God and the mystery of the Trinity in Christian contemplation except through the Incarnation of Christ. The concepts used in the doctrine of the Trinity too often ring hollow when divorced from the relations of Christ with the Father and the Spirit, and do not foster contemplation of the divine; at the most they give some satisfaction to the logical mind. On the other hand, perception without concepts is blind, and this applies invariably to that contemplation and interpretation of Scripture which, in the events recorded (whose laws remain valid and cannot be ignored), fails to perceive, hear and touch God's own truth and life. But whether we follow the ideas of St. Paul or of St. John is a secondary matter, since both are forms of contemplation in faith of the God who manifests himself to us in the life of Christ.

"No man cometh to the Father but me." That was of course, known to Origen, Denis the Areopagite, Eckhart and St. John of the Cross. Being touched by God, they strove for the veiled vision of the divine being. But, whatever the process of thought, whatever the theoretical arguments they used in their endeavour, they always acted as believers, disciples of the Son whom they followed, and, in their "vision" of the Father in the Holy Spirit, they knew themselves to be on the way of Christ and within the framework of the laws of his discipleship. It is not in by-passing or soaring above him that Christian contemplation strives to reach the *speculatio majestatis*. That would be a form of gnosis, a vain clutching at the void. And when it dies to all sensible and intelligible forms, renouncing seeing, hearing and touching, in order to attain the divine reality that transcends all form, that too is to follow the Son. For if the Son ceases to be a subject of contemplation, it is only to incorporate the contemplative more fully in Christ's own inward state and allow him an active participation in Christ's death and resurrection. Indeed, the mystical night of the senses and the spirit, however solitary the person experiencing them, is always something that bears on the Church, something deeply embedded in the order of the Incarnation. Theology can demonstrate the fact, whereas the mystics, describing their experience of the night, necessarily dwell on the feeling of being alone; that is why they do not always avoid the temptation of using the categories of Platonism to describe their experiences.

The contemplative, and not only the specially favoured, will inwardly experience something of the night of the soul if his prayer be the expression of a real following of Christ in faith. That will be a sign that he is on the way of Christ, and so a consolation, although it will have the form of a withdrawal of consolation. There is a kind of consolation generally meted out to beginners as a kind of advance payment, "sensible" consolation in which the senses and faculties of the soul rejoice at discovering a divine meaning and presence in the words and events of Scripture. It must, sooner or later, be withdrawn for an indefinite period from those who have made some progress; for God is found only on the road of his Son's death and resurrection. The spirit must die in the flesh for the flesh to rise again in the spirit. This death has already taken place in principle, sacramentally, in baptism; and the contemplative ought to be grateful that it is being worked out through the acts he elicits in his intercourse with God.

An important part of this death will consist of personal penance, penance for past sins in which, listening to the voice of the flesh, he was disobedient to the spirit; penance as painful detachment from the senses and faculties of the soul, so that they come to learn what Christianity really means; for the same senses and faculties cannot claim to enjoy both the divine and its contrary, concurrently or turn by turn, or to detach themselves from what is not divine through joy in divine things (as the Jansenists held). Aridity and absence of consolation, emptiness and boredom, disgust and the feeling of uselessness, which, from time to time come to every contemplative and may last a long time, constitute a real "purgative way"; they are a severe and irksome discipline, provided they are accepted wholeheartedly and the affliction they involve is not just the inevitable consequence, psychologically, of indifference. But, since this purgative way has a christological and ecclesial reference, it cannot be wholly described in terms of psychology and discipline. It may, in fact, be imposed anew and more heavily even on someone who does not need it for his own individual good. The cross has many meanings, appropriate to all times and to every period of life. It may, perhaps, be imposed in view of particular or general conditions or necessities of the kingdom of God; the individual is then a representative of the community. This is often the case with the prayer of the contemplative orders. It may be a grace of God, who, for his own glory, graciously accepts the offer, explicit or implicit, to be consumed as a sacrifice before him, and makes the perfume of this sacrifice fill the whole house of the Church on earth and in heaven. Accordingly, we must take care not to impose any kind of hard and fast rule of succession on contemplative states, or claim that they have universal validity. God uses the contemplative as he pleases; he regulates the states he judges necessary and right for him to experience. No sequence is irreversible, the termination of a period of aridity or darkness is no guarantee that a fresh, and severer, one is not to follow. The classification of purgative, illuminative and unitive ways should be used, as we have already insisted, with discretion. A Christian, who has been led in advanced unitive ways and has experienced a beatific, nuptial union with God, may conceivably at death feel himself abandoned by God. This may, indeed, be a form of the highest union with the Lord, who ended his earthly existence in a night of the senses and spirit.

Of course, contemplation need not invariably begin by taking Christ as its object, in order to ascend with him to the Father through the Spirit. It is part of the liberty of the children of God to have direct access to all the goods of God, by contemplating God's majesty in creation and, especially, his own being and attributes. Yet, objectively speaking, the procedure takes place within the order of salvation : contemplation is the act of a believing Christian, and he never imagines himself free to dispense with Christ in making his way to God or to be capable of gaining experiences of the Godhead by his own efforts and without any intermediary. The Christian knows, though often without fully realising it, that even now, after the resurrection, all access to the Father is through Christ, the mediator between God and man. He knows that the Son's human nature with its senses and faculties transfigured and glorified, raised by the Father to be Lord of the cosmos, is the medium through which the mystical body makes contact with God, now and for eternity. The bold, and perhaps too rash, idea of certain Greek mystical theologians, that the soul striving to reach God must become "equal to Christ", so as to behold the Father with the eyes and heart of Christ (Isochristism), contains, if understood in reference to the Church and to the cosmos, a core of truth; for Christian contemplation to be acceptable in the sight of God it must be performed within the frame-work of Christ's contemplation. But in Christ on earth, and still more in heaven, we see the extreme tension between "spirit" and "flesh", between a direct vision of the Father and the remoteness demanded by obedience, and brought by obedience to the extreme point of God's abandonment of him on the cross. However we interpret the first, it certainly did not annul the second, the ordinary human way of experiencing God, as superfluous; nor did it lessen its hidden character and its efficacy for salvation, or disable the Son from accomplishing his obedience to death with all his faculties of soul and body. The Church's contemplation takes place within that tension and between the extremes of the vision of God and abandonment by God; the same is true of the individual member, sharing in the Church's contemplation and contributing to its vigour and life.

CHAPTER III

HEAVEN AND EARTH

THERE IS a mysterious polarity in creation, indicated by the terms used in the very first verse of Scripture—"In the beginning God created heaven and earth." This opposition, as the subsequent course of the history of salvation shows, has not only a cosmological, but a theological, significance. It contrasts God's being and place (in the world) with the being and place of man. What it brings out especially is that the earth is not heaven, even before the fall caused a spiritual divorce between man and heaven. Before the fall, there were times when God was openly present walking in the "afternoon air". And, subsequently there are frequent mentions of Jahweh coming down to the world (Gen. XI. 5-7; XVIII. 21, etc.): Jacob's ladder ascending and descending, God "looks down" on the earth, and inhabitants of the earth are carried up to heaven (Elias, and "in spirit" Isaias, Ezechiel, Daniel). As the story of revelation proceeds, God's heaven appears, in increasing detail, in man's representation of it, and, at the the same time, its cosmological opposite declines in importance, and comes to be seen as merely symbolical of it. The prophets make bold to direct their gaze to heaven, and what they see is so compelling that a new movement arises in Judaism. By following the steps of these seers, men try to become acquainted with the heavenly world, to scale the ascending spheres to the world above them by human effort; and this desire to contemplate heaven gives rise to a luxuriant growth of apocalyptic doctrines.

But this is not the way along which God wills to reveal the secrets of heaven. The Son himself "descends", and with him heaven

becomes accessible to the understanding earth. "He that seeth
me seeth the Father." "You shall see the heavens opened and the
angels of God ascending and descending on the Son of man."
Man's longing to see into God's dwelling-place is abundantly satisfied through God's coming to live in man's abode and "sup with
him" (Apoc. III. 20). This is a first, secret descent, and what it
shows is simply the self-abasing love of God and nothing else;
what the mystics of the late Middle Ages called the poverty of
God, something so wonderful that it should make us forego, for
the time being, all curiosity about the splendours of the world
above. In Christ, heaven is no longer a piece of imagery, but a
person; it is God's love capable of being loved in a human form,
as a being like one of us. And this personal being dies for you and
me, and, when he lies dead, heaven too has died for us. Holy
Saturday is the contemplation of the lost heaven, precipitated
into the horrors of the world beneath. But the Son rose from the
dead, and during the forty days which he spent among us, he laid
the foundations of the lasting Christian feeling about life. God, the
object of our love, the heaven on earth who sued, while on earth,
for our love—and to whom we only gave it when he had died for
our sakes—is now earth in heaven. For forty days he showed us
this earth transformed into heaven, as if to intensify our love for
him, and then suddenly to carry this love with him, on his ascension to the right hand of the Father in heaven.

We will try and bring this home by an example. Suppose I have
a friend I love more than anyone else, in whose company I discover my real self, apart from whom my life seems to have no
meaning at all. He dies for my sake and I am inconsolable, rooted
to the spot where he left me; I pine away in the memory of him,
and centre my whole life on his place of burial. Then one day he
reappears, more vigorously alive than ever, converses with me,
walks, eats and drinks in my company. He avows his entire love
for me anew, in a renewed and nobler form. The new life we lead
together has nothing exaggerated, or *exalté* about it, of the kind
that is bound to wear off in time; it is the fulfilment of all that

went before, yet so far above earthly measure that it can no longer be called heaven on earth (since then all the shadows and limitations of the earth would cling to it), but earth in heaven. But after an interval he disappears, not, however, celebrating his departure beforehand—as he did the evening before his death—but making me understand that he will not show himself to me again in the same way as before; that he does not withdraw from me; that everything remains as it was, only in a mode of being truer, more profound, more fixed and final. It is precisely this that arouses a longing to see him again, for he is not far from me; though the fact is that I am not yet so far as he. This longing consumes me the more because it is not a longing for something past or in the future, but for something that *is*, because I have already experienced it, something not temporal and past but eternal, which it has been granted me, earthly and transient that I am, to have contact with for a moment. Something of the sort is the Christian's longing for the second coming of the Lord. The believer lives a life of heaven on earth with the beloved, lives it anew each day in prayer, the sacraments, the Eucharist, the whole life of love. All this is life in the Lord and life by him; it is his presence among us, gathered together in his name and celebrating the memory of his death and the memory of his spirit, which we try through him to make prevail in us. Yet this is not all, for, after his resurrection and ascension to his Father's right hand in his kingdom, he has shown us heaven so open to us as to make us, still on earth, participators in it along with him. The disciples themselves were with him in heaven; for who does not feel, in reading and reflecting on the accounts of the resurrection, the breath of eternal life, the atmosphere of heaven, more pervasive there than in the most stirring of the visions of the prophets? We have been granted access to heaven, not by being taken there physically, nor in imagination or vision, but by an act of grace on the part of the Redeemer, one wholly internal, utterly changing our entire being, transplanting it, uprooting it from this earth and embedding it in the soil of the kingdom of heaven; he makes us "pilgrims and

strangers" on earth, because "citizens of heaven." St. Paul and the
other apostles were intimately aware of this, and so too were all
the saints of the Church. The paradoxes St. Paul boldly employs
in this connection simply express the fact that Christ, our Head,
is in heaven, now that he has appeared to us as risen and has conversed with us; this would not have been possible, unless he had
imparted to our love a heavenly quality, and unless, as St. Paul
says, we had risen with him and ascended into heaven (Eph. II. 6;
Col. II. 12). So then not only Christ, but also our love for him, is
already in heaven; at the Mass we receive him in heaven, in prayer
and contemplation we seek and find him in heaven. Even
in the ordinary practice of fraternal charity we meet with him in
heaven. For the time being, all this remains hidden from our
earthly senses, but, when the Lord comes again, it will appear together with him as something that was present all along. St. Paul
says so expressly : "If you be risen with Christ, seek the things that
are above, where Christ is sitting at the right hand of God; mind
the things that are above, not the things that are upon the earth.
For you are dead, and your life is hid with Christ in God. When
Christ shall appear, who is your life, then you also shall appear
with him in glory" (Col. III. 1-4). It is by no means inconsistent
with this that the elect, whom the author of the apocalypse
sees in heaven following the Lamb, are persons still living on
earth.

The epistle to the Hebrews brings out the theological circumstances and effects of the ascension of the eternal high priest, and
proclaims to all Christians : "Having therefore a great high
priest that hath passed into the heavens . . . . Let us go with confidence to the throne of grace" (Heb. IV. 14-16). For we are those
who "have tasted the heavenly gift and were made partakers of
the Holy Ghost, have moreover tasted the good word of God and
the powers of the world to come" (VI. 4-5), and in the Christian
hope possess "an anchor of the soul, sure and firm, and which
entereth in even within the veil" (VI. 19-20). The whole epistle
leads up to the absolute necessity of perseverance in faith, of per-

sisting in the standpoint of the eternal and unchangeable. For that is the life of the Church : "You are not come to a mountain that might be touched . . . . but you are come to mount Sion, and to the city of the living God, the heavenly Jerusalem, and to the company of many thousands of angels, and to the church of the first-born who are written in the heavens, and to God the judge of all, and to the spirits of the just made perfect, and to Jesus the mediator of the new testament" (Heb. XII. 18, 22-24).

Finally, the apocalypse of St. John, which concludes the New Testament, is distinguished from all that precedes it in that it is the "revelation of Jesus Christ, which God gave unto him, to make known to his servants the things which must shortly come to pass", of Christ, "the first begotten of the dead and the prince of the kings of the earth, who hath loved us and washed us from our sins in his blood, and hath made us a kingdom and priests to God and his Father" (Apoc. I. 1, 5-6). In the letters to the Churches we hear the voice of the Incarnate Son speaking from heaven to his bride, the Church. The visions contain the truth of the Old Testament heaven, but now with the Lamb of God in the centre of history, which ultimately becomes the revelation of the eternal marriage of the Lamb with his bride, the "woman", the "Church", the heavenly Jerusalem. Apocalypse, indeed, means the revelation of what took place in the Incarnation, hidden in a humble form. The cry of longing in which the book ends is for a present that still hangs back, not for a future that is not as yet. St. Paul too, who had not known the Lord on earth, or shared the forty days' intercourse with him, but had communed with the glorified Lord of heaven on the road to Damascus and on many occasions (Acts. XVIII. 9; XXII. 17-18), spoke from the same experience as the other apostles, and shared the same eschatological longing.

The mode of existence we speak of is one which the Son himself inaugurated while on earth, since, though living fully on earth, he did not leave the Father's heaven. He lived in uninterrupted contemplation of the Father, but, though real vision, it was not the same as that given him by the Father after his ascension; for it was affected by the gulf separating "earth" from "heaven", a gulf existing from the beginning of creation and widened by man's sins. It is not sufficient to say that the Son possessed the open vision of God, where man has only the obscurity of faith. There are two things we must add : first, that both have their love in heaven and keep it on earth because of their heavenly love and the missions entrusted to them; indeed they love the earth, mankind, all their transient relationships and tasks, and are sustained by a "food you know not" (John IV. 32). The second is that something of the concreteness which the Father always retains in the open vision of the Son is carried over into the concreteness that the risen Son takes with himself into heaven for eternity, and which springs from his living and loving intercourse with the Church after the resurrection. His bride, the Church, will never forget those days; and all the visions, in their various degrees of clarity, that heaven gives to earth throughout the centuries are for the purpose of keeping alive her memory and rekindling her desire—"where thy treasure is, there is thy heart also".

In considering the Son and the discharge of his mission, we can see that the Church, though her eyes are turned heavenwards, is not hindered from fulfilling her mission on earth loyally and exactly. This plain Christian truth is independent of the disagreements between the masters of the spiritual life on the relationship between contemplation and action; it forms part of the description of the Christian life in general. If having one's "heart in heaven" were not a foretaste of eternal happiness with God, then the present life, torn and made restless between heaven and earth, could only seem tragic. Looked at from the outside, that is what it seems. Even considered from within, it can be so, if love and faith decline in vigour and vitality. The Christian life demands, at one and the same time, the maintenance and elimination of the gulf between heaven and earth—for it is eliminated in principle by the ascent of the human Christ to heaven, and he has taken our own humanity along with him mysteriously but really. The resulting tension enters into the whole Christian life, and particularly into the life of contemplation.

The teaching of the Fathers and of St. Augustine in particular, follows from this. According to them, contemplation consists in bringing out and realising the heavenly dimension and truth of the Christian life, while action is the application of that truth in the present transitory sphere which hastens to its end. Contemplation is Mary, oblivious of time, sitting at the feet of the Master and performing the "one thing necessary"; while Martha is active, distracted by the temporal demands of loving service to others and has to bear the Lord's reproof. St. John is the contemplative; he sees the Word at the beginning and encounters the eternal word of life "hearing, seeing and touching", and in the apocalypse, sees the eternal form of the Word with head white as snow and voice like the sound of rushing water. Peter is action; he serves the flock committed to him in its passage through time, feeding it till it reaches the sphere of eternity. Contemplation anticipates the joy that will never end (*delectatio*); action is involved in the distress that will one day cease, and is endured by virtue of the power drawn from contemplation and its promises. The Middle Ages saw the active life so dependent on the contemplative that in its theology, politics and art, it held the kingdom of God on earth to be the transitory image of the abiding kingdom, the object of contemplation. The cathedrals were the visible expression of contemplation and could only be understood by those prepared to devote themselves to the contemplation of the things of heaven. The same might be said of the political ideas of the time, whose ideals were far above their distortions and inadequacies in the practical sphere, and of the great Summas and Scriptural commentaries; also of the attempts at a theology of history, all, in some fashion, expressing a view of the world from the standpoint of heaven such as we find in the Apocalypse.

This idea of contemplation can easily be purified of its Platonic accretions and in its simple form harmonised with the Gospel. It will then be valid for our time. The Platonic misconception consists, not so much in the exaggerated estimate of contemplation as the vision of the eternal ideas, as in the depreciation and contempt of action, of work on earth, which educated Greeks regarded as beneath their dignity. Christianity overthrew that view by teaching the humility of the carpenter's son who, even in his own spiritual mission, dwelt with us as "one who serves". Our own times have emphasised the Christian conception of work. Even more than the Fathers, we look upon action as sharing in the spirit and value of contemplation, convinced that the earthly life of the Christian, whether in ordinary family life or in politics or culture, contributes, in hidden fashion, to the building of the eternal cathedral, the heavenly Jerusalem. For all that, the value of contemplation is neither diminished nor reversed, but enhanced and deepened. It means that the burning desire for heaven felt in prayer extends into our ordinary life and kindles our actions with the fire of eternal love. St. Paul would frankly have preferred to die and be with Christ; but, in his love for Christ and his work on earth, for Christ's brethren and members, he chose to remain and fulfil his mission.

During the first Christian centuries the contemplation of heaven, as the hidden setting of the Christian life, was rightly emphasised. But it was fitting that prominence should subsequently be given not to the contrast between the "joy" of contemplation and the "weariness" of action but to the joy of the redeemed life under our glorified Head, a joy that flows out into the active life. At first contemplation was regarded as an individual matter. This was the legacy of Greek thought, according to which the human community is something earthly, and so pertains to the world of action, while the contemplative goes to God in solitude and enters into the society of the angels. This view has given place in modern times to a fuller understanding of our membership of the Church, even in the sphere of contemplation. For it is not so much the individual as the bride who is the "body" dependent on the "Head", and calls longingly to the bridegroom in his spirit (Apoc. XXII. 17); she is the widow left behind "in the desert" (Apoc. XXI. 6-14) but sustained by his secret presence in the sacraments and the word, and, ever watching with ardent desire, she gives to all contemplatives the form and substance of their prayer.

Any stress on the ecclesial element in contemplation must be accompanied by a corresponding emphasis on the role of Mary. Mary is the archetype of the Church as she turns to heaven in contemplation, and applies its fruits to her action of bearing and fostering her offspring. The knowledge that Mary was taken up bodily to heaven gives added strength to our hearts' longing for the spiritual realm where the union of bride and bridegroom, the marriage of the Lamb, is already fulfilled in anticipation. It gives a concreteness and reality to our share in that union which, in so far as we are the Church, is, in fact, ours.

This change in the relationship between contemplation and action is accompanied by a more conscious realisation of the antithesis between contemplation as an end in itself and as related to active life on earth. The patristic period viewed contemplation as a participation in heaven, as an end in itself, and considered ordinary Christian living as little more than a preparatory phase, a means of attaining the necessary purity of heart, while the Middle Ages regarded it as a kind of inferior receptacle into which the exuberant riches of contemplation discharged themselves. In modern times, there is an equally onesided tendency to subordinate contemplation to action, to see it as a means to recollection, to a fuller awareness of the mysteries of faith, which would bring greater calmness, clarity and more abundant grace to the work of the apostolate. Hence our concern to give each exercise of contemplation a definite practical application. The true conception lies between these extremes. Our mission, our assent to God's personal will in the concrete, springs from the contemplation of God's eternal truth and our assent to it. Isaias, in heaven, absorbed in adoration of God, heard the word "Whom shall I send, and who shall go for us?", and said; "Lo, here I am. Send me" (Is. VI. 8). In Christianity, contemplation on the plane of essence necessarily includes realisation on the plane of existence, for heaven becomes earth for us, the daily round—though never a function of earth. Heaven is form penetrating the whole of life, and can only produce its effects on a grand scale if it retains its original "breadth and length and height and depth".

With the passing of the world-picture of former times, the cosmological remoteness of heaven has itself been superseded, and, with it, a certain feeling that the contemplative, if he is to rise in spirit to heaven, must do so in a definite series of gradations, must turn away from the terrestrial world, and penetrate to the "purely spiritual" world. The psychological barriers too have fallen, which might hinder us from entering, contemplatively, directly into the things of heaven.

We strive, it is true, to reach from earth to heaven, but that is not all. It is equally true that in our love and faith as Christians, we are essentially with God, while for those in heaven who look on us from "above", we already belong to heaven, being redeemed and endowed with grace, although we cannot be assured of this by our senses. The Eucharist is the presence among us of the Lord of heaven, though he does not "come down from heaven", as at his birth, but on an equal footing, from his heaven into his Church. The Church is already with him, but he cannot remove the veil of faith from her eyes, since her purifying and testing must continue till the end. In sacramental absolution the action of the priest is one with the action of the Lord in heaven, and the reconciliation of the sinner with the Church is one with his reconciliation with God, for the Church is God's heavenly court, and God, since his incarnation, does not will to be treated in isolation from his brethren. In Christian love, which embraces all our suffering brethren on earth, the godless and the despised, the bond is perhaps still closer. For love knows that all the brethren, those filled with charity, and those void of charity, are images and sacraments of the Son abandoned by God on the cross, who "became sin for us, that we might become in him the justice of God" (2 Cor. V. 21). Fraternal love is, without knowing it, something done in heaven—"Hospitality do not forget, for by this some, being not aware of it, have entertained angels" (Heb. XIII. 2); indeed, with hearts burning within them, yet unknowing, they have entertained the very Lord of the angels (Luke XXIV. 29; Gen. XVIII. 1 ff.). And why should not life lived in the Church and according to the truth of her being be, apart from its earthly covering, a life lived within what is eternal and imperishable? Why, too, as we re-enact all these eternal mysteries in our life should our prayer and contemplation not be in heaven, though, for the time being, only in the way in which the giver of a picture is depicted in it, an insignificant figure on his knees, his hands joined, gazing on the mystery it represents? When St. Ignatius makes his contemplation take place "in the presence of the whole court of heaven" he is not using a fanciful or exaggerated expression, nor is he translating a purely mystical expression into terms all can understand. He is contemplating the truth in its own surroundings; he has come, in the words of St. Paul, "to the city of the living God" (Heb. XII. 22).

The same thing is true when we contemplate the history of salvation. Christian contemplation begins at the point where the meaning of the swiftly flowing surface of earthly events is broken to reveal their relation to heaven. That mysterious and alluring element which impels us to adore, is not put there by the person contemplating; it is detected by the eye of faith—whether present in the simplest parable, the most natural, perhaps even unrecorded, action of the Lord, or a casual piece of information such as that St. Paul had left his cloak at Troas—the cold was bitter in the prison at Rome, before his execution, and Timothy was to bring him his cloak and with it the love of Christ. Contemplation does not aim at remoteness from the earth; the apostles and saints were not visionaries who rejected the world and lived in fairyland. The Acts of the Apostles is a serious and sober historical reality, inspired by the Holy Ghost, who breathes on the faithful when he will, and is seen by them, in their plans and decisions, as the principal agent and accepted as such. Contemplation must be realistic; it does not scale the reality of heaven by dissolving and allegorising the reality of earth, but supports the span which links the two together, and that can only be upheld in virtue of the union of the two natures in Christ. The tension between heaven and earth, then, is made possible only by Christ, and not by the unaided effort of man or by contemplation as such. Christian contemplation alone preserves this tension, seeing heaven plainly in what most plainly pertains to earth. It is not an aesthetic contemplation of earthly reality to which is no doubt added an indefinite range of overtones whose meaning—as in the cosmic contemplation of Rilke—extends into the idea and reveals affinities with the world below and above man. Nor does it see earthly reality as a mere shadow, or maybe a screen shrouding the world of heaven—as the Alexandrians were in danger of thinking or, on a different plane, a "seer" like Swedenborg held.

The distance between heaven and earth takes the contemplative deeper and deeper into the mystery of the Son, both in its form and its content. The ultimate longing for the full manifestation of heaven—the eschatological impulse—draws its force from the desire the Son felt on earth to see the heavenly fire he came to light on the earth blazing over the whole world. But it is also the Church's response to the desire of Christ in heaven to have his body and all his members fully redeemed and glorified along with him. That longing is our longing for the rest of the Sabbath, so that we only need to wait till the mystery of eternity prevails over the earth (Heb. X. 13); though it is, at the same time, active and vigorous and labours to make the kingdom prevail (1 Cor. XV. 25), and fights fiercely to that end (Apoc. XIX. 11 ff.).

Who could describe the rhythm of this alternation between the eternal Sabbath beyond the conflicting forces of this world (experienced by Denis the Areopagite) and involvement in the dramatic struggle of the world moving towards the Sabbath, in which the Word of God himself fights with two-edged sword (Heb. III. 7—IV. 13)? Who could, in contemplating Christ himself, discover the laws of the movements by which heaven opened on the Son of man on Thabor, and, immediately after, there stood "Jesus alone" before the disciples in the earthly form that hid him, and yet told them as much of heaven as the splendour they had just seen? "Thou hast made him a little lower than the angels; thou hast crowned him with glory and honour . . . thou hast subjected all things under his feet . . . . Now we see not as yet all things subject to him; but we see Jesus, who was made a little lower than the angels, for the suffering of death crowned with glory and honour" (Heb. II. 7-9). Glory, abasement, exaltation; the alternation is not purely temporal, since temporality is but one of the factors; it is neither in the Lord nor in us, who are his "holy brethren, partakers of the heavenly vocation" (III. 1), but abasement is itself the manifestation of glory, earth is the manifestation of heaven, to the end that our earth, together with Christ, may become worthy of heaven. It is not a rhythmic alternation between the "unchangeable" and the "changeable", as if the unchangeable were itself subject to the rhythm of change, but "the translation of the movable things as made, that those things may remain which are immovable. Therefore receiving an immovable kingdom, we have grace, whereby let us serve, pleasing God. . . ." (Heb. XII. 27-28). It is we who enter into his rhythm. He, the heavenly man, who comes from above (1 Cor. XV. 47), forms us after his image; indeed, becomes for us, as the Word of God, a mysterious food, through which we, striving from earth towards heaven, are endowed with the grace coming down from heaven to earth. "For it is best that the heart be established with grace, not with meats . . . . We have an altar, whereof they have no power to eat who serve the tabernacle" (Heb. XIII. 9-10). In Christ's rhythm, set up by his word, it is possible that the remoteness from God of our life on earth may itself become the form and expression of life in heaven, and the experience of abandonment by God be the expression of a love impossible to understand on earth, and only explicable in heaven.

CHAPTER IV

CROSS AND RESURRECTION

HEAVEN, THEN, in which we can already participate, informs our life on earth and gives it its meaning; and, in like manner, the resurrection determines our relation to the cross, setting up a second and final "soteriological" tension. We are Christians, because the Lord has risen; if he had not, our faith would be vain (1 Cor. XV. 14). Christ suffered for the sake of glorification and took on himself the cross, the confession of the cross, that he might obtain absolution from the Father. We are not at first entitled to go with Christ on the way he walked; otherwise there would be no qualitative difference between him and us; he would only be *primus inter pares,* and we could be literally called co-redeemers. But "God commendeth his charity towards us because when as yet we were sinners according to the time Christ died for us . . . . When we were enemies, we were reconciled to God by the death of his Son" (Rom. V. 8, 10). If we walk with the Son, it is because we are carried along by the grace of the redemption accomplished by him. The sentence that decided our destiny in principle was pronounced on Christ as representing all sinners. In him we were crucified and condemned to death; in him justified and accepted as sons. In him, without any action on our part, God's wrath against us has changed into solicitous love. So then we have to bring to full reality in our temporal life on earth what is already true in Christ and through him in heaven with the Father.

In the New Testament what we have to do follows from what we are. We are justified, and must act accordingly. We are dead, buried and risen with Christ, and have to live our lives in view of this. We are no longer to live to sin; we are henceforth to look on the "old man", who *is* dead as dead in fact, daily oppose his resistance to the sentence of death, make him die daily (Rom. VI). One might say that in order to exalt the resurrection St. Paul upsets the equilibrium between the old and the new eon, the old and the new Adam, cross and resurrection, fear and hope. From now on the first member of each pair of antitheses is comprised within the second; the cross, in the Christian life, is borne in the strength of the resurrection already accomplished. "In all things we suffer tribulations but are not distressed. We are straitened, but not destitute. We suffer persecution, but are not forsaken. We are cast down, but we perish not. Always bearing about in our body the mortification of Jesus, that the life also of Jesus may be made manifest in our bodies . . . . For which cause we faint not; but though our outward man is corrupted, yet the inward man is renewed day by day. For that which is at present momentary and light of our tribulation worketh for us *above measure* an *eternal weight* of glory. While we look not on the things which are seen, but at the things which are not seen. For the things which are seen are temporal, but the things which are not seen are eternal" (2 Cor. IV. 8-10, 16-18).

For that reason, St. Paul can always present his own sufferings, though so great and continuous, as a proof of the power of the risen Christ, never as a kind of rival with his passion. He does so even when asserting that he bears Christ's sufferings in his own body (2 Cor. IV. 10), that he has the marks of Christ's wounds on his body (Gal. VI. 18), that he is crucified with Christ (Gal. I. 20), and that he fills up those things that are wanting to the sufferings of Christ in his flesh for Christ's body, the Church (Col. I. 24). All this was only possible in virtue of his election by the risen and ascended Christ, whose will it was to manifest his power in him and to "show" him how much he must suffer for the name of Christ (Acts. IX. 16). Consequently, the servant has nothing to boast of, but only does his duty (1 Cor. IX. 16), when he offers himself for the Father to reveal his Son in him (Gal. I. 16).

This basic fact of the redemption means that there is no other starting-point for the imitation of Christ than the resurrection. It is the ascended and glorified Head of the Church and of humanity who distributes the charismata and assigns the missions which constitute the following of Christ (Eph. IV. 7 ff.).

Out of the fulness of his victory the Son gives each individual a special kind of participation in his passion on earth and in the profound mystery of judgment accomplished on Calvary. The participation granted in virtue of his victory may, by the will of the Lord, reach the point of an extreme powerlessness, an experience of inner darkness, abandonment and reprobation; and because it is a sharing in the cross, it surpasses anything naturally experienced and endured, even to the complete loss, subjectively, of all spiritual light, of any view or hope of a future redemption and resurrection. Yet this darkness most certainly proceeds from that light and presupposes it objectively, even subjectively, for the light is never withdrawn from any believer without his knowing it beforehand and his giving his consent to that loss, at least implicitly.

Thus the contemplation of the cross is comprised within that of the resurrection (for all faith is faith in the resurrection), and, further, in the contemplation of the cross the contemplation of one's own and the world's sins finds its true place. For, from the Christian point of view, the contemplation of sin is only profitable when done in view of confession, and the source whence confession springs is the cross. Only in the light of the cross and of that judgment on sin can the sinner gain any sort of understanding and estimate of his own sin. Even a good conscience, as it is called, in contradistinction to a bad, does not suffice for this, necessary though it be; for the essence of sin is falsehood, a darkening of the inner sight. It is easier than we think to evade conscience and to accommodate oneself to the judgments of the "world". On the other hand, there is a kind of total despair arising from the abyss of one's sins, and this, in the way we experience it, is not willed by God, but results from our own attitude as affected by sin. It is from the cross that the sinner learns the right kind of objectivity (the insight into guilt that God wills) and of subjectivity (the experience of contrition, conversion willed by God), and the cross imparts a proper sense of fear of judgment. An unrestrained fear of judgment disregards the fact of the cross, and is quite unchristian. For all that, the contemplation of sin in the presence of the cross is dialectical; only in so far as I look on my Redeemer can I understand what I have really done. Face to face with his redemptive love I feel that I could be, that I am, the hangman of eternal love, deserving damnation. While I contemplate the work of the supreme love between Father, Son and Holy Spirit, the work that was done for me from whom love was absent, I know that I am a stranger to it, and have no love in me, and so I feel deserving of eternal wrath, of annihilation and rejection from the whole divine order :

"Cry of astonishment and heightened emotion. Take in turn all creatures, and wonder how they could have let me go on living, and kept me in life. The angels, the sword of divine justice, have yet borne with me and protected me and prayed for me. The saints, how they have bethought themselves to intercede for me. Heaven, the sun and moon, stars, fruits, birds, fishes and animals. The earth, which might well have opened to swallow me up and make new hells for me to suffer in for ever" (*Exercises*, 60).

Admittedly, St. Ignatius separates the meditation on sin (first week) from the meditation on the passion (third week). None the less, he sets the consideration of sin, both sin in general and personal sin, in the theological framework of redemption, and leads each exercise in contemplation to the "colloquy of mercy" with the "Lord present hanging on the cross", whose love shows me "what I have (not) done for Christ, what I am (not) doing for Christ, what I shall (not) do for Christ". The hell I have deserved should also come to my view in the context of this colloquy ("like friend with friend or servant with master"). The thought of hell remains fantastic and fanciful, and cannot be taken with proper seriousness, so long as it is not given form by contrast with the love that redeemed us. Only in this connection is the sinner's mouth finally "stopped" (Rom. III. 19); otherwise he can always raise some objection to the real possibility of God abandoning a man.

Thus the contemplation of hell, like that of sin in general, preserves its dialectical element. It is carried on in the presence of the Son's abandonment by God and of his descent into the darkness of Hades. The severity of the Father's judgment—for who but the Son really knows what it means to be abandoned by God?—is something I can only understand in the Son, who bears not his sins but mine. It is my "descent into hell" that I am looking upon, which, God knows, I have merited, and from which I cannot dissociate myself in contemplation, behind the secret feeling that my own skin is safe enough because eternal Love is suffering ignominy in my place. Such a feeling would argue complete absence of love, the crudest egoism, a coldness of a heart unmoved by the Son's agony, and which, for all we know, could bring down on itself the heightened, inescapable wrath of the Father. There is only one course for the contemplative who sees that his own sin is being judged, to be present where his matter is under jurisdiction, to be present as the kind of person he really is; as the sinner who, in fact was not there, who betrayed as Judas did, denied as Peter did, and fled like all the rest. He must be present as one who is guilty of all, and cannot evade sharing the condemnation of the judge and the victim's cry of dereliction. That, indeed, is the truth; that is what he has deserved.

The dialectic consists in this: the believer, because he believes (that the world's redemption and his own is happening), because he loves (and cannot dissociate himself from the Son), is obliged to recognise the Father's condemnation of the sinner (which is what he is). The faith and love that impel this contemplation are what subject him to the judgment of the Father. No doubt that faith and love expect all good from the Father, being graces proceeding from the redemption and resurrection now achieved. But they include in this expectation of the good an assent given to their just condemnation. If God had to condemn them, then he would be perfectly right; for he certainly did right when he abandoned in darkness the Son who bore and embodied my sins. Yet it is really faith and love, and they alone, that impel this contemplation, and which express the recognition of their own deserts in the presence of the redemption from hell, and of that unique happening from which they derive. But at the same time, a genuine, living faith and love, cannot accept the idea of condemnation from the mouth of God, because the Son, Love itself, has borne it in my place. So it is that the strange utterance of the saintly Cardinal Bona is perfectly Christian, and has its proper place in the theology of faith and love : "In thee, O Lord, have I hoped; in eternity I shall not be put to shame. Even should an angel from heaven tell me for certain that I have been rejected from thy presence, I would not believe him. Even were you yourself, God almighty, to say : I have condemned thee for eternity, I would not listen to thy word. Forgive me, Lord; in this I would not believe thee, for even were thou to kill me and cast me to the depths of hell, I would still hope in thee" (*Via compendii in deum*, c. 12, *decas* 9).

Apart from this twofold aspect, impossible for human understanding to grasp, but clear and imperative to the eye of faith, there can be no contemplation of mortal sin and its punishment. Where the vitality of faith and love that flows from the resurrection of Christ makes itself felt, the fear of hell cannot be paramount at the same time and in the same respect. But where faith and love are engulfed in the abyss of the cross, and the light of the resurrection is no longer seen, and we are plunged into the darkness that overwhelmed the soul of Christ, the contemplation of hell has its rightful. It must not be looked on as "co-suffering" with Christ, but must be carried out, as the truth demands, the sinner holding himself apart, just as Peter "went out" to weep in solitude; nor can it occur to the mind that it should be reckoned for our redemption along with Christ's sufferings, sufferings the

238

sinner himself caused and intensified. From this it becomes evident
that the contemplation of hell is applicable to the individual, and
so—at least in practice—to the sphere of the "closed room". In the
light of living faith, I can never believe, fundamentally, in anyone's damnation but my own; as regards my neighbour, the light
of the resurrection can never be so obscure for me, as to allow or
compel me to cease hoping for him.

Yet even this strictly personal contemplation of damnation is
not so exclusively monological in character as not to retain an
element of dialogue, for it is contemplation in faith. Even the concrete and existential contemplation of hell that St. Ignatius places
at the end of the first week of the Exercises is dialogical : "In colloquy with Christ, Our Lord, call to mind the souls who are in
hell . . . . thanking him that he has not made me fall into it by
cutting short my life, and that he has so far treated me continuously with great mercy and grace" (*Exercises,* 74). This
"dialogue", when carried out existentially at the highest pitch of
intensity, is the "dark night of the soul". It is a participation in
Christ's abandonment on the cross, in a love deprived of light and
incapable of judgment or discernment; but as regards this love
the dialogue is finally resolved into a monologue without answer.
Yet the "night" is something granted by the risen Christ, who
directs its course and assigns its limits.

The dialectic as described turns again into the dialectic of consolation and desolation, inasmuch as the tears which the contemplative sheds in representing to himself the passion are considered by St. Ignatius as a consolation ("Likewise, when someone
sheds tears which move him to the love of Christ, whether he does
so out of grief for his own sins or on account of Christ's passion. . . ."
Exercises 3, 16). This leads logically to the idea that even the dark
night of the soul, the total absence of consolation, is a form of consolation. And it is so objectively, in contrast, for instance, with
that form of tepidity, dryness and separation from God, which the
person praying has to ascribe to his own negligence.

The same dialectic that takes on so pronounced a form in mystical prayer prevails, fundamentally, in ordinary Christian prayer and in the whole Christian life. We can see this from the fact that the feeling of sorrow is both sweet and bitter, and that the bitterness accepted liberates, purifies, and clears the way for faith and love to enter. Peter's tears, when he went out struck by Christ's looking on him, and when he was made chief shepherd, after Christ's love had recalled to him his denial, were on both occasions Christian, and not essentially different. In the second instance, it is very evident how they were used by the risen Christ and called forth by the necessities of love and how from them came the promise that harked back to Calvary, the promise that he would follow Christ to the Cross.

Since all that a Christian can accomplish in the way of imitation of Christ is done in virtue of the risen Christ, he cannot accompany Christ in his act of redemption. Consequently, the contemplation of the Passion, however intense and whole-hearted, can never make, or even aim at making, the person who prays join Christ in carrying Christ's own original cross. On the contrary, the fuller his participation in Christ's passion, the more conscious he becomes of the difference. The Lord suffers, but as an innocent man; I suffer, but as one guilty of his sufferings. The bitterness of feeling himself alone has, for the person praying, the added pain of feeling cut off from the presence of Christ in his Passion through his denial and betrayal of Christ; he is fully conscious that if he tries to bridge the gulf, he will incur the reproach of the Lord to the women of Jerusalem, lamenting him on the way of the cross: "Weep for yourselves and your children". It is true that this rejection is objectively a form of participation in Christ's way of the cross, for the Lord took our rejection on himself and endured being abandoned by the Father in outer darkness. But we must never interpret it subjectively, as though we were on the same way, and experiencing a common anguish. There will be fellowship once again at Easter; during the Passion, what predominates is loneliness endured individually by each person, which will be seen as community only in heaven and valued accordingly. Mary was separated from her Son when she was committed to the care of John; the cord which bound her to the sufferer on the cross was cut, and another relationship set up which was no substitute for the former. The same may be said of St. John, who represented both the apostles and all Christians who suffer.

Everyone who gives himself to the contemplation of the Passion derives a sense of liberation from this separation. The idea that I could, in spirit, unite my insignificant sentimental activities to the mystery of the Redemption is so remote from the truth as to be spurious. Whether I shed tears or follow the scene dry-eyed with the gaping crowds and the soldiers affects the situation very little. Contemplation of the Passion demands self-abasement, adoration without self-regard, the simple consideration of the scenes, happenings and the inner states of the suffering Christ. We move from station to station, prostrating ourselves *"Adoramus te, Christe"*; or, as in the adoration of the cross on Good Friday, we approach with repeated genuflections and humbly kiss the wounds. At this particular moment, my guilt appears so evident and conspicuous that it does not need to be brought to the light; and, on the other hand, in so far as it is mine it is insignificant, because only the burden it has placed on the Lamb of God is visible and of consequence.

This does not mean that there is no place for a serious purpose of amendment, but the situation is no different from other forms of contemplation; there is no question of the individual's amendment making the Redeemer's original cross easier for him. I have been shown, primarily, what *is*, and I have to be satisfied with the reality and try to face it, and not aim at using my good resolutions to make it more endurable. The fact that I see the Passion from the standpoint of the Resurrection means that the whole of it, its form, greatness and burden, are fixed and confront me for eternity. "Nothing may be taken away nor added" (*Ecclus.* XVIII. 5). That is the first point, and nothing subsequent can affect it. The second point is, certainly, my own participation; but I participate both as sinner and as believer, both in augmenting and mitigating it. And the mitigation consists, first of all, in the full recognition of what really was and is, and in letting this reality operate in me.

It is true that the believer who faces this reality is brought by grace, in a hidden and incomprehensible way, into the redemptive work as originally achieved. Mary, who was sinless and is an image of the Church, stood beneath the cross; John, too, who was a sinner, and the women. Together with Mary and the two thieves, they formed the nucleus of the Church. The sacrament of the Eucharist had been instituted, and the shedding of blood "for you" and the giving of the body "for you" were accomplished in a new, unprecedented community in which all sinners and all the just are included. Yet this incomprehensible work of common suffering, even as first accomplished in bloodshed, is only achieved by the grace of incorporation which the contemplative must never take for granted. He must contemplate the source of this grace which incorporates him into the Passion in its purity and uniqueness; and the more truly he is led by grace in his contemplation of the Passion, the less difficulty he will find in distinguishing between the sufferings of Christ and his own state of being better or worse. The Church alone as the bride, symbolised by the Virgin Mother who suffers with the Son, precedes the rest of mankind in taking her place by the side of the Son; she is the way of entry, for the rest, the sinners who are to share the Passion. Yet even she is only there through a grace of "pre-redemption" imparted from the beginning.

All these considerations bring out once again the relations between dogma and contemplation. Contemplative prayer is the reception of revealed truth by one who believes and loves and therefore desires to apply to it all his powers of reason, will and sense. Consequently, the form of the truth itself must always determine and prescribe the mode of reception. Knowledge of the basic truths of theology helps contemplation, for theology, by formulating precisely what the contemplative experiences personally, enables him to avoid being led into false or devious paths. Conversely, anyone practised in prayer will welcome all the central insights he gains from theology as a means of enriching his own prayer.

In considering the passion the contemplative starts out from the fact of the resurrection and this means that his basic disposition is one of gratitude. The Paraclete sent us by the risen Christ makes the world conscious that there is sin, justice and judgment (John XVI. 8). The tremors that shake the earth and cleave it to its depths are forms of the grace of the Paraclete by which he stirs it. In fact, what to the earth appears only a judgment passed in justice is itself a beginning of the resurrection, for the splitting of the earth opens hell, and the upturned graves liberate their bodies to resurrection (Mt. XXVII. 51). The darkening of the sun (*desolatio*), the withdrawal of the Father's favour—for it is the Father who makes the sun shine on the just and the unjust—is also a sign of the coming judgment, of the dawning of the "day of the Lord", the day on which Israel had placed its entire hope. The dramatic culmination of the passion and resurrection was the sudden transformation of darkness and perdition in death and hell into eternal redemption and heavenly glory. These two extremes are thus inseparably conjoined, and the descent of the light of heaven into the depths of hell itself indicates that this spiritual light breaks through and prevails.

This mystery of the unity of God's concealment and his manifestation, his withdrawal and his closeness, was known of old to the faith of Israel. The psalms of abandonment, the bitter reflections of Jeremias and Job, are an authentic form of the revealed word, and are to be understood, not only psychologically, but theologically; they represent stages on the way to the cross. But these patches of darkness only have significance as shadows in a picture where light prevails, in the general image of Jahweh's concern and fidelity to his people, and, in that people, to mankind. Indeed, even in the Old Testament they were felt only as a bewildering, incomprehensible element in a marvellous history of faith. They were always accompanied with questions, reproaches, complaints against the God of the covenant, whose nature it is to be the consolation and support of those who believe in him. The darkness is the effect of a pre-existing light, itself imperishable.

The same dialectic is developed in the sapiential books to illuminate and evaluate the world as a whole. It is the wisdom of God's nearness, such as that of Ecclesiasticus and the book of Wisdom, which sees the entire creation filled with the wisdom of God everywhere visible, a wisdom which is not transient like the day to which night succeeds (Wisdom VII. 29). This wisdom shines forth in nature as clearly as in Israel's history, so that we can see in creatures the living Creator and have no need of images. Even for these contemplatives God's wisdom is unfathomable and utterly inaccessible to the natural man, but God gives it to those who fear and love him and beseech him for it. "He set his eye upon their hearts, to show them the greatness of his works . . . . Their eye saw the majesty of his glory, and their ears heard his glorious voice" (*Ecclus.* XVII. 7, 11). But man sees too that the splendour of the divine that is seen is little by comparison with that which does not appear (*Ecclus.* XLIII. 27-33).

It is here that the reversal takes place. Wisdom now proclaims God's hiddenness and non-appearance in the world. Ecclesiastes describes the wisdom of God's remoteness from the world, its emptiness of God, and Job, in the chapter on wisdom, describes the unfathomable character of wisdom itself. "Man knoweth not the price thereof, neither is it found in the land of them that live in delights. The depth saith : It is not in me; and the sea saith : It is not with me. . . . It is hid from the eyes of all living". What appears is only vanity, uselessness, finiteness, and these are but a weariness to man. God's great promises sound very distantly to the ears of Ecclesiastes; he is unable to hold on to them, they say nothing to him. He feels himself cast into the desert of a false wordly eternity, an evanescent "eternal cycle", from which one thing is always alien, the true eternity of the divine Being.

That too is a contemplation of God in his world, who is yet

greater than the world; but it is the prayer of a tired man, whose joy in reaching out to God has left him. With the disappearance of the living God wisdom itself becomes dialectical: "Behold I have become great, and have gone before all in wisdom that were before me in Jerusalem. And my mind hath contemplated many things wisely, and I have learned. And I have given my heart to know prudence, and learning, and errors, and folly; and I have perceived that in these also there was labour and vexation of spirit. Because in much wisdom there is much indignation, and he that addeth knowledge addeth also labour" (Eccles. I. 16-18). And instead of a life spent in an effort to reach God by withdrawal from the world, the wise man commends one which, conscious of its own futility, rejoices in nothingness and vanity: "Live joyfully with the wife whom thou lovest, all the days of thy unsteady life which are given to thee under the sun, all the time of thy vanity; for this is thy portion in life, and in thy labour wherewith thou labourest under the sun". "He that observeth the wind shall not sow; and he that considereth the clouds shall never reap" (Eccles. IX. 9; XI. 4).

There is also in contemplation an ultimate indifference, from the standpoint of God, whether one finds God in prayer or not; whether he deigns, like the risen Christ, to manifest himself, or hides himself and remains silent, as he did for Christ crucified; whether he speaks or not; whether he is the God of his creatures, who, drawing near to them, fills their vain, transient world with his presence and draws it to himself, or the God who is sufficient to himself (which he always is) and holds sway, seen by none, in his own region of light inaccessible. For this reason, the mystics of Eastern Christianity are not wrong in making the days of the Passion, Good Friday, Holy Saturday and Easter Sunday, serve contemplation of the whole relationship between God and the creature—God's transcendence and immanence, the necessity of death for every spirit, indeed its burial, so as to rise beyond itself, on the unknown land of God (so Bar Sudaili, Evagrius, Maximus, Gregory the Great). But, taken in the sense of Ecclesiastes, this tension within the Christian life need not be looked on as solely or primarily mystical. It can be experienced in ordinary life, at any rate analogously, with its joys, trifling indeed but legitimate.

Yet, in the New Dispensation, these "vain joys" are taken over by the joy of a life redeemed in God, and so by the joy of the resurrection and the joy, though veiled, of heaven, a joy entirely situated in God, one by which the Christian lives, rejoices and suffers. It is impossible for the Christian to escape from the tension of heaven and earth, cross and resurrection, into a purely natural mode of living; he is too thoroughly formed by the word of revelation, which has touched him once and for all and made him what he will remain for ever. But *how* the Word forms him, whether it makes him as one dead or risen, as one who still lives on earth or who has his being already in heaven, or one who goes down with the Word to the world below—is ultimately no concern of his. The contemplative leaves it to the Word to decide in which state of the Word he is to live during his pilgrimage on earth, the life he lives in alienation from the world, and not yet in possession of heaven.